Japanese Communication

Japanese Communication

Language and Thought

in Context

Senko K. Maynard

University of Hawai'i Press
Honolulu

07 06 05 04 03 02   8 7 6 5 4 3

Library of Congress Cataloging-in-Publication Data
Maynard, Senko K.
    Japanese communication : language and thought in context / Senko
K. Maynard.
        p.   cm.
    Includes bibliographical references and index.
    ISBN 0–8248–1799–0 (cloth : alk. paper). — ISBN 0–8248–1878–4
(paper : alk. paper)
    I. Title.
PL665.M39 1997
302.2'0952—DC21   96–46386
                                                        CIP

Design by Jean Calabrese

To the memory of my mother,
Harue Kumiya, of Yamanashi, Japan

Contents

Preface

In this book I attempt to characterize ways of communicating in Japanese. Based on these characterizations, I describe some language-associated ways of thinking and feeling in Japanese. Any language is indirectly and diffusely associated with the ways its speakers think of themselves and their societies. To understand how Japanese people think and feel, knowledge of the Japanese language becomes critically important. My concern is with how the Japanese language communicates, how Japanese people think and feel in their language, how they give the language its meaning, and how, through language, they manipulate and create the social reality that defines Japanese culture.

Defining cultures in simple terms is a trap one must avoid. Careless descriptions of societies can and often do result in negative stereotyping. Overemphasizing differences may breed ethnocentrism; ignoring them may lead to cultural colonialism. Hinting that Japanese modes of speaking and thinking differ from American ones could disturb some critics. But Japan's differences from other cultures, including that of the United States, cannot be ignored or pushed aside. Questions remain about how Japanese people communicate, think, and whether they are similar to or different from Americans in the ways they communicate, think, and feel. Although my primary focus is on exploring ways of communication in Japanese, I contrast the Japanese situation with the American one when useful.

This book is for those who have a basic knowledge of Japanese language and culture and are curious about how Japanese people interact through language. Students who have studied or are currently studying Japanese language and culture will benefit from reading my discussions of Japanese communication. Japanese-language instructors, who might be interested in learning more extensively about Japanese language and communication, should also find the book useful. One way to learn the language efficiently is to know how it works to foster certain modes of communication and certain (sometimes contradictory) orientations of thought. Such knowledge enables one to form a cohesive vision of Japanese communication. Professionals in all fields with a basic knowledge of the Japanese language who are interested in learning more about Japan and the Japanese people will also benefit from this book. For graduate students and language specialists who conduct research in Japanese-language studies, especially Japanese discourse analysis and sociolinguistics, the book can serve as a general introduction. It touches on many research areas in the field that the reader may find worthy of further study.

The pictures of Japan and Japanese ways of communication given in this book are only some of many possible interpretations. I hope that the interpretations will prove useful either as points of reference or as an introduction to further study. Many of the assertions need further discussion. The reader is encouraged to refer to studies mentioned in the text and listed in the references.

Contrary to the widely held assumption that the Japanese language is difficult—some people even call it the "devil's language"—it is not. English is just as difficult for Japanese people as Japanese is for Americans, but no one calls English the devil's language. Despite the convenient excuse that the Japanese are "inscrutable" and cannot truly be known, one can, through effort, come to understand them—just as with effort we come to understand all peoples of the world.

An understanding of the Japanese language, its rhetoric, and its use in social interaction can lead to insights about orientations of Japanese thought. I explore this line of inquiry, revealing that although Japanese modes of communication are similar in many ways to those of other languages (and however tempted we may be to emphasize similarities and find comfort in the sameness) we cannot deny the existence of some profound differences. I hope to assist the reader, in some small but important ways, to gain a better understanding of what it means to speak, think, and feel in Japanese.

Since it is impossible to list all the relevant works that have inspired me in writing this book, I take this opportunity instead to express my respect and admiration for past scholarly achievements in Japanese linguistics (especially discourse analysis and sociolinguistics) and related fields (anthropology, communication studies, and so on) including and beyond those mentioned in this book.

I gratefully acknowledge permission given by Mito Orihara, Jitsugyoo no Nihonsha, Ltd., and Shuueisha to reproduce comic excerpts contained in this book; Edwin International, Inc., for the reproduction of the Edwin jeans ad; and Mick Stevens and the *New Yorker* for the reproduction of a cartoon. I am grateful to Rutgers University and the Department of East Asian Languages and Cultures for making funds available to secure the use of the *New Yorker* cartoon.

I thank my long-time friend, Linn Henderson, for her editorial assistance, especially for her patience, knowledge, and generous support. I am also grateful to Nancy Woodington for her careful and thoughtful copyediting. I wish to express my sincere gratitude to Pat Crosby, editor at the University of Hawai'i Press, for her faith in me as she has continued to offer encouragement and support for this project.

As always, my special thanks go to my husband, Michael, who, with his optimism and encouragement, makes it possible for me to do what I truly love to do.

Note on Romanization

The romanization used in this book generally follows the Hepburn style, but long vowels are marked by doubling the vowel rather than by a macron.

Introduction

Japanese Communication

Japanese is spoken by some 124 million people, most of whom reside in Japan. It has little in common with the major European language families, Romance and Germanic, and has no linguistic link to Chinese. Some have suggested that Japanese is distantly related to the Altaic languages (e.g., Turkish). Word order in Japanese is usually subject-object-verb, and sentence structure is dominated by the topic-comment relationship, where the topic, what is being talked about, is followed by the speaker's comment on it. Although in the structure of a Japanese sentence the agent is grammatically functional, other elements (such as topic) are just as important. Along with other linguistic features, this gives some Japanese expressions a nonagent orientation (knowing the agent of an action is less critical). Nominal clauses and nominal predicates appear frequently and offer a means for expressing the speaker's comment toward the nominalized clause, which enhances, along with other features, what I call a "rhetoric of commentation."

Japanese is classified as an agglutinating language, one that contains many separable elements—particles, auxiliary verbs, and auxiliary adjectives—attached to the words. Particles express not merely grammatical relations but also personal feelings. And, of course, the Japanese language is known for its system of respectful and humble forms as well as its variety of strategies for marking politeness. As one can easily imagine, however, Japanese speakers are not always polite. Conflict naturally occurs in the so-called harmonious society. Likewise, although Japanese is known for its indirectness in

1

communication, Japanese expressions are not always indirect. On the contrary, Japanese speakers find ways to express emotion directly, for example, through a variety of attitudinal adverbs.

What do these characteristics have to do with how Japanese people think and feel? Well, in a word, everything. Language lies at the root of culture and society. The idea that languages differ and that such differences are closely associated with different ways of thinking is neither new nor surprising, but it can be, and has been, somewhat muddled. For example, the Sapir-Whorf hypothesis, credited to the American linguist Edward Sapir (1884–1939) and his student Benjamin Lee Whorf (1897–1941), endorses this idea, although not without controversy. The controversy stems from a vague formulation of their ideas and originates from differing interpretations of the Sapir-Whorf hypothesis. At least two interpretations are recognized: an extreme notion (language "controls" thought) and a more moderate belief (language "influences" thought).

Neither Sapir nor Whorf, however, drew the sweeping conclusion that certain culturally defined ways of thinking exist. Nor did they believe that such a culturally limited reality directly corresponded to such specific grammatical categories as tense, gender, and number in a given language. Interpretations of Sapir and Whorf out of context have taken the "control" theory to the extreme and hastened the growth of belief in an unsubstantiated connection between language and thought. For example, consider the myth that the rich vocabulary related to snow allegedly used by Eskimos reflects their "culture." According to Geoffrey K. Pullum (1991), such characterization is a case of "the great Eskimo vocabulary hoax." The truth is that "Eskimos do not have lots of different words for snow, and no one who knows anything about Eskimo (or more accurately, about the Inuit and Yupik families of related languages spoken by Eskimos from Siberia to Greenland) has ever said they do" (Pullum 1991, 60).

What Whorf (1956) had in mind, and the idea I find most convincing, is that some ways of analyzing and reporting experience have become fixed, readily available, and favored in the language. Ways of interpreting experience through language, which Whorf calls "fashions of speaking," suggest that language as a whole (not just a vocabulary item or a certain grammatical structure) encourages certain ways of viewing the world.

In this regard, another important aspect must be considered. Since one cannot fully interpret meaning in cognitive terms by referring to words and grammar alone, one must pay attention to how cultural relativity is likely to influence the ways language is used for communication. Language usage is revealed in socially defined interactions, and linguistic relativity must be interpreted not only in cognitive but also in social terms. One must carefully observe as many aspects of language and its use as possible before drawing conclusions about the "fashions of speaking" of a particular speech community.

Another tradition addressing the relationship of language to thought comes from the work of the Russian psychologist and semiotician L. S. Vygotsky (1896–1934). Vygotsky addresses the relationship of language, thought, and society in the context of child development. According to him (1962), a child achieves cognitive development through a process of internalizing language whose result is "inner speech." The child first uses language for the purpose of socialization with other individuals, but reaches higher psychological and mental stages by internalizing the speech experience. Vygotsky emphasizes that an individual's developmental process reflects the social process, particularly through sign systems, one primary example being natural language. Vygotsky maintains that human "psychological nature represents the aggregate of internalized social relations that have become functions for the individual and form the individual's structure" (Wertsch 1981, 164).

Here again, as in the case of the Sapir-Whorf hypothesis, a careful reading is called for. As James V. Wertsch (1991b) warns us, it is not so much that there is a direct correlation between a specific item of language and a particular way of thinking. Rather, what Vygotsky is saying is that (1) there are specific structures and processes of thinking common to individuals who share similar social experiences, (2) there is a close connection between these structures/processes and those in each individual's mind, and (3) the common structures and processes give rise to the connection.

Wertsch (1991a), incorporating M. M. Bakhtin's work (1981), discusses the concept of social language, which is a way of speaking characteristic of a particular group in a particular sociocultural setting. Although to Bakhtin social language primarily means social dialect, professional jargon, generational languages, and so on within a single national language, it is also possible to view each national language as a social language. As Wertsch (1991a, 95) summarizes, "Speakers always use social languages in producing unique utterances, and these social languages shape what their individual voices can say." Following Vygotsky and Bakhtin, it seems reasonable to conclude that a social language plays a part in influencing what one expresses in thought and in language.

Obviously human beings are capable of thinking across sociocultural boundaries, and yet we possess the social language defined and endorsed by a specific society. Wertsch characterizes the association between language and thought by stating that "certain patterns of speaking and thinking are easier, or come to be viewed as more appropriate in a specific setting than others" (Wertsch 1991b, 38). It is not so much that language controls thought as that a certain kind of thinking is encouraged by a certain language. That is, the coding categories of a specific language encourage a speaker to engage in specific, readily available ways of thinking. This idea of "thinking for speaking," as mentioned in an article by John J. Gumperz and Stephen C. Levinson (1991) is, I think, a reasonable way to understand the concept of relativity prompted by language.

In discussing language, Whorf concentrated on grammatical structures, while Vygotsky conducted psychological experiments primarily about word meanings. Vygotsky was interested in how language functions in the sociocultural context; Whorf was more concerned with the concepts and knowledge referred to by grammatical structures. I combine their approaches in my exploration into the relationship between the Japanese language and language-associated thought. I also include in my discussion aspects of language that function to create and maintain interpersonal relations in communication.

The aim of this book is twofold. First, I introduce varied aspects of Japanese communication in the hope of encouraging the reader's interest and curiosity by some of the topics introduced. Second, I present three basic elements of communication—context, language, and thought—in a coherent and meaningful manner through use of the underlying notion of "relationality"—specifically, the "society-relational" orientation. While not unique to Japan, relationality serves as a framework for understanding the Japanese sociocultural context, rhetoric of language, and related orientations of thought. Relationality does not, of course, explain everything about Japanese language and society, but it does offer a prism to direct our understanding. These three basic components of communication—context, language, and thought—interact indirectly, and they influence each other in defining the Japanese self, society, and culture. Through specific examples I hope to provide further illumination of the interrelationship of context, language, and culture.

This book should also serve as a source for reevaluating our view of language and thought. Because our understanding of language depends on the characteristics and the use of language, different languages bring different issues to the fore. Theories of language must also be reevaluated so that they account for the phenomena of varied languages, including such nonwestern languages as Japanese. I make no claim that available sociological, anthropological, and linguistic theories in the West are strangers to the idea of relationality and to the significance of meaning based on the society-relational orientation. Some of the works cited in this book prove otherwise. But the view of language that this book presents may play a part in the needed reevaluation of some of our dominant theoretical paradigms.

In part 1, I present the cultural and social milieu within which we understand Japanese communication. To describe how the Japanese language operates, it is useful to contrast it with another language, and for this purpose I have chosen the language and culture of the United States. The reader may not be an American, but whatever one's background, American culture is so widespread that most people are familiar enough with it to understand my examples.

First, I reflect on two mythical figures representing Japanese and American cultures—the samurai and the cowboy—focusing on the ways they identify themselves in their societies. Proceeding from these archetypes, I discuss the concept of relationality. I then examine sociocultural concepts often associated with Japan—group, as in *uchi* 'in-group' and *soto* 'out-group,' as well as *amae* 'dependence'—from the perspective of relationality. Toward the end of part 1, I explore basic concepts that we confront when discussing language and thought in society, namely, self and society, specifically as each relates to Japan.

In part 2, I introduce various features and characteristics of the Japanese language in their social and cultural contexts. Each of the four segments focuses on the language from a different perspective: (1) styles and varieties, (2) phrases, (3) sentences, and (4) communication strategies.

To analyze and discuss various aspects of the Japanese language and communication, I draw from recent developments in Japanese-language studies, especially from Japanese discourse analysis, conversation analysis, pragmatics, and sociolinguistics. I include both the results of my own research and the research findings of other scholars. My hope is that part 2 will serve as an initial guide to Japanese-language research—primarily within the framework of discourse analysis—in which the functions and meanings of language are examined in sociocultural context.

In part 3, I answer another essential question of this book: How do people think and feel in Japanese? Here I identify some of the Japanese ways of thinking that influence, and are influenced by, the Japanese language—a world intricately defined by a particular kind of relationality. The Japanese view of the world is presented as having a characteristic tendency to "become." Certain thoughts are formed and expressed without reference to the concept of the agent. Ideas may be grouped into topics to which the speaker adds a personal commentary.

Japanese thought is also influenced by how the Japanese view their own language. The image of their language held by Japanese-language scholars in Japan differs markedly from its characterization by western scholars. For the Japanese, language captures the "event," and it expresses, through various linguistic strategies, "voices from the heart," which readily respond to the constraints and forces of its social context. Profiles of Japanese thought associated with these observations include the conceptualization of scene to which the speaker offers commentary, and the speaker's self-understanding reflected in the personal narrative he or she tells by the act of speaking and writing. All these orientations suggest Japanese ways of thinking that respond to, and that express accordingly, the shifting relational context created in part by the Japanese language.

Part 4 considers Japanese communication in its global context. First, I contrast samples of Japanese and English discourse, both written and spoken. Second comes an examination of Japanese-American intercultural discourse, which is followed by a brief discussion of the involvement of the media in the manipulation of information from a global perspective. Finally I offer some thoughts on how similarities and differences in language and thought across cultures may be understood by appealing to the awareness of relationality.

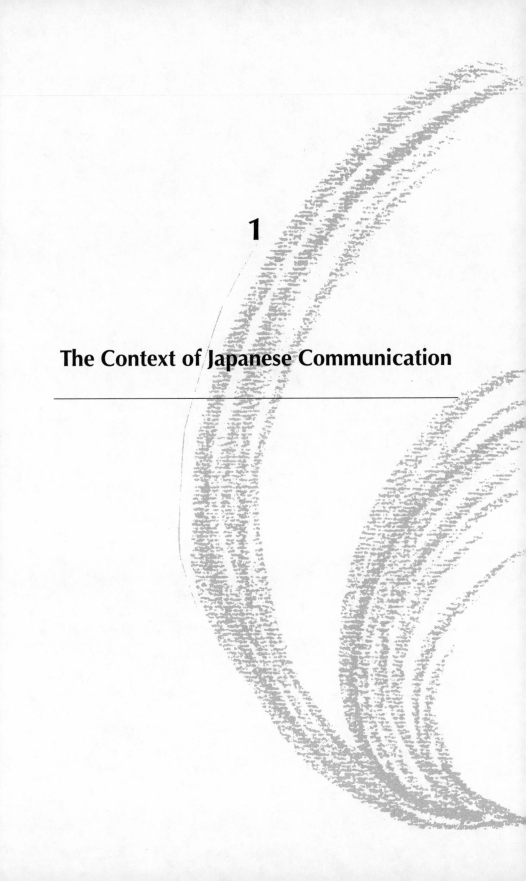

1

The Context of Japanese Communication

1 Cultural Myth, Self, and Society

In this introductory guide to Japanese ways of communication, a few words about the cultural context are now in order. Language is the source of culture; no artifact, custom, ritual, or rite can truly have value or meaning without being expressed in language. Though language, culture, and society form a seamless web of identity, language is the most fundamental. So let us think, for a moment, of the word "samurai." It is one of the most familiar Japanese words to people inside and outside Japan, and it evokes one of the stereotypical Japanese cultural myths. What does it mean? What sociocultural roots does it have in delineating the Japanese psyche? To avoid analyzing the image of the Japanese samurai in a vacuum, I compare it with the American image of the cowboy. These two figures help place some of the salient characteristics of Japanese society in high relief, providing a context for Japanese language and thought.

A note of caution is in order here. Although masculine pronouns are used in discussing the samurai and the cowboy, they do not reflect an intent to exclude females. A female could well be a samurai and a cowboy, if only in spirit. I wish to emphasize not the masculine physical image but the human will and spirit represented by these idealized heroes. And although I use stereotypical images of Japanese and American mythical figures, I do not intend to endorse harmful cultural stereotyping. Instead I reexamine the images so that we recognize both similarities and differences between them, especially as they confront the dilemma of self-identification in their respective societies.

9

Picture a scene where a samurai prepares for ritual suicide. He is about to end his life for the sake of the samurai code and to remain loyal to his lord and to himself. It is simultaneously an ultimate act of self-denial and self-justification. There is stark beauty in this tragedy—life lived not as an ordinary given but as a mission. Now picture a cowboy as he rides off into the sunset, fading into a diminished silhouette in the distance. In the typical scenario, he has just delivered a herd of cattle to the roundup; now it is time to leave his temporary family. At this moment he personifies freedom and independence. There is poetic beauty in this lonely image of the American West.

There is a similarity between these heroic, if not tragic, mythical figures of Japan and America. Both show a commitment to code and belief; both abjure what is considered normal life—life that offers emotional security and material comfort. In each case we witness an expression of loyalty—"the willing and practical and thoroughgoing devotion of a person to a cause," as described by Josiah Royce (1920). Both the samurai and the cowboy confront the contradictory forces of human desire—to be committed to one's cause and so to sustain one's integrity, or simply to surrender to the comfort of living an ordinary life. In the end both the samurai and the cowboy decide to pursue a life that makes a strong yet muted individual statement supported by an inner strength.

Self and Society in Japanese and American Cultural Myths

Besides the similarities, there are deep-rooted differences between these brave and poignant images of Japanese and American archetypal heroes. The Japanese figure is anchored in society but aspires to find his own self, while the American figure is anchored in his awareness of self but aspires to societal approval.

The samurai was deeply integrated into Japanese society. By his complete commitment to his lord he helped sustain the social hierarchy of feudal Japan. According to *Hagakure* (the warrior philosophy), the essence of the samurai way of life is in dying. Modern civilization finds this disturbing. Since the violence in the act of *hara-kiri* or *seppuku* runs so contrary to today's standards of decorum, the usual reaction is to condemn it. A samurai's death, today considered a bizarre act of self-destruction, was never meaningless in the context of his time. According to Tetsushi Furukawa (1957), the samurai must think of dying and being born every day; he must live life as if death is constantly with him. In Furukawa's words, "The possibility of human existence increases qualitatively and quantitatively in proportion to the fierceness of how a person faces the possibility of death, and also with what degrees of sincerity a person lives his or her life. Therefore, by dying every morning and every evening, and being always in the state of mind of as-if-dying, one is able constantly to face the limit of one's existence and to maximize the possibility of one's life" (1957, 160; my translation). And when death finally comes, the samurai must be brave enough to face this essentially solitary act. Honor demands that he overcome fear and accept death with tranquillity and, above all, find an inner serenity on his own terms.

Although a samurai was integrated into society and was a full participant in it, he was constantly striving toward a unique, individual expression of his loyalty. The ideal samurai was not a mindless automaton of the feudal age who willingly committed suicide at his lord's whim, but a man who aspired to an inner serenity of individual self-control and spiritual peace. Here we witness the image of a person who is socially integrated and yet trying to realize his own identity—a social person becoming an individual.

Now think of the American mythical figure. Perhaps no other image captures the archetype of the American hero better than that of the cowboy riding off alone into the sunset. The essence here is that the cowboy is a solitary figure, demonstrating to others that he rides into town and solves problems on his own. For the cowboy, riding off into the sunset may be a reasonable—or in fact the only— option when his work is finished. Yet his rootless life as a loner leaves much to be desired from the community's point of view. The cowboy's satisfaction is short-lived, and he lives his life struggling with the desire to be simultaneously socially connected, and yet disconnected.

The cowboy who settles down loses his identity as a cowboy. To retain that identity, he must always be on the periphery of society, where he symbolizes the American myth of complete self-reliance and freedom. For an American cowboy, the highest achievement seems to be to make it "on his own," to be "on the move," to be forever "free." But since the archetypal cowboy hero is usually not a rancher, farmer, or entrepreneur, he has to participate in society at some level to sustain himself. As James Oliver Robertson (1980) puts it, a cowboy was an employee—a hired hand. Once one job is done, he must choose another. In Robertson's words, "Whether villain or hero, . . . cowboy[s were] usually without a future. . . . They had two choices once they had performed their services for civilization: they could join civilized society and settle down, or they could move on. They could, in short, continue to be what they were and thereby reject society, or they could join society and reject what they were" (1980, 164).

The cowboy has a second tenuous connection to society. He is often portrayed as a man who does "the right thing," facing and fighting authority and power as he defends the weak and the unfortunate. The cowboy in this sense is society's hero—a man praised on the basis of his ethical standards. During his defining moments, the cowboy wins what he secretly cherishes—the approval of others.

The cowboy, also representing the western individual vis-à-vis the eastern establishment society, symbolizes a rugged, aggressive, and to some extent, an anarchic resistance to power. This mirrors American destiny, the creation of a New World through defiance of the Old. Unlike the samurai, who plays an integral part in the feudal order, the American cowboy refuses to play a part in the established order. The image of the American cowboy is that of an independence-seeking man who resists the establishment and yet cannot completely deny his society. He is an independent individual secretly seeking social approval.

In the samurai and the cowboy myths we find some opposing cultural forces between Japan and the United States. Japanese myth advocates a psychological direction from-society-to-self, while American myth moves from-self-to-society. The samurai seeks to be an individual self despite being deeply integrated into society, even as the cowboy wishes to be socially connected despite his independent selfhood. The different cultural obsessions are demonstrated by the samurai's social dependence even during his struggle to become psychologically independent, whereas the cowboy, socially independent, seeks to become psychologically dependent.

What Cultural Myths Can and Cannot Tell Us

The above discussion is not presented to argue that all Japanese and all Americans through time have the psychosocial profiles as depicted by the images of the samurai and the cowboy. In today's world we no longer find the genuine samurai or the authentic cowboy. Yet the spirit of the samurai still lives on in the moral values of contemporary Japan, in subtle and sometimes different manifestations. Consider, for example, the sense of loyalty and devotion encouraged in the Japanese corporate world. Admittedly, someone's loyalty may be motivated by self-interest and the knowledge that such behavior is positively evaluated within the corporation. Certainly it is not my intention to draw a picture of corporate Japan, or Japanese society, as being one big happy family. There is little doubt, however, that Japanese business staff places importance on work-related achievement and devotes much time to the good of the group.

The image of the loyal samurai persists. For example, an actor dressed in samurai attire singing *Japaniizu bijinesuman* 'Japanese businessman' in Japanese-English in an early 1990s Regain beverage television commercial for Taishoo Seiyaku (a pharmaceutical company) depicted the coalescence of the traditional and the contemporary samurai. And the myth of the American cowboy also remains very much alive. Examples of cowboy images appearing in the most urban of contemporary America are the Marlboro Man, as depicted in the successful advertising campaign for Philip Morris, and the corporate cowboy, J. R. Ewing, of the 1980s television series "Dallas." The cowboy lives on even in the visual image of former President Ronald Reagan, whose pastimes are known to have included riding through his California ranch dressed as a cowboy.

Why do these images continue to engage us? Every culture cherishes its myths because they seem to explain not-so-easily explained aspects of the culture. Myth often surrounds a hero or a heroine who lives the familiar life filled with all of life's familiar contradictions. The public continues to embrace myth because it captures a truth. The samurai myth encapsulates Japanese conflict, dedication, and the realization of independence and inner serenity. The cowboy myth illuminates "American loneliness, independence, conviction, and the need for approval" (Robertson 1980, 6).

Myth often comes with countermyth, a story that advocates the opposing view. One can perhaps understand these opposing cultural values from a psychological perspective in the human awareness and desire to behold different, even opposing, values simultaneously. The image of the independent loner is also portrayed in Japanese heroic stories. A strong individual rendered in the series of Saho Sasazawa's *Kogarashi Monjiroo* stories is a case in point.

In this well known fictional series, Monjiroo, the hero, operates alone. Monjiroo is a tall, gaunt, thirtyish homeless *toseinin*, a gambler-rambler-swordsman of the Edo period. Just like a cowboy, Monjiroo leads a solitary life at the fringe of society, denying any personal attachment to others. Sasazawa's description of Monjiroo follows:

> His face wore no expression. His cheeks were hollow as if someone had sliced them off, and this made his face look even more angular—his thin and long face was featured by accented [prominent] eyes and nose. His eyes were nihilistic; but they were sharp, as if piercing through everything. And somehow he looked gloomy and sad.
>
> His eyes were dark and deep. They expressed the sense of refusal by which he seems to turn his back on society as a whole; one could feel in him this masculine detached coldness. His emotions seemed lifeless. No one could tell what he was thinking. And that was, in a sense, the reason he impressed others with his fierceness. (1983, 59–60; my translation)

Although Monjiroo is portrayed as a social outcast who refuses to interact with society, he cannot entirely deny his humanity. The motif of his cruel childhood (which led him to flee from his home, vowing never to return) is interwoven in the text so as to show that Monjiroo still struggles with his desperate determination to detach himself from all human emotion. When he is vulnerable, he, like the American cowboy, is portrayed in the "sunset." In one episode, for example, Sasazawa (1983, 342) has Monjiroo say in reference to a girl named Osute (lit., "abandoned"): "Osute was looking at the sunset for a long time. That is something a person often does—a person who either has no knowledge of the hometown, or who has left the hometown forever." And at the end of the episode, Monjiroo climbs down from the mountain peak under the red evening sky.

We must also remind ourselves that the lone antisocial image is not the only one associated with American cowboys. Think of the Cartwrights of the 1960s television series "Bonanza," in which the cowboys as a family are shown to lead rather civic and community-minded lives. Ben Cartwright, and the Cartwright brothers, to varying degrees, commanded respect as good social citizens of their time. In fact the Ponderosa was a place where individual rights were respected. At the same time it was a place where priority was put on doing what was good for the community.

The sense of loyalty associated with the samurai is not unique to Japan. According to Royce (1920), America strongly believes in the importance of loyalty. Royce emphasizes that the kind of loyalty he advocates—the willing devotion of a person to a cause—must be chosen freely. The loyalty described in *Hagakure*, the warrior philosophy, differs in a fundamental way: A samurai cannot freely choose the cause, although he may willingly devote himself to it. And yet one cannot deny that Japanese and American cultures are alike in their sensitivity and vulnerability to social belongingness, social approval, and loyalty as well as independence, individual will, and freedom. In terms of possessing contradictory feelings, Japan and America are very much alike.

2 Relationality and Communication

Relationality as Context

Discussion of the samurai and the American cowboy, who are part myth and part reality, offers a background from which to work toward an initial understanding of language and thought in Japan. The ambivalent feelings the samurai and the cowboy hold toward self and society can be sorted out by understanding the kind of relationality adopted in the two societies. "Relationality" refers to the reciprocal influence exerted by two different elements that are reflexively characterized by each other. More specifically, it refers to the mutual relationship that language—as well as thought—comes into contact with in sociocultural and situational contexts. For example, linguistic strategies and social context are interrelated; the use of linguistic expressions (e.g., politeness strategies) is determined in part by the context in which they are used. In turn, the use of linguistic expressions itself determines in part the changing and mutually renewing social context.

By recognizing this influence of relationality in communication involving two or more parties, one is able to focus on its type, its frequency, and its relative importance in a particular speech community. Obviously, every language operates in relation to its context. Characteristics of Japanese language and thought, however, reveal themselves most clearly when they are examined in terms of the mutual influence they share with the social context. The dynamic force of relationality operates on various levels within language, thought, culture, and society, as well as among diverse elements across these domains. I think that many sociocultural and communication-related characteristics of Japan (particularly in contrast with those of the United States) can be comprehended in terms of differences in the role of relationality observed in different societies.

Japanese society and culture cannot be directly characterized in terms of the labels often attached to them, such as Japanese "group" as opposed to American "individual." Rather, as we saw in the mythical images of the samurai and the cowboy, both desire social integration and independence, but with a different orientation and emphasis. Differences between Japan and the United States become apparent in how one understands and comes to terms with the relationship between self and society.

The starting point for the Japanese experience lies in society, while the starting point for Americans lies in the concept of self. By "starting point" I mean the primary and deep-rooted self-concept one is encouraged to identify with early in life. In Japan, social accommodation, responsiveness, and cooperation are the dominant, although not the only, training one receives in the socialization process. The relationship one identifies as one's psychological foundation is based on, anchored to, and defined in relation to society. The Japanese, however, express individuality more as they mature and achieve comfort within society. The direction of opposing forces between society and self in Japan is from-society-to-self, that is, society-relational.

For Americans, the concept of self is fundamental. Socialization presupposes social relationships with others in society, but more importance is placed on exercising individuality than on learning to accommodate others. This tendency can be labeled from-self-to-society, that is, self-relational.

A note of caution should be sounded here. What I describe are general tendencies that influence the behavior of members of the speech community as a whole. The prototypical American I discuss may prove to be most characteristic of the middle-class American with a European cultural background. Given the diversity of contemporary Japanese society, and even more of American society, however, one must keep in mind that no description of a group of people can completely escape overgeneralization. Still, Japanese and Americans seem to find themselves holding opposing values from the beginning as they both struggle toward what turn out to be opposing goals. The Japanese are more likely to be trapped in the self-imposed concept of society; Americans are more likely to be shackled by faith in self. Yet we all find some balance between these opposing forces.

The relationship between self and society characterized here can shed light on various aspects of Japanese life. No one is completely separated from society. Human existence is partially defined by it, and society, in turn, is partially defined by its constituents. Self and society feed on each other, define each other, contradict each other—and yet always coexist. These associations create the different kinds of relationships that characterize the Japanese view of life.

The Japanese preference for *amae* 'dependence' is a case in point. *Amae* is frequently identified as a cornerstone of the Japanese psyche (Takeo Doi 1971, 1976). *Amae* presupposes at least two individuals and their psychological and emotional interrelationship. The person who wishes to indulge in emotional dependence must find a willing counterpart who shows signs of cooperation as the supporting one in the *amae* relationship. This psychological interplay depends on the willingness of both parties, or more accurately, on the relationality supported by the willingness of each.

In this context several sets of often-cited terms come to mind— Japanese "dependence-indulging" versus American "independence-seeking," Japanese "group-oriented" versus American "individual-oriented," and so on. When these terms are assigned to whole societies, they tend to polarize them. Exaggerated, dichotomous interpretations proliferate—almost as if these terms had a will of their own. Unfortunately, in some cases scholars, in their zeal to find flaws, criticize established scholarship based merely on their impressionistic interpretation of the terms. By using the concept of relationality, I try to avoid the hazard posed by these potentially divisive terms.

Another possible pitfall of such dichotomous labeling as "group consensus" versus "individual will" is that, without qualification, one may be considered more advanced than the other. For example, Americans think Japan lacks the most important (as it is often believed to be) American value—individual freedom. Although characterizing Japan as lacking an important human trait may comfort some Americans, the reality in both countries is far more complex.

Relationality as a Source for Interactional Cues

In addition to finding different kinds of relationality as social context, we also observe different ways that relationality plays a part in influencing personal and interpersonal behavior. Differences are especially evident in communication behavior, since relationality exerts different influential forces when operating as interactional cues.

Every language is equipped to express relationality, which is universal to human interaction, but languages differ in their approach. Some have many language-explicit devices that respond to relationality-based cues. Others lack language-explicit means to respond to relationality cues and instead possess persuasive strategies that are conventionalized as part of the communicational style. Japanese and American English fall into the former and the latter categories, respectively. Lest the reader misunderstand, I am not saying that Japanese people are more sensitive or relationally accommodating than Americans, only that the Japanese language is coded with more explicit expressions that convey relationality. Americans use different linguistic and extralinguistic means to express relationality.

Japanese contains devices and strategies that reflect and express the society-relational tendency toward object(s) described and person(s) to whom a message is addressed. It is equipped to respond to relationality cues in abundance and with specificity. Politeness-level distinction is a good example. In Japanese, each and every verbal expression is bound by the relationality cues of the particular situation. Cues may be grammatical, stylistic, or interactional. In other words, Japanese modes of communication are closely tied to the way participants locate themselves in the relational context.

Differences in how relationality influences communication behavior are not limited to cross-cultural factors alone. We can speculate that relationality-based stylistic choice is exercised with different intensity depending on the types and the purpose of communication. How one understands and uses relationality as a source for interactional cues is in part genre—and gender—specific. Certain aspects of relationality become primary in some genres but not in others. Such speech style differences as those in masculine and feminine utterances illustrate that relationality is interpreted differently within a single culture. Among Americans, women are said to seek the feeling of community more strongly than men, while men seek a sense of contest more strongly than women.

Relationality and the Rhetoric of Language

The rhetoric of the Japanese language is influenced by a particular kind of Japanese understanding of relationality. The topic-comment structure and nominal predicates are cases in point. Although Japanese sentence structure defines referential meaning by the grammatical relationship of subject and predicate (who-does-what-to-whom), just as important is the function of offering comment by means of the topic-comment structure (what is being talked about in what ways). Likewise, although verbal predicates occur in Japanese (again describing who-does-what-to-whom), nominal predicates are also prominent, where the event as a whole is portrayed in a nominalized expression, and the speaker's personal evaluation and attitude are added as comment. These features of Japanese indicate that relationality plays a part not only in how participants behave in communication but also in how participants form concepts.

Through indirection and diffusion, rhetorical features of the Japanese language including those described above are connected with the society-relational context of Japan at least in two ways. First, by making the who-does-what-to-whom portion of a sentence a topic, the speaker distances himself or herself from the event. At the same time the speaker expresses, in comment, his or her attitude toward the event by such relationality cues as formality and politeness levels. Second, expressions chosen for comment create communication strategies that respond to a variety of interactional relationality cues, for example, collaborative strategies for persuasion. Because the Japanese kind of relationality encourages these characteristics, Japanese rhetoric can be called a rhetoric of commentation.

In contrast to the society-relational characteristics of Japanese, in English, the human agent often appears as the grammatical subject and explicitly identifies who-does-what. The rhetoric of commentation so prominent in Japanese is notably absent in English.

Modes of American communication are, however, far from being rhetorically insensitive to, or incapable of, the expression of society-relational elements. To a greater degree than the Japanese, Americans use extralinguistic cues for expressing human relations and personal emotions. They employ a variety of communication strategies including, but not limited to, the use of intonation, facial and other nonverbal messages, the incorporation of jokes, puns, quips, wisecracks, and so on. These cues are not part of the language structure per se. The American view of the Japanese people as inexpressive of their emotions may stem in part from looking for the wrong cues. Human emotions may be expressed either through linguistic codes, as in Japanese, or through other means, as in English.

Relationality in Contrast to Related Concepts

It is important to stress that my concept of relationality differs from other related concepts. Two terms introduced by Takie Sugiyama Lebra and the concept of context, as characterized by Edward T. Hall and Mildred Reed Hall, can help to explain the difference.

Lebra (1976, 1–21) introduces two relevant terms, "social relativism" and "interactional relativism." She points out that Japanese actions are governed by something far removed from unilateral determinism: "The Japanese Ego acts upon or toward Alter with the awareness or anticipation of Alter's response, and Alter in turn, by responding according to or against Ego's expectation, influences Ego's further action" (1976, 7). Lebra calls this orientation "interactional relativism" and continues: "In interactional relativism, an actor acts in a certain way not because he is forced to do so by an external prime mover such as an environmental force, not because he is driven by an internal prime mover such as an irresistible passion or desire; his behavior is, rather, a result of interaction and mutual influence between himself and his object" (1976, 7–8).

Lebra combines this concept of interactional relativism with the concept of the "social preoccupation" of the Japanese people and refers to the combined concepts as "social relativism." By "social preoccupation" Lebra (1976, 2) means the Japanese sensitivity to social objects, particularly other human beings. And when a Japanese individual experiences inner feelings, he or she tends to be preoccupied with his or her relationship to some *hito* 'person(s).'

Both interactional relativism and social relativism are closely associated with the concept of relationality. In fact relationality is an extension of Lebra's line of thought. Granting that the Japanese practice interactional relativism or a broader orientation of social relativism, I explore the characteristics of the relationship itself and the ways in which relationality serves as a cue for influencing communication behavior. Since a sensitivity to relationships exists between Lebra's Ego and Alter, by setting up a framework of relationality I can focus on how relationships reveal themselves in Japanese language and thought.

Relationality also offers a framework within which to analyze different societies and cultures. The terms "interactional relativism" and "social relativism" are used to characterize Japanese patterns of behavior, which tend to focus on the difference between Japan and other societies. Unfortunately, it is also true that these labels are subject to misinterpretation. They are frequently polarized by critics. The term "relationality" is readily applicable to all cultures. By examining different tendencies of relationality in their nature and degree, one can retain commonality while placing differences in comparative perspective.

Another concept relevant to relationality is the characterization of Japan by Edward T. Hall and Mildred Reed Hall (1987). These authors identify Japan as a case of a "high-context" culture in comparison to the "low-context" culture of America (especially white American culture). According to Edward T. Hall (1976), a high-context communication or message is the type in which most of the information is already known to the person. Very little is coded, explicit, or transmitted in the message. A low-context communication is just the opposite. Low-context speakers, according to Hall and Hall, include Americans, Germans, Swiss, Scandinavians, and other northern Europeans. Although the distinction between high- and low-context captures how important context is in a culture, it fails to clarify how context and culture interact. The concept of relationality allows a clearer focus on the culture-context relationship as it is revealed in communication and thought.

My effort also differs from the Halls' approach in the following sense. When Japan is characterized as a high-context culture, the label obscures the fact that much information is coded in language, although the encoding differs from that of European languages. The aspects of communication that become important differ in Japanese and in English. When Hall and Hall state that Japan is a culture in which little information is coded in the message, they may be referring only to certain kinds of messages. Comment and the interpersonal aspects of information are abundantly coded in the most ordinary of Japanese expressions. To understand Japanese language and culture, not only from the outside observer's viewpoint, but also from as near a native speaker's point of view as possible, the concept of relationality is key. Relationality has the potential to illuminate some of the psychological and philosophical forces underlying Japanese ways of communication.

3 Competing Orientations within Relationality

Typological differences exist across cultures in the concept of relationality. But how are the opposing forces between society and self within and across cultures dealt with psychologically? As our task is to understand language and thought across cultures, we should ask whether it is possible to shift one's orientation of relationality. To answer this question, let us turn once again to our mythical images of Japan and the United States, the samurai and the cowboy.

In this regard Philip Slater's insight offers special significance. Slater (1970, 8–9) recognizes "three human desires that are deeply and uniquely frustrated by American culture."

1. The desire for community—the wish to live in trust, cooperation, and friendship with those around one.
2. The desire for engagement—the wish to come directly to grips with one's social and physical environment.
3. The desire for dependence—the wish to share responsibility for the control of one's impulses and the direction of one's life.

The irony of this characterization of American culture lies in the fact that Americans are, too often and too quickly, labeled as strong proponents of independence and freedom. As important as independence may be, human beings also long just as much—or possibly even more—for dependence.

And Japan, a country characterized as fostering dependence and subordination of the individual to the welfare of the group, is haunted by contradictory forces. As we saw in the samurai's inner thoughts, there is a desire for independence and freedom—often freedom from the bonds of human relationships. Japanese people seem to seek out every possible nook and cranny in their fairly tightly woven society to find solitude—being distant from the crowd and being free from (sometimes forced) dependent human relationships.

The heroic and tragic images of the samurai and the cowboy reside in our consciousness regardless of our individual cultural heritage. They simply reflect the human emotional tug-of-war—the simultaneous desire to foster a relationship and to sever it. In this sense the fiercest battle between two different values takes place in each individual's heart.

Competing Values in America

Such a battle may be represented in a public forum. According to Donal Carbaugh (1988/1989), contemporary American discourse often takes the shape of individual and self fighting against society, as is depicted most clearly in the television talk show "Donahue." After examining "Donahue" discourse, Carbaugh observes that the terms "self" and "society" are used with strong semantic force, and a deep agony is enacted in American speech as the "cultural symbols of 'self' are asserted against the cultural symbols of 'society' " (Carbaugh 1988/1989, 181). He states:

> Consider the following: (1) "self" is divisible (unique) from others, yet in so being, enacts a cultural person, and thus enables identification with others; (2) "society" is unity (uniformity) with others, yet so bound, gives perspective to uniqueness and motivates "self" acts of extrication and separation. Treated together, the cultural and social functions may thus be summarized: "self" provides a cultural model for individuation and division, but is held in common, thus displaying a social outcome of unity; further, since "self" symbolizes division from others, acts seeking unity are motivated; "society" provides a cultural model of unity, but since it is de-valued, social outcomes of division are sought. With "self," a common sense of the divisible person motivates unity; with "society" a unified sense of sociation motivates division. Such is the complexity of the social and cultural tensions that are activated when American life is discoursed through a deep agony. (1988/1989, 204)

This agony, displayed daily on American television, reflects today's inner conflict. As Kenneth Burke aptly puts it, when a person identifies with another, he or she is substantially one with that other. "Yet at the same time he remains unique, an individual locus of motives," and therefore "he is both joined and separate, at once a distinct substance and consubstantial with another" (Burke 1950, 21).

Tipping the Scale of Competing Values

The ancient battle for priority between self and society will continue on every level of human life. This universal conflict, although acted out differently in different cultures, is the primary opposing value—both within and across cultures. Although it seems that this difference in values can be reconciled only by the victory of one, with the annihilation of the other, in reality opposing cultural values remain at near equilibrium in the heart. Slater explains: "An individual who 'converts' from one viewpoint to its exact opposite appears to himself and others to have made a gross change, but actually it involves only a very small shift in the balance of a persistent conflict" (1970, 8).

The characteristics of Japanese communication—both in language and in thought—that I identify through my discussion of relationality may, in reality, be less particular than at first assumed. Cross-cultural understanding may not be as difficult as it seems. Indeed, understanding Japanese communication is not as difficult as it is often made out to be.

4 Relationality Cues in the Sociocultural Context of Japan

Language is never spoken in a vacuum, and its potential meanings are realized only when their interpretations are endorsed by social conventions. These social conventions, which are imposed on our communities, thrive because they are continuously reaffirmed. We derive much of what we know and believe from these socially constructed conventions. At their root lies society's collective point of view toward itself and its members. The key Japanese concepts that I review are based on the society-relational orientation in Japan. They can be viewed as specific relationality cues that influence how participants in Japanese communication behave.

Group Theory and Its Criticism

Many observers characterize Japan as a culture that emphasizes social hierarchy, group membership, harmony, modesty, and obligation. Indeed, over time a long list of adjectives has accumulated. These modifiers presumably define the character of Japan and its people. The list usually includes the following:

1. "group-oriented" (versus American "individual-oriented")
2. "shame-oriented" (versus western "guilt-oriented")
3. "intuitive/emotional" (versus western "rational/logical")
4. "harmonizing" (versus American "confronting")
5. "high-context" (versus western "low-context")

There is some truth here. These models, however, have been criticized for their inability to account for some of the defining aspects of Japanese society (see, for example, Ross Mouer and Yoshio Sugimoto 1986). While recognizing the usefulness of employing a framework or a model in explicating Japan, it is also important to evaluate some of the accepted positions. The most prominent model is often referred to as the "group model" (versus the American "individual").

Undoubtedly the group model is the dominant characteristic associated with Japanese society. While more than a few scholars have argued for the group orientation of the Japanese people (for example, Edwin Reischauer 1970), it is Chie Nakane's work, *Japanese Society* (1970), that has made a decisive impact. According to Nakane, Japanese society is characterized by hierarchical organizations whose group membership is determined in terms of "frame" rather than "attribute." For example, a Japanese person identifies himself or herself as a member of a particular organization or an institution ("I work for Sony"), while a typical American identifies himself or herself by a universal attribute such as profession ("I am an engineer").

The Japanese group is led by a sympathetic and paternalistic head who provides for the social and emotional needs of the members. The frames may be currently in place, such as one's family and the company where one works. The groups may be based on one's past, such as one's birthplace or school, the prefecture one's family is from, and so on. An individual is likely to belong to several of these groups simultaneously. The group is led by a head with established seniority, and members are bound by a vertical relation in which individuals are linked to a chain of higher-ranking members. Despite, and because of, the clear ranking differences, the relationship between leader and subordinate is one of mutual dependence.

While this "group" interpretation offers general guidance in understanding the social behavior of some Japanese, it fails to explain many other related aspects of Japanese society. Let us follow Harumi Befu's criticism of the group theory. Befu (1980) lists the following points.

1. The paternalistic leader may be exploitative rather than protective.
2. The loyalty and harmony themes often implied in the group model do not accurately reflect reality. "Loyalty and cooperation

[of workers] are realized only because and to the extent that each worker stands to gain by being loyal and cooperative, and the management dispenses 'benevolence' insofar as such dispensation is profitable to the management."(Befu 1980, 179–180)

3. The group model cannot account for relationships among groups, since only the group's internal structure is put in focus.
4. There is some evidence that the group model is an ideology promoted as an official statement. Scholars have tended to confuse the ideology of the society as a whole with the behavior of individual members.
5. Some individualistic behavior by the Japanese cannot be explained by loyalty to the group alone, but by reference to *seishin* 'one's inner spiritual strength.'

Based on these inadequacies, Befu proposes a descriptive alternative that incorporates three perspectives: (1) group ideology, (2) social exchange, and (3) *seishin*. This alternative approach endorses (1) a view of the group model as an ideology rather than a social reality, (2) the belief that loyalty and cooperation are motivated by a fair exchange of benefits, and (3) the hypothesis that the Japanese people's inner strength originates not so much from a concept of loyalty but from *seishin*, the individual's inner strength, which results from character development and self-discipline.

Another factor promoting the popularity of the group theory is the concept of "Orientalism" (Said 1978). The group model is useful for setting aside Japan as being different, if not unsophisticated, and therefore viewing it as America's (or the West's) "other."

Beyond the points specifically raised by Befu, Nakane's thesis cannot escape the criticism of being representative of the elite male model. This model conveniently excludes from discussion women and men whose jobs are much more precarious than Nakane's description, leaving only those men working for large to midsize corporations. While recognizing these shortcomings, however, it is reasonable to believe that the average Japanese person is, or at least desires to be, more concerned about his or her primary group than the average American.

I do not endorse the extreme interpretation of the group theory, but I do recognize the importance group membership plays in Japanese culture. I find it preferable, however, to characterize the nature of Japanese social action by focusing on the relationality of

the group members. By focusing on the mutual and dynamic interaction of relationality associated with group theory, I believe we can
gain insight and more accurately understand Japanese modes of
communication and related orientations of thought.

Uchi/Soto and Amae

Closely associated with the group theory are the concepts of *uchi*
'in, inside, internal, private, hidden' and *soto* 'out, outside, external,
public, exposed.' People belonging to an identical group usually
consider themselves *uchi* persons, while they think of those outside
the group as *soto* persons. All cultures offer devices and strategies
(linguistic or otherwise) to make distinctions between those who
are familiar and those who are not. When belonging is relevant, the
Japanese express rather explicitly through strategies of communication that they belong to a particular group.

Uchi/Soto *and* Omote/Ura

According to Takie Sugiyama Lebra, this *uchi/soto* dichotomy,
together with another dichotomy of *omote/ura*, defines Japanese
social situations. *Omote* refers to 'front, exposed, light side' and *ura*
to 'back, hidden, dark side.' The two dichotomous variables create
four possible combinations. Among the four, *uchi-omote* 'inside-
exposed,' because of its contradictory tendencies, is highly unlikely
to occur. The three remaining possible combinations define social
situations in Japan as follows (Lebra 1976, 112–113):

1. *omote/soto* 'front/out'   ritual
2. *ura/uchi* 'back/in'   intimate
3. *ura/soto* 'back/out'   anomic

Ritual occurs when (1) two interacting persons do not belong to
the same group (consider themselves *soto* members) and (2) the
action is performed with the awareness of an audience. It should be
added that ritual occurs when participants think a conscientious and
dutiful effort is necessary to conform to social rules and conventions. The intimate situation occurs when (1) two interacting persons are in a close relationship (are *uchi* members) and (2) the
behavior is protected from public exposure. I should add that even
when the behavior is exposed to the public, if the atmosphere is
such that the persons wish to express intimacy, and this does not

breach social etiquette, intimacy, rather than ritual, is acknowledged. The anomic situation is when (1) two people identify themselves as *soto* members and (2) they are unaware of an audience
watching their behavior.

Of course Japan is not the only place where people behave differently depending on whether their relationship is intimate or
whether they are exposed to the public eye. Among the Japanese,
however, changes in behavior—especially communication strategies—depending on social contexts is linguistically explicit. Japanese speakers and listeners change their ways of communication in
reference to *uchi* and *soto* situations. What triggers a specific style
lies in the kind of personal and situational relationality that a person identifies in a given social situation. The style chosen, in turn,
influences the kind of relationality mutually mobilized by the participants, thus continuously changing and defining the context of
interaction.

Uchi and *soto* worlds shift on the basis of interactional perspectives (see Bachnik 1994 and Bachnik and Quinn 1994). This changing but defining location of social space offers the primary
organizing focus for Japanese communication. Participants in Japanese communication use society-relational cues, including *uchi* and
soto, extensively to find appropriate ways of expressing themselves.
In Bachnik's words, "In the Japanese case, indexical meaning should
be the primary focus, so that referential, denotative functions of
language—or, the 'patterns' and 'ordering' of social life—can be
viewed as indexed by social participants interacting in social context" (1994, 16).

Amae *and Social Interaction*

Another concept often associated with the group theory is its psychological base, *amae* 'psychological and emotional dependence,' as
explained by Takeo Doi (1971). The desire for *amae* motivates one
to belong to a group or groups. The term *amae* is a noun related to
the verb *amaeru*, for which Doi gives the English translation 'to
depend and presume upon another's love' (Doi 1988, 100). *Amae* is
also etymologically related to *amai* 'sweet.' Think of the feelings of
warmth and security a child feels in its mother's arms. The dependence associated with *amae* echoes the sweetness of all-forgiving
and all-embracing parental love. *Amae* above all involves the desire
to be (passively) cared for by another. Again, think of the feelings of

warm camaraderie and the strong sense of trust found among intimate group members. Among them you can be foolish, crazy, rude,
or whatever, and you know you will always be accepted as you are.
According to Doi, worlds where *amae* is allowed and encouraged
have "the function of seeking to 'melt down' others by *amae* and
make them lose their *tanin* 'other' quality" (1971, 76; my translation). It is as if belonging to a group makes a Japanese person feel
totally comfortable and secure because he or she does not have to
face a strange and unknown other. One can avoid the vulnerability
of exposure to unknown others, which may cause social injury.

Doi's concept of *amae* has been criticized (for example, by Yasuhiko Taketomo 1988) for a lack of clear definition. I agree that
there is danger in resorting to a set of "untranslatable" Japanese
words when explaining Japan to people with no knowledge of Japanese. This process often frustrates and angers readers because the
words remain ambiguous and obscure. But as Doi (1988) himself
has responded to this criticism, the concept of *amae* defies easy
translation. It involves a variety of emotions, and although it is conveniently translated into English as "dependence," Doi confesses
that it is perhaps better to insist on using phrases like "to depend
and presume upon another's love" (1988, 100). Also, using the Japanese term is useful in understanding the concept from the native
speaker's point of view.

Advocates of the *amae* concept, misreading Doi, may unneces-
sarily accentuate the "uniqueness" of Japan. Such an interpretation
has encouraged criticism of Doi's approach, especially among the
critics of *nihonjinron* 'discussion of the Japanese people.' *Nihonjinron* adheres, through an array of publications, to the idea that
Japan is uniquely distinct from other cultures. For example, Peter
N. Dale (1986, 125) characterizes Doi's theory of *amae* "as an
explanation of the image of emotional, group-dependent relations
among the Japanese" and criticizes that it is "dependent on a Japanese kind of psychoanalysis" that is "inaccurate and incomprehensible in Western terms."

Doi, however, does not intend to claim that *amae* is unique to
the Japanese. In his words, "I am saying that the vocabulary of *amae*
is unique to Japan; I am not saying that the *amae* phenomenon is
observed only in Japan. I emphasize the simple fact that because the
vocabulary of *amae* occupies a special place in Japanese it is perceived explicitly and apparently" (1988, 111–112; my translation).

I find it particularly important to recognize this point. The desire for *amae*, or at least the feeling resembling it, is universal. But the degree of intensity and society's attitude toward it differ from culture to culture. How *amae* is expressed and manipulated also differs from culture to culture.

One aspect of the *amae* emotion that distinguishes it from its American counterpart is the pervasiveness of *amae* among adults. In America, dependence is most frequently associated with childhood and therefore immaturity. Emotional dependence is thought to be something a person should grow out of. The sooner the child becomes independent of parental indulgence, the better off the child. Although very generally speaking, this social tendency can be seen in the United States, we must also be aware that the American notion of independence is part myth. Many readers know experientially that Americans enjoy warm camaraderie with colleagues and friends—often resulting in all-forgiving *amae* love.

Although the term *amaeru* has a distinct feeling of sweetness and is often used to describe a child's love-and-attention-seeking behavior toward his or her parents, in Japan it is encouraged and sustained in many facets of daily life throughout one's lifetime. For example, think of a group of businessmen who are treated by their boss at an evening outing. They get drunk and complain to the boss about what happened at the meeting the week before. The boss simply listens and lets his subordinates express themselves. They need emotional support, recognition, and all-supporting love and attention. Here the boss plays a role of *amayakasu* 'accept another's (desire for) *amae*.' Although one may witness somewhat comparable scenes in the United States, the dynamic does not appear to work in the same way. Adult professionals in contemporary America are not expected to let down their guard as much as Japanese often do.

Amae can be seen as that part of the social contract that allows emotions to be freely expressed with approval. For *amae* to happen, at least two persons must be involved; one to seek the other's dependence, and the other to accept it. Being aware of this, a Japanese person may seek *amae*, since he or she recognizes a sign from someone else who desires to accept it. Consider a situation where you ask your aging father's opinion about your life's choice, although you have made up your own mind already. It is your love toward your father that makes you do this; your father feels needed and depended upon, thereby sanctioning the father's role. Your father knows what you are thinking, but gives his opinion anyway. After all, he must accept your love to make you feel important. *Amae* is often observed in this feeling of reciprocal, dependent love.

Japanese ways of interaction change markedly depending on the degree of *amae* allowed in a situation. Because of its pervasiveness, its encouragement throughout one's lifetime, and the importance it plays in determining social and communication style, the concept of *amae* remains important in understanding Japanese ways of communication.

The concept of *amae* also operates in other, although somewhat indirect, ways. The appropriate mode of communication—presumably reflecting the corresponding level of *amae*—can help create or nurture social relationships of *amae*. In other words, *amae* not only serves as an indexical cue but also, indirectly through the *amae*-based linguistic choice, helps create or nurture the *amae* relationship even when *amae* is absent or is experienced only minimally.

5 Relationality and the Concept of Self

The Concept of Self

The concepts of self and society shape all other sociocultural concepts. For this reason we cannot ignore how these notions are understood in Japan. But before we begin, let me quote from an American anthropologist, Clifford Geertz, because what he has to say is relevant to my position on self and society.

> The concept of person is, in fact, an excellent vehicle by means of which to examine this whole question of how to go about poking into another people's turn of mind. . . . The Western conception of the person as a bounded, unique, more or less integrated motivational and cognitive universe, a dynamic center of awareness, emotion, judgment, and action organized into a distinctive whole and set contrastively both against other such wholes and against its social and natural background, is, however incorrigible it may seem to us, a rather peculiar idea within the context of the world's cultures. Rather than attempting to place the experience of others within the framework of such a conception, which is what the extolled "empathy" in fact usually comes down to, understanding them demands setting that conception aside and seeing their experiences within the framework of their own idea of what selfhood is. And for Java, Bali, and Morocco, at least, that idea differs markedly not only from our own but, no less dramatically and no less instructively, from one to the other. (Geertz 1984, 126)

The case of Japan is no exception. Although similarities exist in the Japanese and American concepts of self and society, we also face some profound differences.

The differences in the concept of self that I am going to discuss should not be viewed as differences in the civilizations' level of sophistication. Unfortunately, differences between the United States and Japan—or more broadly between the West and the East or the North and the South—have been viewed as different stages of civilization. For example, one may think of the Japanese self as something that should be encouraged to mature so that it resembles more closely the view of self in the West. The concept of the American self has tended to be viewed as something more valuable and readily justifiable. The cultural differences that I discuss in this book do not arise from one culture's superiority or its greater value or sophistication. The differences must be viewed simply as differences.

Japanese Selves and American Self

To start with, let us look into the etymology of the term for "self" in Japanese, *jibun*. *Jibun* literally means "portion given to self," that is, a portion appropriately distributed to a person out of a larger whole, a piece of a pie, so to speak. At the level of etymology, *jibun* implies that the self is not an autonomous entity disconnected from society. The Japanese self is a part of society, perhaps a concept existing only in relation to society. Here one must be careful not to view self and society as opposing entities, as Americans tend to do. Self and society can be viewed as interacting and complementary, and placing importance on their relationality is useful for understanding Japan.

Belief in the tendency of the Japanese to view the self in relation to others is widely accepted. Tetsuroo Watsuji's position of defining self in "betweenness" is a case in point. In his work Watsuji (1937) develops the concept that the social human relationship is that of *aidagara* 'betweenness.' The term *aida* 'betweenness' refers to the distance separating two items. Watsuji developed the concept of space that makes the notion of betweenness operative earlier, in his work *Fuudo* (1935). In *Fuudo*, Watsuji proposes that a person is realized as he or she closely interacts with *fuudo* 'climate (and mores),' and that this process of interaction and integration serves as the basis of human ontology. For Watsuji, a person is also a betweenness in the social network, as the Japanese word for person, *ningen* (lit., *nin* 'person' and *gen* 'between') implies. Watsuji emphasizes that the concept of self cannot be defined without sufficiently considering the social relationship between the self and others, which in fact are definable only in their betweenness.

Watsuji's suggestion that a direct causal relationship exists between nature and culture is perhaps too simplistic. As Augustin Berque points out, Watsuji's severely limited understanding of nations outside Japan leads him to oversimplify the nature-culture relationship. And one may rightfully criticize Watsuji's method of interpreting phenomena based on "a logic of identification" (Berque 1992, 101) as too metaphorical and lacking in reason. Still, I believe there is evidence (linguistic or otherwise) that the Japanese tend to make a relatively strong emotional and psychological investment in the enhancement of relational selves.

Arimasa Mori advances the notion of the non-autonomous self even further and defines the Japanese self as "thy thou." First Mori develops the concept he calls *nikoo kankei* 'binary combination' or 'binary rapport' (1979, 66). According to Mori, in binary combination two persons construct an intimate relationship, and that relationship serves as the ontological basis for each person.

> I mentioned earlier that among "Japanese," "experience" defines plural persons—more specifically two persons—or the relationship between them. What does this mean? This view of "defining two persons" leads us to conclude that it is impossible for us to analyze our experience to the extent that it defines an experience as an "individual" experience. . . . Essentially, among "Japanese" what opposes "thou" is not the "self." Instead, what opposes "thou" is also a "thou" from the point of view of your "thou." . . . For example, if we consider a parent as "thou," it might seem obvious to consider the child "self." But this is far from the truth. The child is not the "self" that has its ontological root in its "self." Rather, the child experiences self as "thou" from the perspective of the parents, who in turn are "thou" from the child's point of view. (Mori 1979, 63–64; my translation)

For Mori, what opposes "thou" in Japanese is not "self" but rather, a "thou" from the point of view of your "thou," thus defining Japanese self as *nanji no nanji* 'thy thou.'

Mori's characterization of the Japanese self antedates a similar view discussed by Mara Miller. Miller, in her discussion of Japanese selfhood and subjectivity, introduces the concept of "gender-independent co-subjectivity." Japanese men and women are, regardless of gender, constructed as "Subjects" in a relationship between two Subjects (co-subjectivity) rather than in a relationship between

Subject and Object. According to Miller (1993, 482), in Japan "sub-jectivity seems to co-exist routinely with a genuine sense of shared identity," which yields co-subjectivity, "the formation of the Subject through identification with a group or community."

Robert J. Smith (1983, 74), following the work of David W. Plath, also supports the idea of an "interactionist self." Plath (1980, 3–5) contends that the Japanese interactionist self emerges in social relations, and that awareness of self is endlessly re-created as one lives on and responds to the responses of others. In fact, Plath warns that to label the Japanese self immature is no more than an example of western stereotyping.

> Furthermore the stereotypes may, however unintentionally, amount to an ethnic snub. For the person who is "dependent," whose self is "submerged," who has "weak and permeable ego boundaries"—phrases applied to the Japanese—is by Western measures immature. He can scarcely be acknowledged to be "his own man," gliding about with Emersonian self-reliance. Such images fail to take account of the expanding awareness of the world and the self, the ripening capacity to care for others in their terms, the increasing ability to apply one's own experience, that are hallmarks of the mature person in Japan as elsewhere. (Plath 1980, 4)

I must hasten to add that the image of the Japanese self por-trayed here is not unique to the Japanese. Scholars have suggested that many other cultures—Asian, African, Latin-American, south-ern European—exemplify the interdependent view of the self. In a review of these ideas, Hazel Rose Markus and Shinobu Kitayama state: "We suggest that for many cultures of the world, the Western notion of the self as an entity containing significant dispositional attributes, and as detached from context, is simply not an adequate description of selfhood. Rather, in many construals, the self is viewed as *inter*dependent with the surrounding context, and it is the "other" or the "self-in-relation-to-other" that is focal in individual experience" (1991, 225; emphasis in original). The concepts of independent and interdependent selves bear a significance, far beyond the Japan–U.S. framework.

The Construction of Japanese Selves

More concretely, though, what constitutes the self in Japan? Along with Nancy R. Rosenberger (1992, 67), I take the position that self is not "transcendental with an ultimate meaning within itself." The meaning of self, or more appropriately "selves," derives from its interrelationship with others. Furthermore, Patricia J. Wetzel (1994) contends that the concept of situationally dependent *uchi* with fluid boundaries is critical for understanding Japanese selves. According to Wetzel, rather than the "I" of Indo-European languages, it is the *uchi* relationship that serves as an anchor for identifying Japanese selves. Self is not rigid, stable, constant, and standing alone. It is a changing, forming, fluid awareness based on social relationships, and it bears meaning in relation to one's thought, to other people, and to contexts.

Takie Sugiyama Lebra (1992) describes these variable Japanese selves as "the interactional self," "the inner self," and "the boundless self." In the interactional self, Lebra singles out two polar orientations, "presentational" and "empathetic." "Presentational" is the self that consists of "continuous reflexivity between performance by self and sanctions by the audience" (1992, 106). "Empathetic" is the "awareness of self as an insider of a group or network, or as a partner to a relationship" (1992, 108). In contrast to this interactional self, the inner self is a "precarious, vulnerable, relative and unfixed" kind (1992, 111). In the center of the inner self is the *kokoro*. *Kokoro* can be translated as 'heart, mind, emotion, and spirit' and occupies the most private part of Japanese being. *Kokoro* ordains a person's sincerity, purity, and moral standing. It enables communication. In *kokoro*, *seishin*, one's 'soul'—or in Harumi Befu's (1980) translation, "one's inner spiritual strength"—lives. This is a space not easily violated or influenced by others; it is where one can always find one's inner self, however precarious and vulnerable that self may be.

The "boundless self" is what one must obtain to be free from the self. Lebra states:

> In self-other relationship, we have characterized the interactional self as relative, multiple, and variable in accordance to where and how self stands vis-à-vis other; a less relative, more stable, fixed self is captured in the encapsulated inner self—the world of pure subjectivity. Now, in the boundless self, relativity is overcome by the mutual embracement of self and other, subject and object. Far from being actively assertive, self is supposed to be absolutely passive and receptive, and passivity entails the state of being empty. The ultimate self then is equated, paradoxically, with the empty self, non-self, non-thinking, mindless, or nothingness. Self-awareness itself is to be transcended. (1992, 115)

Although the boundless self or the inner self may be reached, Japanese people face a dilemma about how much selfhood to express in their daily lives. Certainly the Japanese self is socially non-autonomous, but how much autonomy should be claimed even in the inner self? Here, like Americans, the Japanese face inner forces pulling toward both dependence and independence.

The Construction of the American Self

Let us turn our attention to the concept of self in the United States. The term usually associated with self in the United States is "individual." Interestingly, the Japanese word for "individual"—*kojin*— often has negative meanings attached to it, sometimes even analogous to "selfishness." In *Habits of the Heart* by Robert N. Bellah et al. (1985), Americans are described as believing "in the dignity, indeed the sacredness of the individual." Anything that violates Americans' right to think, judge, and live their lives as they see fit is considered not only morally wrong, but "sacrilegious" (1985, 142). Americans hold dear the dignity and autonomy of the individual. They subscribe to "an individualism in which the self has become the main form of reality" (1985, 143). As symbolized by the image of the American cowboy, American individualism calls for the hero who must leave society in order to realize the moral good on his own terms. This connection between moral courage and a lonely individualism seems to be at the root of the American ethos.

Yet because their emotions pull them toward both dependence and independence, Americans remain ambivalent in their pursuit of the autonomous self. They seem to be aware that radical individualism is a dead end.

> The inner tensions of American individualism add up to a classic case of ambivalence. We strongly assert the value of our self-reliance and autonomy. We deeply feel the emptiness of a life without sustaining social commitments. Yet we are hesitant to articulate our sense that we need one another as much as we need to stand alone, for fear that if we did we would lose our independence altogether. The tensions of our lives would be even greater if we did not, in fact, engage in practices that constantly limit the effects of an isolating individualism, even though we cannot articulate those practices nearly as well as we can the quest for autonomy. (Bellah et al. 1985, 150–151)

Charles Taylor also warns against the extreme individualism that makes the individual's self-fulfillment paramount. He alerts us by saying that "a total and fully consistent subjectivism would tend toward emptiness; nothing would count as a fulfillment in a world in which literally nothing was important but self-fulfillment" (1989, 507). And "a society of self-fulfillers, whose affiliations are more and more seen as revocable, cannot sustain the strong identification with the political community which public freedom needs" (1989, 508). Taylor claims that significant others are not external to a person; they help constitute his or her own selfhood. This echoes Mori's characterization of the Japanese self.

Ambivalent Selves in Japan and the United States

One cannot escape feeling that both Japanese and Americans share a deep ambivalence about self and society. Parts of the samurai and the cowboy reside in all of us. We all wage internal battles between self and society. The simultaneous pull toward dependence and independence is a universal experience, but it differs in how self is sought in relation—or as opposed—to society. While a Japanese person is often forced to seek the inner and boundless selves in relation to society, an American considers that he or she is endowed with self and is often encouraged to seek self as opposed to, or at the expense of, society. A Japanese person finds balance between self and society by moving from "social dependence" toward "psychological independence." An American finds balance between self and society by moving from "social independence" toward "psychological dependence." Cultural forces in Japan and the United States sustain opposing directions within the relationality of selves and society.

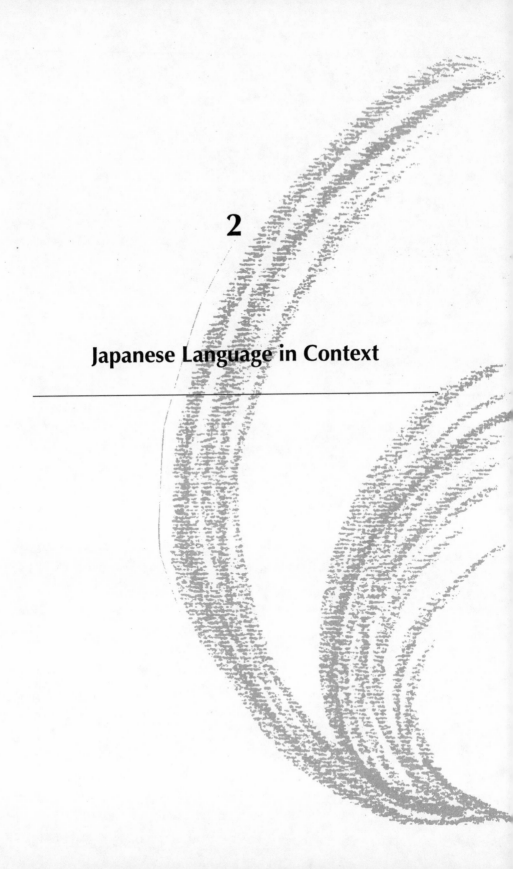

2

Japanese Language in Context

Notes on Japanese Data and Presentation

Although I have tried to keep Japanese-language samples to a minimum, in some cases they are necessary to the discussion. When they appear, word-by-word translations are given immediately beneath the Japanese transcription. English translations are also provided. Some extended texts whose linguistic aspects are not essential to our discussion are presented in English translation only. Japanese transcriptions of these examples in romanization are presented in the appendix.

For grammatical items, note the following abbreviations: BE (various forms of the verb 'be'), COM (command form), COND (conditional expression), HBL (humble form), IO (indirect object), IP (interactional particle), LK (particle linking nominals), NEG (negative marker), NOM (nominalizer), O (direct object), PASS (passive marker), Q (question marker), QT (quotative marker), S (subject marker), T (theme marker), VOL (volitional form).

The following notations are also used.

1. A recognizable pause is marked by /.
2. Listener response is given in parentheses. Listener response occurring immediately following the previous turn is expressed by a connecting latch mark.
3. Simultaneous utterances are marked by a large square bracket connecting their starting points.
4. H represents head nod (vertical movement); S represents head shake (horizontal movement).

5. Identification numbers for the authentic sample are given in parentheses; identification numbers for fabricated and/or manipulated sample appear in square brackets.
6. An asterisk (*) placed at the beginning of a sentence means ungrammatical and/or inappropriate expression.
7. Triple hyphens (= = =) indicate deletion of phrases or sentences.

The Japanese conversational data presented in this book were collected in Tokyo in May 1985. All the subjects were university students studying in Tokyo. Proper nouns appearing in the sample are altered to protect the privacy of those involved. Each conversation was performed by two speakers of similar age (between nineteen and twenty-three) and the same sex. Twenty pairs (ten male and ten female), for a total of forty speakers, participated. All conversations were video- and audiotaped in a controlled situation. No outsider was present, and there was minimal guidance. The statistical information presented is based on sixty minutes of conversation—three minutes taken from each conversation.

The American English conversational data presented were collected earlier in New Brunswick, New Jersey, in February 1985. Each conversation was performed by two speakers of similar age (eighteen to twenty-two, with the exception of one thirty-two-year-old speaker) and the same sex. Twenty pairs (ten male and ten female) participated. The video- and audiotaping conditions were similar to those in Japan, and statistical information is again based on three minutes from each conversation. (For those interested in more detailed information, see Maynard 1989.)

Sources for other samples presented in this book are given with the samples. Written materials from which some samples are drawn are listed in the references.

6 Styles and Varieties of the Japanese Language: Responding to Social Needs

In part 2 we examine the Japanese language in detail in four areas: (1) styles and elements, (2) phrases, (3) sentences, and (4) communication strategies. All languages provide different styles, for example, regional dialects, occupation-based jargons, formality levels, gender-based varieties, and so on. Japanese is no exception. In comparison to American English, Japanese offers more varieties that are explicitly different in their linguistic forms. These include varieties based on genres, speech situations, relative social statuses of speakers, foreign influence, and gender-based style.

The availability of variation built into the Japanese language system points to its society-relational orientation. A Japanese speaker is expected to choose a linguistically distinct style and a tone of speech appropriate in a given sociocultural context. It is often only in the appropriate style and to the extent the particular style allows that the Japanese speaker exuberantly expresses himself or herself. I do not imply that the Japanese speaker cannot or will not easily express his or her own thoughts or feelings. But for the Japanese, choosing a style is a more compelling task than for those whose language varieties present fewer explicit stylistic differences. In Japanese the commitment a speaker makes in his or her choice of variety conveys serious meaning, and when the stylistic differences are linguistically explicit, that information becomes more obvious in communication.

Genre-Specific Styles

Within the range of genre-based styles, one can easily find very different tones of expression and levels of formality. To witness the variability, I contrast samples from four genres. To retain some of the stylistic effects English translations have been made more or less literal. The Japanese transcript appears in the appendix. The samples given are from (1) a scientific text (Kamikawa 1992, 23); (2) a newspaper (*Asahi Shimbun* Oct. 24, 1993, 22); (3) a girl's comic book (Orihara 1992, 122–123; see figure 1); and (4) a work of contemporary literature: tanka and essay by Tawara (1988, 153).

(1)

Scientific text taken from *Reezaa-igaku no Kyooi* ('The wonder of laser medicine') by Kiyo'o Kamikawa (1992, 23).

Electromagnetic Waves

Around the nineteenth century light and electromagnetic waves were thought to be two separate elements. It was found, however, that both light and electric waves are transmitted at 300,000 kilometers per second, and Maxwell predicted the following. First, that "waves in electric and magnetic fields are transmitted through the air at the same speed as light," and second, that "light is one kind of electromagnetic wave." The content of the first point is illustrated in chart 1–5.

(2)

Asahi Shimbun, October 24, 1993. (Specific details have been changed to protect the privacy of those involved.)

A Taxi Driver Stabbed to Death
At Kashiwa, Chiba. Burned Taxi Found Nearby.

On the 20th, about 10:00 P.M., a 119 emergency call was made reporting "a white automobile is burning" near the Tone River at Bentenshita, Kashiwa City, Chiba Prefecture. Police officers from the Kashiwa Branch, Chiba Prefectural Police, found a private taxicab completely burned and a male body floating in the canal approximately seven meters from the burned automobile. The body was identified by the surviving family to be that of a taxi driver, Masaru Kanayama (age 60), of Ookubo 7-chome, Narashino City, Chiba Prefecture. Since Kanayama was found to have suffered stab wounds in his neck, the police, having determined that he was murdered and his body abandoned, set up investigative headquarters on the 21st.

(3)

Girl's comic titled "Voice of the sea, song of the sky" by Mito Ori-hara (1992, 122–123). Words in quotation marks appear in speech balloons.

Nanami:	That's Koota for sure!
Nanami:	"Oh, uh, Koota, it's me . . ."
Koota:	"Oh, you." "I was wondering who and it turns out to be you Nanami *(yo)*." "You still are a country bumpkin, aren't you? *(naa)*"
Nanami:	What?
Koota:	"I couldn't find a girl quite like you in Tokyo *(na)*." (giggles)
Nanami:	Koota! "That's not the Koota I know." "He was much nicer before!" "He got changed because he was in Tokyo *(n da)*."

The italicized phrases are interactional particles and sentence-final manipulations that express the speaker's subjective and emotional feelings.

(4)

Collection of tanka (a type of poem consisting of thirty-one syllables) with an accompanying essay by Machi Tawara (1988, 153).

> Deciding that this is the one,
> Fast along the seaside highway,
> To the tune of "Hotel California," driving, you are.

Why is it "Hotel California"? Why is he determined so? I wonder, he has his reasons—perhaps memories of past romance? What memories? Memories with whom? I now see his profile—listening to this song with feelings that I cannot see. This song that connects him to his past, this song that connects me to my future.

The background music outlines memories. One day I will also look back and find today in a distant memory. And I will perhaps then listen to "Hotel California." Alone, I will think of this white seaside highway in the summer light—the highway we are driving now. So for that day I'm listening to "Hotel California."

As with English, but even more clearly in Japanese, depending on the different genres of language, different aspects of communication are prominent. In scientific text and straight news reporting,

Figure 1. Excerpt from *Voice of the Sea, Song of the Sky* (Orihara 1992, 122–123)

the expected communicative goal is the transmission of information (presumably "facts") as objectively as possible. The use of emotionally loaded words and expressions—exclamatory words, interactional particles, expressive affixes and so on—is normally avoided. Such words and expressions are more prominent in literary discourse, where they appear in order to stir human feelings. Ordinary everyday discourse also includes many expressions that appeal to the emotions. Like written language (including written language depicting speech as in dialogues in comic books), styles in spoken Japanese also vary. Formal speech, for example, when compared with casual conversation, displays fewer intimacy-appealing expressions.

Although the characteristics of a particular language present themselves in various genres, I find that characteristics appearing in the most ordinary discourse types—everyday language—are the most significant. Because of its ordinariness and its closeness to our daily lives I have chosen to concentrate on this style while investigating the Japanese language. A discourse genre such as scientific text is expected to show greater similarity across languages and cultures, since the purpose of communication is more uniform and predetermined than, say, that of ordinary conversation. In the discourse of mathematics and science, for example, Japanese employs mostly common cross-cultural symbols and technical terms. By comparison, ordinary daily communication, where interpersonal and emotional stakes are high, contains much more socioculturally motivated use of language suitable to its speech situation.

Mixture of Styles

Although I have presented different styles as genre-specific, in reality, mixture of styles sometimes occurs. For example, in a television news program, a variety of speech styles is used, including different levels of formality. This seems reasonable when we observe that in a news program different kinds of interaction take place with reporters, interviewers, interviewees, news anchors, voice-overs, and the audience.

When the news anchors read prepared news copy addressed directly to the audience, the standard style chosen is formal (*desu/masu* style) without interactional particles. When the anchors talk to each other, offering commentary on various facets of the news stories, although the formal style is maintained, particles like *ne* and sentence-final expressions like *janai deshoo ka* 'isn't it the case?'

appear. When the reporters/interviewers talk to children, they adopt a style appropriate for doing so. Adult interviewees may answer in a friendly casual speech style. Sports and weather reporters seem to express friendliness as if they are talking to the audience, using primarily formal style, but with limited casual speech markers. Separate news report segments (such as background narrative and documentary report) often use informal written styles (*da* and *dearu*).

For example, in a small portion of television news (taken from New York's Fuji Sankei *Suupaa Taimu* 'Super time' news broadcast, November 11, 1994) where the anchor, a reporter reporting live from overseas, and a background narrator (voice-over) interact, three distinct styles are mixed. The anchor uses formal speech consistently, the voice-over uses *da*-style, and the reporter uses formal speech with particles and the nominal predicate *n desu*. So although styles may be genre-specific, certain genres consistently incorporate style mixtures as well.

Another mixture is that of spoken and written styles. In contemporary Japanese writing, a speechlike writing style appears that goes beyond the common practice of incorporating spoken styles in direct quotations. For example, fashion and lifestyle magazines targeting young men often use the colloquial male speech style in their feature articles and reports. Magazines for teenage girls mostly take on girlish colloquial spoken language. Romance novels for girls are written in what may be called conversational writing, which often features a first-person narrator speaking to the reader in confessional style. Writing as if talking in these genres adds to the friendly tone, giving the impression that the writer is speaking directly to the reader.

Likewise, personal letters and personal and informal essays particularly favor the incorporation of spoken styles, thereby increasing a feeling of openness, frankness, and friendliness. Styles are not static; manipulating them through choice and mixture is a dynamic process for realizing rhetorical effects.

Politeness

Politeness is universal. Virtually all speech communities use respectful forms, address terms, pronouns, and speech formulas as well as general rules of etiquette and protocol to express various levels of politeness. American English offers a variety of strategies for expressing formality, respectfulness, and general politeness. Politeness is required in every society, and all languages provide for different styles and variations to accommodate it. But the strategies used, as well as the level of intensity and overall importance of conventions of politeness, differ from one language to the next.

Japanese people are usually characterized as polite. Although the Japanese language has a built-in system of politeness strategies that requires a choice of appropriate politeness levels, this does not mean that the Japanese are always polite. As a casual peek into a karaoke bar or other such place for dining and drinking reveals, Japanese people, given the right place and the right time, engage in casual conversation that may seem to a foreigner quite impolite, tactless, and even downright rude. The myth that the Japanese are always polite has much to do with who is doing the observing; to an observer who is outside the *uchi* group, the impolite side of the Japanese is scarcely ever expressed. Only if participants are engaged in a blatant verbal argument (which is more prevalent than some would have you believe) do Japanese speakers drop the expected marked level of politeness and formality toward the *soto* person.

Each individual is simultaneously a member of several social groups—family, university, workplace, and so on. Depending on the context, one of these groups is emphasized over the others. Within the two contrasting and yet constantly shifting social territories, *uchi* and *soto*, a different social orientation and behavior is observed. In *uchi* relations, where the psychological distance among the participants is minimized, politeness is usually avoided, and intimate and less formal expressions are nurtured. In *soto* relations, where the psychological and social distance is accentuated, appropriate levels of politeness must be maintained.

Social Comfort

Why is it important to be polite? Perhaps because we seek comfort or try to avoid social embarrassment. In normal situations humans seek to maintain mutually comfortable feelings. In America, such a comfortable level is achieved by providing a relaxed atmosphere— by being friendly, by creating the impression that people are on equal terms, by showing interest in others, and so on. One of the most obvious strategies Americans use is calling each other by first names, which conveys that they are (or want to be) friends. People overtly make use of this practice by saying, for example, "Call me Bill." When a person's name is unfamiliar (as happens with foreign names), Americans specifically ask how he or she would like to be called. Even when there is a noted difference in social hierarchy between the persons involved, Americans feel more comfortable minimizing that difference. Of course the social hierarchy does not disappear simply when one calls a superior by his or her first name. But being on a first-name basis gives that impression and provides a comfortable feeling that a kind of social equality has been mutually constructed.

In Japan the management of social comfort includes the recognition and expression of situational and social differences among speakers. Japanese people normally try to achieve a comfortable level of interaction by physically and emotionally accommodating others, by giving gifts, by repeatedly expressing gratitude, by making others feel important and appreciated, by humbling and often blaming themselves in order not to upset others, and so on. Using polite expressions is one strategy for expressing feelings of respect and admiration. When Japanese speakers wish to achieve greater intimacy with a person to whom they should show social deference, they avoid overuse of politeness expressions or mix the polite style with other expressions of endearment. Still, even in fairly close relationships social deference is expected to be acknowledged.

Wakimae: *What Society Expects*

If the motivation for politeness is seeking for comfort, the general framework associated with politeness strategies is *wakimae*. *Wakimae* 'discernment' was introduced by Beverly Hill et al. (1986) and explicated by Sachiko Ide (1992). *Wakimae* refers to sets of social norms of appropriate behavior people must observe to be considered polite in society. The manipulation of politeness strategies is a concrete method for meeting the social rules of *wakimae*. Both American and Japanese speakers must behave according to the *wakimae* code. We can think of *wakimae* on at least a micro and a macro level. According to Ide, on the micro level *wakimae* involves "sense of place in relation to situational context" (1992, 300), and on the macro level it refers to "sense of place in relation to society" (1992, 301). Although both Japanese and American speakers wish to make their interactions comfortable by meeting *wakimae* standards, how they arrive at their comfort zones differs. While Americans make an effort to diminish social deference, Japanese make an effort to recognize deference and follow the *wakimae* conventions by choosing differentiating expressions.

Another aspect associated with *wakimae* is that Japanese society assigns stereotypical speech styles to certain occupations and social statuses. For example, university professors are expected to make liberal use of expressions with honorifics at formal conferences. Department store salesclerks are expected to use correct polite expressions to all customers, since the consumer has power over them. Salespeople at a mom-and-pop fish store, however, are expected to use a casual, energetic, and often informal speech style mixed with politeness. The seemingly rowdy speech heard in the produce market helps create a friendly atmosphere.

Checklist for Stylistic Choice

The list below gives categories for which Japanese speakers make stylistic decisions. Under normal circumstances the type of person who is first in each pair claims higher status and expects polite expressions from the second type of person. Regarding the situation and topic of conversation, the first in each pair requires relatively politer style than the second.

1. Demographic factors

   male/female
   old/young

2. Social status and relationship

   more prestigious occupation/less prestigious occupation
   high ranking/low ranking (within an organization)

3. Social and personal relationship

   soto/uchi (relation)
   past history (intimate past history nullifies social deference; a person who has performed a favor ranks higher to the person receiving the favor)

4. Situation

   formal (official or public situation)/informal (unofficial or private situation)
   in front of large audience/dyadic

indirect communication/direct communication (letters tend, for example, to be more formal than face-to-face speech)

5. Topic of conversation

   technical/personal

   official/personal

   traditional/new, foreign

Expressions of Politeness

One of the most common ways for expressing politeness in the Japanese language is to use formal verb endings, the *desu/masu* style. This is the style people normally use in formal, institutional, and official situations—for example, businessmen meeting in corporate offices, bank tellers interacting with customers, professionals attending conferences, and so on.

An informal, casual style is used among social equals. Extremely casual style is reserved for close friends. The levels of politeness expected from speakers representing different social levels are not reciprocal. Friendly informal speech from a social superior does not properly evoke a response in the same style. Among speakers of different social statuses, however, if the speech situation is personal and informal, as during casual talk while drinking sake, the style is likely to be informal. Choosing the appropriate style in different social encounters obviously requires experience, and even native speakers sometimes find it difficult.

Beyond verbal strategies, politeness in Japanese often requires a prescribed set of behavior as well as certain avoidance behaviors. For example, when making a request, the Japanese tend to apologize repeatedly. Adding apologetic phrases to one's request is an integral part of the politeness strategy. Tone of voice, level of hesitancy expressed, even facial expressions—such as smiling apologetically when asking a favor—make a decisive difference in persuading another to comply.

Honorifics

Beyond the formal/informal stylistic choice of verb forms to express politeness, Japanese honorifics generate another set of strategies. Honorifics are a group of linguistic expressions marking social deference, and in Japanese use of honorifics involves two separate strat-

egies. Besides formal and informal forms, the verb has the further
dimensions of respect and humility. Respectful forms are used when
addressing or talking about someone whose social status is relatively
higher than the speaker's. In the same situation, humble verb forms
may be used in reference to the speaker's own action and state of
mind. By humbling one's action, social differentiation is achieved.

Although the speaker's choice of honorific forms and formal/
informal endings depends on a combination of sometimes conflicting values assigned to various social, psychological, personal, and
situational variables, five situations occur most frequently and
demand the appropriate level of politeness.

1. The speaker and the listener share social, psychological, and
   emotional closeness (i.e., are *uchi* persons), the referent is someone of a lower or of the same social level, and the situation is
   informal and casual:

   The verb form is plain-informal: *kuru* 'come.'

2. The speaker and the listener may be either *uchi* or *soto* persons,
   the referent is someone on the same or a lower social level, and
   the situation is formal:

   The verb form is plain-formal: *kimasu* 'come.'

3. The speaker and the listener are *uchi* members, the referent is
   someone superior to the speaker, and the situation is informal
   and casual:

   The verb form is respectful-informal: *irassharu* 'come.'

4. The speaker and the listener may be either *uchi* or *soto* members, the referent is someone superior to the speaker, and the
   situation is formal:

   The verb form is respectful-formal: *irasshaimasu* 'come.'

5. The speaker and the listener may be either *uchi* or *soto* members, the speaker refers to his or her own action toward someone superior to the speaker, and the situation is formal:

   The verb form is humble-formal: *mairimasu* 'come.'

A Japanese person may choose several different speech styles
during a day. An example of how the choice is made is given by
Ide (1992). A professor is holding a graduate seminar in a Japa-

nese university. The students listen to the professor, silently nodding but rarely trying to take the floor. When the professor finishes, the students speak, observing *wakimae*, by selecting allowable topics and content. Students must use honorific forms in this situation. The honorifics indicate that the speaker is in a formal classroom situation and is a person who is expected to show deference toward the professor. The professor also speaks in a formal style, often with honorifics, indicating his or her sense of place in the formal setting and expressing respect for the situation. The professor may speak without honorifics outside class, but students do not reciprocate with nonhonorific forms even in an informal setting. Among themselves, students who enter the university in the same year tend to speak in a casual style that borders on rudeness. This intimate style reaffirms feelings of camaraderie and solidarity.

The choice of speech style does not depend solely on the social, psychological, and situational contexts described so far. One may always choose a speech style or a mixture of styles in order to create the atmosphere of intimacy/distance, equality/dominance, respect/disdain, and so forth. When using style as a persuasive strategy, the speaker's understanding of the social values associated with given styles plays a role and reflects the speaker's sociolinguistic ideology.

American Politeness

Although English does not possess verb changes, Americans use a variety of expressions to convey different degrees of formality, politeness, and candor. Polite expressions, of course, play a major role when asking favors. Think of a situation where one wants to borrow a pen. Let us compare how this request is negotiated in Japan and in the United States. (The following discussion is based on Hill et al. 1986.)

Americans use a number of expressions. Among them are more polite expressions, as shown in [5], and more abrupt ones, as shown in [6].

[5] Would it be all right if I borrowed your pen?
[6] Give me a pen.

Japanese people also use a variety of expressions, the most polite being [7] and the most abrupt being [8].

[7] Okarishitemo   yoroshii   deshoo ka.
    borrow-HBL   permissible BE   Q

Is it permissible if I could (humbly) borrow?

[8] Aru?
    there is

Is there?

These observations lead Hill et al. (1986, 359) to conclude:

1. There is a smaller difference in degree of politeness among the English request forms than among the Japanese request forms.
2. In the United States, there are fewer differences in the degree of politeness owing to the various person/situation categories than there are in Japan.

Differences in Japanese and American Politeness

A feeling of uneasiness in social settings is often caused by not knowing where one stands. Japanese speakers tend to mark linguistically where they stand in social settings in order to reduce social uncertainty. In strictly formal situations, Japanese honorific and formal forms are (socially) obligatory. Politeness expressions in American English, though important, are not obligatory, although, of course, polite forms are more expected under certain circumstances. Politeness can be more easily omitted in the United States without causing serious offense, because in many cases the volition of the speaker determines the level of politeness. When persons of different social status in Japan engage in formal conversation, however, the use of honorific and polite expressions becomes obligatory. Maintaining the appropriate stylistic register, which is often non-reciprocal, is necessary for successful communication. However candid or intimate they may wish to be, Japanese speakers must mark deference linguistically, if only minimally, in certain situations. It is the expected code for carrying on appropriate conversational interaction. Being obligatorily polite in Japanese under the right circumstances does not imply a lack of candor, friendliness, or intimacy. The proper politeness can actually enhance these sentiments.

Some American readers may find this asymmetric linguistic marking of social differentiation uncomfortable since it violates their ethic of "equality." For Japanese, using appropriate politeness strategies does not necessarily presuppose subordination to another's power or acquiescence in a rigid code of inequality. Above all, Japanese are concerned with making the encounter comfortable. To them, expressing deference through honorifics and formal expressions puts everyone at ease and makes people feel comfortable with each other. The user of these social conventions finds comfort in knowing that he or she is socially educated and follows *wakimae* rules. The receiver of polite expressions also feels comfortable because the deserved respect and deference Japanese society has taught Japanese to expect are reinforced through their continual usage.

Learning to use Japanese honorifics correctly does not come easily. Normally only when a person becomes a full-fledged member of society (as when holding a job for the first time) does the serious need to handle appropriate honorific forms arise. Honorifics are learned at home and at school, but the real training is often offered at the job site. Employers provide special training for this purpose. Books on how to handle social situations requiring honorifics also tend to proliferate. Knowing how to use correct honorific forms is a sign of being well educated. The fact that a person, especially a woman, can use honorific forms with ease, even in casual situations, indicates good breeding and enhances social status. For example, a woman may incorporate honorific and formal expressions when talking to her neighbor, not necessarily to mark social deference, but to show off somewhat indirectly that she has mastered a difficult and elaborate task and therefore comes from a high social class. Women are also inclined to use polite expressions more frequently for aesthetic effect. Language graced with honorifics and presented with politeness, unless egregiously excessive, is considered beautiful and elegant. Expressions used for their aesthetic effect are called "beautification honorifics." They bear little relevance to social deference.

Violation and Avoidance of Honorifics and Politeness

What happens when a Japanese person violates the rules of politeness? In general, noncompliance with the rules of linguistic politeness creates a negative impression. The violator is thought to be childish, unsophisticated, and lacking in common sense. Anyone who defies the social contract for speech pays a steep price and will be, as a rule, a person not to be treated seriously. It is also important to understand, however, that no Japanese person gains unlimited respect simply by using honorific and formal expressions correctly.

Avoidance of excessive honorifics and politeness is as significant a communication technique as is their use. One who chooses a formal speech style that is not required creates a greater social distance. It is as if Bob suddenly (and seriously) were to address his friend Al as Mr. (Allen) Johnson. Bob's behavior puts his and Al's otherwise intimate relationship into question. In a relationship where *amae* is allowed and honorific and formal forms are routinely avoided, the use of too polite forms is a violation of the relationship. The use of casual, almost rude, forms of speech in the appropriate context actually functions to reinforce the *uchi* relationship.

For example, a Japanese person reunited with an old friend after many years will revert to the speech style shared in the past, which situates both parties instantly in the old relationship. They are once again "buddies," and their speech reaffirms the continuing spirit of *amae*. Evoking a shared *uchi* language engenders feelings of solidarity and camaraderie. It has an effect similar to what a person experiences when using ethnic, social, and regional dialects to enhance a solidarity based on the same ethnic, social, or regional background. Although both situational and interpersonal context determine speech style in Japanese, a speaker can, through choice of speech style, purposefully create and manipulate the situation in order to highlight interpersonal meanings required for a particular encounter.

As Motoko Hori (1985) states, the standard *desu/masu* formal endings may also be thought of as the most noncommittal. When one cannot quite figure one's position in a relationship, *desu/masu* style is most likely to be chosen. *Desu/masu* style works like a "bubble" (Hori's term) that surrounds a person's private space.

Japanese speakers also get by sometimes without using honorifics. For example, as explained by J. V. Neustupný (1983), Japanese speakers may avoid repetitious honorific endings by not completing a sentence or by presenting talk as if it were a monologue (although the speaker is conscious of having an audience). Akiko Okuda (1977) also discusses what she calls the "boomerang effect," where two intimate speakers speak in a casual style, avoiding honorifics, as they indirectly address a third person. In such a situation the speakers can convey their message without using the required honorifics and without violating *wakimae*, since the message "comes back" to the third person like a boomerang returning to its starting point. This is not unlike situations when a mother speaks to her child in front of another adult, knowing that the content of her talk is indirectly addressed to that adult.

Japanese speakers do have room to maneuver among and within politeness levels, but maneuvering strategies must in general follow the rules of *wakimae*. Overall, there are fewer volition-based choices available to speakers of Japanese than to speakers of American English.

Japanese people, of course, sometimes violate the rules of *wakimae*. Think of people who are infuriated. They can follow *wakimae* only so far as they can control their tempers. As an example, let me reproduce here three utterances made by the character Sato, a junior high school boy in the novel *The sunflower diary* by Yuu Asagiri (1992), written for teenage girls.

(9) "Anta ga kimeru n   janai!   Ore no   mondai da.
    you S decide NOM BE-NEG my LK   trouble BE

Ore ga kimeru n   da!"
I   S decide NOM BE

That's not something you decide (abrupt)! It's my business, I decide (abrupt)! (Asagiri 1992, 96)

(10) "Sensee, ore,   ichikoo   ukemasu."
     teacher I   the First High School   take (the exam)

Teacher, I will take (the exam of) the First High School (formal). (Asagiri 1992, 206)

(11) "Sensee, ukatta.   Ore, ukarimashita."
     teacher passed the test I   passed the test

Teacher, (passed the test) made it (abrupt), I made it (formal)! (Asagiri 1992, 211)

All three examples are addressed to his teacher. According to the *wakimae* rules, Sato should speak as he does in (10), in a formal style. In (9), however, he is angry because his teacher had decided for him which high school he should attend, and Sato expresses his anger in abrupt endings. In (11), Sato is on the phone reporting to his teacher that he has passed the high school entrance exam. In his excitement he first reports it with an abrupt ending, but, almost as if regaining awareness of the fact that he is addressing his teacher, he repeats it a second time with a formal ending. The choice of style depends on the speaker's psychological and emotional condition. Though violations of *wakimae* occur, they are always understood as violations because society recognizes and sanctions the norm.

Obviously, both Japanese and American speakers must manipulate different speech varieties depending on each society's *wakimae*. In general, however, the need to make the correct choice of speech style while meeting the obligatory *wakimae* is more acute in Japanese. Choices must be made depending on the relationality between the speaker and the listener, between the speaker and the referent, between the speaker and the speech situation, and so on. While Americans strive to show friendship and intimacy by emphasizing equality in their choice of verbal expressions, Japanese strive to show closeness, deference, consideration, and admiration by appropriately manipulating different speech styles. Although there is some room for a Japanese speaker to choose a speech style as a self-motivated communication strategy, there is a significant difference in the practice of politeness strategies between these countries. More room is allowed for American speakers to behave based on their personal choice. Although both Japanese and American speakers strive for comfort, both the concept of comfort and the methods for achieving it remain different.

Loanwords and Made-in-Japan English

Beginning with China in the Nara period (A.D. 710–794), the Japanese people have borrowed many words from foreign countries. Chinese words entered the Japanese language over a long period, and many became so much a part of Japanese that they lost their status as foreign loanwords. Today, most Chinese words in the Japanese language are written in kanji (Chinese characters adopted into the Japanese writing system).

Around 1600 Japanese started to borrow many western words, particularly from Portuguese and Dutch. The Meiji period (1868–1912) saw the beginning of an influx of German, French, and most of all, English loanwords. Western loanwords are written in katakana, one of two syllabic writing systems developed in Japan. (Katakana is used primarily for transcribing western expressions, while another syllabic writing system, hiragana, is used elsewhere.) Western loanwords are pronounced according to Japanese phonological rules, mostly in the form of the available Japanese syllable structure. Japanese pronunciations of English loanwords are often incomprehensible to native speakers of English.

English Loanwords

Among western loanwords (English, French, German, Italian, Dutch, and Portuguese) English loanwords are by far the most numerous. According to a *Kokuritsu Kokugo Kenkyuujo* (National Language Research Institute) study (1964), English words constitute 80.8 percent of the total loanwords. English loanwords flooded the Japanese language after World War II. According to Kooji Sonoda (1983), more than 10,000 of the 25,000 words listed in the Kadokawa dictionary of loanwords were borrowed after 1945.

Sometimes a homonym in English may appear in Japanese with two distinct pronunciations. In the case of the word "strike," *sutoraiku* means a strike in baseball, and *sutoraiki* means a strike in the labor movement. *Sutoraiki* is often shortened to *suto*. A loanword may have a specialized meaning within the same semantic field as a Japanese word. For example, the word *biru*, a shortened version of the English word "building," normally refers to tall, western-style buildings only, while the Japanese word *tatemono* 'building' refers to other types of buildings. Long foreign words are often shortened, as is shown by *biru, hankachi* 'handkerchief,' *depaato* 'department store,' and so on. Multiple words may be shortened also, often to four syllables: *pa-so-ko-n* 'personal computer,' *ma-su-ko-mi* 'mass communication.'

A more recent four-syllable Japanese English is *ka-a-na-bi* 'car navigation,' referring to a computer-assisted road map/navigation system for automobiles (*Tokyo Walker* 1995, 37). Such related words as *ruuto deeta* 'route data,' *ooto riruuto* 'auto reroute' and *boisu gaido* 'voice guide' also appear.

In contemporary Japan, the proliferation of loanwords in the mass media is especially notable. For example, according to Michael L. Maynard (1993), the occurrence of foreign and loanwords in Japanese print advertising is extremely high. In three men's fashion/lifestyle magazines in Japan—*Hot Dog Press* (Dec. 10, 1992, issue), *Fineboys* (December 1992 issue), and *Check Mate* (December 1992 issue)—a total of ninety-four full- and two-page advertisements was examined. Loanwords in katakana or foreign words in the English alphabet appeared in 97.92 percent of all advertisements. Of course the abundance of English phrases is reflected in the choice of the magazine titles as well—all use the alphabet.

For an example, let us examine the Edwin jeans advertisement shown in figure 2 (from the back cover of *Check Mate* [December 1992]). We find the sentence *Edowin wa, denimu kara umareta* 'Edwin was born from denim' which contains, along with kanji and hiragana, loanwords in katakana. Note also the use of the English copy "Denim is Edwin" and the sign in the background, "Edwin's Coffee and Gas Open 24 hrs." These English words give authenticity to the product. The jeans are made of cotton from the United States, and so on. Note also the play on the English words "EDWIN" and "DENIM." The word "EDWIN" is "born" from the word "DENIM," of which it is nearly an anagram. The *W* is an upside-down *M*.

The reader may ask why so many loanwords and foreign words appear in the Japanese media. In her 1990 study, Kyoko Takashi examined 513 Japanese television commercials on five channels broadcast between January 28 and February 5, 1989, and 406 print advertisements from twenty-four widely circulated magazines and five leading newspapers published between November 1988 and February 1989. She categorized 5,556 tokens of loanwords (4,033 from print and 1,523 from television) according to function. The most frequent usage (45.1 percent) is to create a special effect. Loanwords make a text seem modern and sophisticated. Other functions include use of brand names, loanwords that introduce concepts otherwise nonexistent in Japan, technical terms, and euphemisms.

American (and western) images sell well in Japan. Adding foreign words in Japanese advertisements is a marketing device that makes a product look authentic, sophisticated, and with it.

Made-in-Japan English

Japanese people are fascinated with loanwords, and the number of such words continues to increase. Also substantially common are pseudo-loanwords—phrases of foreign origin (mostly English) created by Japanese speakers with meanings substantially different from the original. For example, *naitaa*, a neologism, is formed from the English word "night" followed by the suffix "-er," and it means

Figure 2. Edwin jeans ad, showing loanwords written in katakana and use of English. (Backcover of *Check Mate*, December 1992)

a night baseball game. Many English words used in Japanese are altered versions of their original meanings, and many are entirely homegrown for domestic consumption. For example, the term *kuuraa* (cooler) refers not to a drink or a food carrier but to an air conditioner, a substantial change in meaning. The term *saabisu* (service), also made in Japan, is used to refer to the custom of giving small gifts to regular customers or giving them a special discount.

The alphabet is more and more frequently used in contemporary Japanese. The nationwide Japanese railway network is called "*JR-sen*" (pronounced "jeiaaru-sen"), and the letters "JR" are its authentic written symbols. Some Japanese brand names that use the alphabet are a source of amusement to English speakers. For example, how appetizing is a powdered cream for your morning coffee called "Creap"? How about an "Ion Supply Drink" called "Pokari *Sweat*"? (Of all possible choices, "sweat" seems exceptionally unfortunate.)

As funny as these phrases are, whether or not they make sense in authentic English is irrelevant. Language is constantly created anew in different situations and cultures, and nobody can claim a monopoly. In this regard Joseph J. Tobin raises an interesting point by saying, "There is a thin line between studying Japanese material culture and ridiculing it" (1992, 36). Although these and other English phrases made in Japan appear funny, to read these words as meaningless, ridiculous, or parodic is to engage in, as Tobin aptly puts it (1992, 37), a "smug orientalist discourse."

English Loans and Made-in-Japan English in Japanese Discourse

The amount of English incorporated into the Japanese language in recent years is phenomenal. I transcribed all the words of English origin, including made-in-Japan terms, that appeared in a fifteen-minute segment of a television program (news program aired in Tokyo between 6:00 and 6:15 A.M. on October 1, 1992, on Channel 10, Asahi Television Network). Below is a list of those words. The tremendous influence of English words in Japanese discourse is obvious. Spoken phrases are marked S; those that appeared on the screen are marked A. Entries marked by both S and A were spoken as well as shown on the screen. Japanese words combined with loans are enclosed in square brackets.

SA	*nyuusu furesshu*	News Fresh (name of news program)
SA	*men's plaza* [*Aoki*]	(advertising headline)
S	*akutio*	(name of a company—seems to be related to "action")
S	*nyuusu*	news
SA	*Nyuuyooku*	New York

SA	*doru*	dollar
S	*puro [yakyuu]*	professional [baseball]
S	*pariigu*	Pacific League (baseball league name)
S	*[Tookyoo] doomu*	[Tokyo] Dome (indoor baseball facility)
SA	*[Seibu] raions*	[Seibu] Lions (name of a baseball team)
S	*[Nihon] hamu*	[Japan] Ham (name of a baseball team)
S	*riigu [yuushoo]*	league [champion]
S	*maundo [joo]*	[on the] mound (of the baseball field)
S	*battaa*	batter
S	*refuto*	left
S	*[naga] shiizun*	[long] (baseball) season
S	*[kon] shiizun*	[this] (baseball) season
S	*[Seibu] nain*	[Seibu] nine (referring to the team)
S	*[Tookyoo] purinsu hoteru*	[Tokyo] Prince Hotel
S	*seriigu*	Central League (baseball league name)
S	*chiimu*	team
S	*iishii*	EC
S	*Yooroppa*	Europe
S	*Igirisu*	England
SA	*Rondon*	London
S	*Denmaaku*	Denmark
S	*Furansu*	France
S	*[soosa] misu*	[operation] mistake
S	*ponpu*	pump
S	*[jin'iteki] misu*	[human] error (mistake)
S	*[tanjun] misu*	[simple] mistake
S	*[kikai koosaku] meekaa*	[machine tool] maker
S	*burokku [betsu]*	[each] block

S	[*issenman*] *ton*	[ten million] tons
SA	*ANN* [*keiretsu*]	ANN (communication network) [related]
SA	*AAB* [*Akita*]	AAB [Akita] (name of a broadcasting station)
A	[*otenki*] *mappu*	[weather] map
A	[*AOKI*] *RENAISSANCE IN ITALY*	(advertising headline)
S	[*Itchaku no*] *suutsu*	[one] (men's) suit
A	[*onsen*] *puuru*	[hot spring] (bathing) pool
A	[*Hatoya*] *hoteru*	[Hatoya] Hotel
A	*san* [*Hatoya*]	Sun [Hatoya]
A	*waarudo suupaa*	world super
A	[*danjo*] *bareebooru* [*taikai*]	[male/female] volley ball [competition]
A	*chiketto Pia*	ticket Pia
S	*suponsaa*	sponsor
S	[*kikai*] *rentaru*	[machine] rental
A	*AKTIO*	(name of a company)
S	*nettowaaku shisutemu*	network system
SA	*akutio* [*rettoo*]	Aktio [archipelago]
A	*JH*	J(apan) H(ighway) (system)
SA	*OA*	O(ffice) A(utomation)
A	*century 21*	the 21st century
A	*guddo estetikku*	good aesthetic (salon)
SA	*TBC*	T(okyo) B(eauty) C(enter)
A	*Tokyo Beauty Center*	(name of a total-body beauty spa)

Masculine and Feminine Speech

How Women Use Language

Although differences between masculine and feminine speech style in formal Japanese are limited, in casual Japanese there are a number of differences. The differences between masculine and feminine speech style I discuss should, however, be understood within the broader category of a more or less blunt versus a more or less gentle style. When the circumstances are right, female speakers sometimes choose a rather blunt style, and male speakers a gentle style. Although I use the terms "masculine" and "feminine," certain aspects of styles are used across genders.

Perhaps the most prominent difference between masculine and feminine speech is the use of different interactional particles. Nobuko Uchida's analysis of twenty pairs of conversations among Japanese college students shows the following distribution of particles (table 1).

Ze and *yo na* are used strictly by males, while *wa* and *kashira* are used strictly by females. Interestingly, particles restricted to males express the forcefulness of the statement; those restricted to females express a softening, hesitant effect.

Beyond particle usage, masculine and feminine speech differs sharply in the following areas:

1. Feminine speech is restricted in the use of abrupt expressions demanding action, for example, the use of the negative demand *na*.

    [12] Sonnani   kangaekomu *na*   yo.
         so much   think   NEG-COM   IP

    Don't think so hard.

TABLE 1.   Use of Particles in Male and Female Speech

Particles	Percentage of Use		Frequency per 10 minutes
	Male	Female	
ze	100	0	0.13
yo na	100	0	0.30
jan	85	15	1.00
yo	81.3	18.7	5.75
sa, saa	77.1	22.9	17.45
no	67.3	32.7	2.45
na, naa	57.5	42.5	11.58
ne, nee	57.3	42.7	39.28
yo ne	39.5	60.5	4.35
wa	0	100	0.10
kashira	0	100	0.23

Source: Adapted from Uchida 1993, 165.

2. Feminine speech is restricted in the use of abrupt expressions demanding an answer, for example, the question expression *dai*.

(13) Dare to   iru n   *dai?*
     who with be   NOM Q

Who are you with?

3. Feminine speech is restricted in the use of utterances with strong statements or utterances insisting on one's position expressed in abrupt form; for example, the volitional form *yoo/oo*.

(14) Soo da na, kimi ni dake wa oshiete*okoo.*
     so BE IP you to   only T   tell-VOL

Well, just you, I'll let you know.

Although male speakers can use the nonpolite abrupt forms listed above to encourage closeness and intimacy, female speakers normally do not. Female speakers are generally expected to express closeness through less abrupt forms.

References to Women

Another aspect of the language and gender issue is how society refers to men and women. Orie Endoo (1993) examined 919 newspaper columns introducing prominent people—721 males and 198 females—from the July 1990 to June 1991 issues of three Japanese newspapers (*Asahi, Mainichi*, and *Yomiuri*). When the profession of the woman interviewed was referred to, it was often marked "female." For example, "female Lieutenant Governor," "female Diet Member," "female manager," "female editor," "female leader," "female treasurer," and "female navigation officer." No marker was attached to a man's profession.

In addition, when a woman was interviewed, information about her family was included much more frequently (see table 2).

Although masculine and feminine styles mostly match the speaker's gender, sometimes styles cross the gender barrier. For example, a young girl who behaves like a boy, or who wants to befriend boys as if she were one of them, may use masculine speech. In a television drama "Kimi to ita natsu" (The summer with you), in which two young men and a young woman spend a summer together, the woman, Asami, speaks to Irie and Sugiya in a masculine speech style. The following utterances (translated into

TABLE 2.   References to Family in Newspaper Columns (%)

Newspaper	Total	Male	Female
Asahi	55.3	51.2	81.5
Mainichi	32.4	26.9	50.1
Yomiuri	22.2	16.7	50.0
Total	35.1	30.2	56.2

Source: Adapted from Endoo 1993, 199.

English, with Japanese style markers in parentheses) depict Asami's speech style. (The transcription of the Japanese text appears in the appendix.)

(15.1) *Sugiya:*   [noticing Asami looking at a photograph] What's the matter?

(15.2) *Asami:*   Sugiya . . .

(15.3)   Doesn't Irie have Keiko's photograph?

(15.4)   This picture. At the office.

(15.5)   The picture of everyone together *(minna no shashin daro?)*

(15.6) *Sugiya:*   Oh, they began dating only a short time ago, so.

(15.7) *Asami:*   I see.

(15.8)   It must be sad *(samishii daroo na)*,

(15.9)   if the situation doesn't change *(kono mama dattara sa)*.

> Transcribed from "Kimi to ita natsu," New York Fuji Sankei, television program, July 22, 1995; my translation.

Asami calls her male friends by their last names only, Sugiya and Irie; she consistently uses the *da*-style, including *daro* and *daroo*, forms normally used by males. Although Asami follows *wakimae* when interacting with other people, her choice of masculine style when interacting with boys seems appropriate for the "just-a-friend" behavior she maintains in the drama. The masculine speech enhances the sense of solidarity; Asami feels like one of the boys.

As is evident from this and other examples, the speaker's gender is not the only determinant for choosing masculine or feminine speech. Gender interacts with other variables including (1) psychological factors (e.g., social identification), (2) social and ideological factors (e.g., power associated with masculine speech), (3) situational factors (e.g., framing of the situation), and (4) discourse factors (e.g., topic). The choice of feminine and masculine speech style is a complex process.

Women's Language in the United States

In Robin Lakoff's 1975 book, *Language and Women's Place*, the author pointed out that both the kind of language women use and how women are referred to in the United States illustrate that women are victims of gender bias. For example, women use (1) special vocabulary ("dart" in sewing), (2) emphatic (but often meaningless) phrases such as "divine," (3) rising intonation for nonquestion sentences, (4) hesitation phrases and fillers such as "well," "kinda," (5) emphatic "so," (6) hypercorrect grammar (they consistently use grammatically appropriate expressions and avoid slang), (7) extremely polite expressions, (8) tag questions such as "John is here, isn't he?" and (9) fewer swear words than men. The overall image of women's speech is one of uncertainty and powerlessness.

Fifteen years later, Deborah Tannen, a student of Lakoff, published the best-seller, *You Just Don't Understand*. In this book Tannen maintains that neither male nor female speech style is better or more correct; they are simply different. Their differences are not dissimilar to those observed in conversational styles within and across cultures. The female style is a product of women's wishing to share intimacy and a feeling of community. The men's style results from their tendency to seek independence and their sense of contest.

Taking Tannen's thesis a step further, I feel that the two different speech styles in the contemporary United States are better described as cooperative and competitive. American women can choose either style depending on the situation and their intentions. What American woman would say "divine" in a corporate boardroom? Male speakers may also choose the cooperative over the competitive style because it may be more effective in some situations.

Freedom to Choose

Speakers of American English usually have more freedom in their choice of style than Japanese speakers. The difference between men's and women's speech in the United States does not lie so much in features internal to the language as it does in the way the language is used for interpersonal effect. For example, as Tannen points out, when a woman talks about her troubles she expects her partner to respond by offering matching troubles. Talk is for rapport, not necessarily for problem-solving. For male speakers, however, a problem or a "trouble" is something to be solved. His first response is likely to be something like, "I'll fix it for you," although this is not what the woman is looking for. The asymmetries of women and men talking at cross-purposes, although difficult to avoid, are not built into English. The Japanese language itself, however, contains certain expressions that are restricted and are intimately associated with the speaker's gender. Japanese speakers have, in general, less freedom in choosing cross-gender styles.

Empirical studies support Lakoff's and Tannen's distinctions between American men's and women's speech. Pamela Fishman (1978), for example, examined seven hours of audiotaped conversations of three couples who were either in intimate relationships or had fairly recently married. Her study shows that women send more supportive listener responses and ask more questions (women asked questions 150 times, men only 59 times), which suggests that women are more accommodating to men.

But when the conversation is between same-gender speakers, differences between men's and women's speech diminish. I examined the American conversations I had collected. During the thirty minutes of female speech (three-minute segments from ten female-female pairs), female participants sent listener responses 219 times; during the thirty minutes of male speech (three-minute segments from ten male-male pairs) the frequency was 209. Female listeners sent listener responses 196 times while the partner was speaking; males, 177 times. These differences do not seem to substantiate Fishman's claim that women's speech is more accommodating. And in my sample men asked questions seventy-three times (compared to women's sixty-nine times), which runs contrary to Fishman's findings.

Men's and women's speech styles in America may have begun to converge between the 1978 and the 1985 data collections, but it is more likely that the archetypal characteristics of men's and women's speech styles are highlighted when speakers are not of the same gender, especially if the speaker's gender is socially significant. In business transactions, men and women are expected to speak in a similar style. But when men and women get together at a bar, men may elect a manly speech style, while women's style is more womanly. Gender-based speech style cannot be adequately understood without considering the speech context.

Further studies are necessary for understanding how masculine and feminine speech styles are used in various facets of communication. Needed are studies that do not neglect the immediate discourse context in favor of such often politicized social variables as gender. We have yet to hear the last word on the existence and extent of gender difference in Japanese and American speech. Ironically, so-called women's language has claimed its difference from men's speech so strongly in the United States that it is almost considered a foreign language, as figure 3 shows.

The distinction between masculine and feminine speech in everyday Japanese points to the society-relational orientation of the Japanese language. In general, (the speaker's gender has a language-explicit value, and gender plays a more prominent role in determining how speakers express themselves than in the United States.) We must be careful not to conclude hastily that all women in Japan are more restricted in their pursuit of freedom and are socially powerless, nor should we conclude that all men are free and socially powerful. But at least in terms of language, despite recognized exceptions of cross-gender styles, masculine and feminine styles differ, and crossing the gender line can result, especially in formal situations, in social disapproval for both male and female speakers.

Youth Language

The language of young people differs from that of the mature population. In recent years some of the features considered distinctive

"Talk to me, Alice. I speak woman."

Figure 3. Women's speech—a foreign language? (Cartoon from *The New Yorker*, 29 June 1992, p. 37. Drawing by M. Stevens; © 1992 The New Yorker Magazine, Inc.)

of the younger generation have taken root in the language of people in their thirties. My discussion is based on Hideo Satake's (1995) work on the language of Japanese youth.

One of the more noteworthy features of sustained youth speech is what Satake calls *han-kuesuchon* 'half-question.' The half-question refers to the rising tone accompanying certain phrases within a nonquestion expression. Satake's (1995, 58) example follows. Upward arrows indicate rising tone.

(16) Ano hito   to   wa   kachikan ↑   ga   chigatteite,
　　 that person with T   value system S   differ

　　 iken   no itchi ↑   ga nai   n   desu.
　　 opinion LK agreement S   BE-NEG NOM   BE

My value system ↑ differs from that person's and there is no agreement of opinions ↑.

The speaker's rising tone at phrase breaks does not pose a question. Rather, it anticipates approval from the listener, permission to continue the talk.

Another noteworthy feature of youth speech includes *janai desu ka* 'isn't it?' *toka* 'and some other things,' *mitai na* (something like), *dashii* (and then), or *tarishite* (such and like) added in utterance-final position.

(17) Watashi wa mainichi inu no sanpo ni iku janai   desu ka.
　　 I   T everyday dog LK walk IO go BE-NEG BE Q

　　 Sono toki ni . . .
　　 that time at

Everyday I take the dog for a walk, right? At that time . . .

Instead of making a statement, *inu no sanpo ni ikimasu* 'I take a dog for a walk,' the speaker ends the first sentence with *janai desu ka*. Here again, the speaker does not expect the partner to answer. Rather than yielding the turn, the speaker simply continues. But at the point where *janai desu ka* is inserted, the impact of the words is softened. This gives the impression that the speaker is solicitous and considerate.

Young Japanese also soften their statements by attaching phrases of uncertainty at the end of the utterance—*toka, mitai na, dashii, tarishite,* and so on. For example, when a young speaker is asked where he or she went for the summer, the answer may be

"*Bali-too toka*" 'Bali and so on,' even when the speaker's summer trip was to Bali only. Likewise, when asked about a new member to the group, a young speaker may respond "*Moo aitaku nai mitai na . . .*" 'Well, like I wouldn't want to meet that person again, maybe, you know.'

The motivation for adding this softening effect, however, is not limited to accommodating to others' feelings. As Satake notes, softening is a rather aggressive strategy that the speaker, vulnerable and concerned with the partner's possible criticism, uses to silence potential disagreement.

According to Akihiko Yonekawa (1995a, 1995b), youth language features extensive word formation, including but not limited to a mixing of English and Japanese words (e.g., *chikin-hada*, meaning *tori-hada* 'goose bumps'), changed expressions (e.g., *okone-mochi* 'person with connections,' instead of *okane-mochi* 'person with money'), created verbs (e.g., *kopi-ru* 'to make copies' and *deni-ru* 'to eat at Denny's'), and deletion (e.g., *saten* instead of *kissaten* 'coffee shop,' *bakkureru* instead of *shirabakkureru* 'to play innocent,' *kons-aba* instead of *konsaabatibu* 'conservative').

Youth language imposes a certain style on written Japanese as well. Salient features are incorporated into writing, as manifested by the frequent use of interjections, onomatopoeic expressions, contracted colloquial verb forms (e.g., *tabe chau* instead of *tabete shimau*), emphatic elongated vowels, and use of nontraditional graphological marks (including ★ and ♥). As an example, let me cite an English translation of a paragraph from a young men's fashion magazine. I give relevant Japanese words in parentheses. The transcription of the Japanese text appears in the appendix.

(18) You, who can hardly wait for the glaring (*gin-gin no*) summer sky. Isn't your body getting antsy wanting to jump into the world of nature?
For this summer's outdoor life, light feeling is the key word.
Just think, even when you ask girls, if you get into a heavy mountain climbing or spend overnight in a sleeping bag (*nante*), no one would come along.

Lunch on the lake, beer on the river bed, nap on the beach.
Light sense (*karuui kanji*), just like you are picnicking, is IN.
Fashion is the same.
Heavy-duty fashion from head to toe is a bit (*chito*) painful.

On top of the usual town wear, add one outdoor fashion item
flawlessly *(bishitto)*, to create the atmosphere.
This light sense; it's cool and you will make it.
You, the summer boys, the bright sunny season is just around the
corner. *(Popeye* 1995, 17)

Many characteristics of youth talk are reflected in this paragraph. First, it is composed of short sentences (sometimes constructed with noun phrases only). Second, it makes liberal use of
katakana (including its use in Japanese words) to create an image of
modernity. (Words in katakana are italicized in the transcription.)
Third, the paragraph plays with language through use of onomato-
poeia *(gin-gin no, bishitto)*, emphatic elongation *(karuui* instead of
karui), colloquial phrases *(chito* instead of *sukoshi, nante* instead of
nado to), and so on.

Young women's language is also known to have a distinct character. According to Katsuaki Horiuchi and Yoshiko Oomori (1994),
in addition to employing the half-question and making comments
laced with uncertainty, young women favor certain in-words and
form words in a manner exclusive to them. Their favorite adjectives
are *kawaii* 'cute,' *suteki* 'wonderful,' *kirei* 'beautiful,' and *puritii*
'pretty.' These adjectives are used selectively depending on what
they modify. Young women may also add a polite note to their
expressions through adding the prefix *o* to many nouns. If the noun
represents something they dislike, however, they drop the prefix.
Depending on the speaker's attitude, for instance, the young Japanese female may say *ii o-mise* 'nice shop' or *anna mise* 'that shop.'
Another word formation particular to young women involves nouns
used as suffixes; *sugure-mono* 'superb quality goods,' *fuka-fuka-kei no
makura* 'soft pillow,' and *moo takusan tte kanji* 'the sense of that's
enough.'

As with feminine and masculine speech, youth language is not
directly indexed to the speaker's age. A young man or woman will
curtail youth speech in formal situations and use it abundantly
among peers, when solidarity is the priority. Psychological, situational, social, and cultural factors interact in a speaker's selection of
speech style.

7 Japanese Phrases:
Expressing Emotion and Speaker's Attitude

Japanese has much in common with other languages in its vocabulary and phrases, but we can also find subtle, yet important, differences. I have chosen phrases that contrast sharply with English to illustrate the semantic characteristics of Japanese phrases.

One of the consequences of being society-relational is that language does not place importance on propositional information alone (that is, the logical relations in a sentence, such as who-does-what-to-whom). Nonpropositional information (various levels of feelings and the speaker's attitude) is also very important. Human emotions find expression through various strategies, both verbal and nonverbal. Japanese is, compared to American English, richer in language-explicit means for expressing the emotional aspects of communication. Presenting accurate propositional information is important in any language. But the Japanese language is also rich in emotional expressions, which are influenced by the speaker's relationship to the psychological, social, and situational context.

Japanese offers a variety of attitudinal adverbial phrases that differ from their English counterparts in the scope of their meanings. The adverb *doose* 'anyway,' contrasted with English "anyway," illustrates the point. Japanese also demonstrates its society-relational orientation by making frequent use of interactional particles lacking in English. Two examples are *yo* and *ne*, compared to English "you know" and the like.

Additional categories of emotional (and sentimental) phrases are examples from aphoristic expressions that Japanese are fond of and words from popular Japanese songs—the kind people love to sing at karaoke bars. Last come swearing and expressions of ridicule. Contrary to the image of the indirect, reserved Japanese, here we find direct bursts of emotion.

Adverbs of Emotional Attitude

Attitudinal adverbs are known to differ significantly from so-called manner adverbs. Unlike manner adverbs, which modify the verb and have a direct bearing on the referential meaning (e.g., "slowly" in "I walked slowly"), attitudinal adverbs modify the entire sentence. Attitudinal adverbs mark the speaker's attitude toward the utterance as a whole. They are linguistic mechanisms that comment on the speaker's attitude or feelings during the speech event, and they function essentially extragrammatically. For example, according to Sidney Greenbaum (1969, 94), "attitudinal disjuncts" (attitudinal adverbs) express "the speaker's attitude to what he is saying, his evaluation of it, or shades of certainty or doubt about it." Perhaps the most famous attitudinal adverb in American culture is "frankly," as in "Frankly, my dear, I don't give a damn," immortalized by Clark Gable in the movie *Gone with the Wind*.

The Japanese Adverb doose

The Japanese adverb *doose*, normally translated into English as 'anyway,' illustrates a speaker attitude not evident from the English word (see Maynard 1991b, 1993a, 1993c, for further discussion). Consider the following:

[1] *Doose* ashita   no paatii wa taikutsu daroo.
    anyway tomorrow LK party T   boring   BE

Tomorrow's party will be boring anyway.

The interpretation process of this Japanese sentence requires evoking its appropriate situational context and attitudinal meaning. By using *doose*, the speaker communicates his or her belief that what will happen at tomorrow's party is predetermined and unavoidable. The word also expresses an attitude of submitting to this inevitability, often with a feeling of resignation.

More specifically, in *doose* sentences, a speaker speculates that what is described is certain to have existed, to exist, to have happened, or to happen because that event is part of how the world operates. Because the interpretation of *doose* is based on a mutual understanding of reality, it is particularly important that interlocutors share a similar worldview. When the speaker assumes that his or her partner already shares this knowledge, this confirmatory action encourages an increased level of rapport. The speaker hopes to strike an emotional chord with the communication partner and achieve a sense of empathy.

Doose *versus English "Anyway"*

At this point let us contrast *doose* and its English counterpart "anyway."

[2] **Doose* Tookyoo e   ikimasu ka?
    anyway Tokyo   to go   Q

Are you going to Tokyo anyway?

In this example, the use of "anyway" in the English translation does not seem inappropriate, since "anyway" can express the attitude of either the speaker or the addressee. In Japanese, however, *doose* is limited to (1) direct discourse and (2) the speaker's expression of his or her own attitude.

An excerpt with English translation from Kooboo Abe's *Tanin no Kao* (The face of another) offers a further illustration of the differences between *doose* and "anyway." At this point in the novel, the protagonist, "I," is looking for someone who can model a mask of his face. He spots a man in a dining hall and asks if the man is willing to do him a favor. The man shows some interest. "I" responds: "That's a weight off my mind. I can still move my seat, but these waitresses are so sullen. However, before I do, I've just one promise I'd like you to make. Since I'll not ask you anything about you or your work, you're not to ask about me." "*There's no work to ask about,*" he said, "*and if I don't know anything I can save the trouble of excuses later*" (Saunders 1966, 73).

The italicized segment is the translation of the original Japanese as given in (3) below.

(3.1) *Doose* kiite-itadaku   yoona   shokugyoo janai.
     anyway have someone hear such as occupation BE-NEG

(3.2) Soreni shiranakya   atode dareka   ni   iiwakesuru
     besides know-NEG-COND later someone IO offer an excuse

tema   mo   habukeru wake   da shi   ne. (Abe 1968, 85)
trouble also   avoid   reason BE and IP

The English translation does not accurately communicate the emotional involvement evoked by the attitudinal adverb *doose* in (3.1). The feeling of being overpowered by fate is reflected to some degree in the English translation "there's no work to ask about." But the emotional response that *doose* evokes in the original Japanese is difficult to locate in this translation. The almost desperate helplessness of not being able to hold a worthy occupation and the attitude of abject resignation expressed in this sentence are not reflected fully by the English translation. By adding *doose*, the speaker hopes to evoke some sympathy from the listener; the speaker indirectly sends the signal that he wants to feel emotionally connected in some way to his listening partner. The feeling invested in this sentence may be expressed as "Heck, don't waste your breath on me. My work isn't anything worth talking about, anyway." "Anyway" involves some emotional attitudinal meaning, but *doose* expresses a sense of doom more intensely than does "anyway."

Admittedly, *doose* is only one adverb, and the reader may question the importance I am placing on the emotional content of Japanese adverbs. But Japanese has many other emotionally loaded adverbs, including *yahari/yappari* 'as expected, at any rate,' *sasuga* 'as might be expected,' and *semete* 'at least, at most, at best' (see Maynard 1991a, 1993a for an analysis of *yahari/yappari*.) Note that the interpretation of *doose* as well as all these adverbs depends on a certain understanding of the world. For example, when one predicts that something will happen for sure (by using *doose*) based on one's view of the world, or when one expresses that something can at least be done (by using *semete*) despite what is normally expected in the world, the crucial information lies in the understanding of what is expected in the world. In using and interpreting these adverbs, one must draw from a common cultural understanding of the world and must position the adverbs in relation to society's expectation. In this sense attitudinal adverbs in Japanese exemplify the society-relational orientation of the Japanese language.

Every language uses certain strategies to express various levels of emotion and of the speaker's attitude. The difference between Japanese and English lies not so much in the fact that English lacks exact equivalents to these adverbs because it is possible to convey the meanings of these adverbs in English, however many words it may take. The real difference is that Japanese has compact words that express the speaker's emotional attitude and that offer easier access to encapsulate, express, and share feelings and attitudes.

Interactional Particles

Among Japanese particles, two types are recognized: (1) those that play a primarily grammatical function, marking grammatical relations within a sentence, and (2) those expressing the speaker's judgment and attitude toward the message and the partner, namely, interactional particles. Interactional particles include the short expressions *ne, sa, no, yo, na,* and the like (along with their variants), attached phrase-, clause-, and sentence-finally. Phrase- and clause-final particles are called insertion particles; the others are sentence-final particles. They appear frequently in Japanese and are especially pervasive in spoken Japanese. For example:

(4) About a pet dog

Soo da ne/ nanka sore mo sa natsu   da kara de sa/
so BE IP like   that also IP summer BE since BE IP

nanka nee/ kekkyoku nee/ mijikaku katchatte nee/
like   IP   finally   JP   short   clip   IP

Yeah, I guess so *(ne)*. Yeah, that was also *(sa)* in the summer *(sa)*, and somehow *(nee)*, in the end *(nee)* they did clip the hair (of a pet dog) *(nee)*.'

We find four occurrences of *ne(e)* and two cases of *sa* in this small segment of conversation.

Japanese provides these particles so that the speaker and listener may communicate with each other in an emotional and empathy-creating way. For example, Haruhiko Kindaichi (1957, 170) has observed that a Japanese speaker deplores letting a sentence end on a note of finality. Adding interactional particles at sentence-final position helps end the sentence with emotional affect. Tazuko Uyeno offers this characterization of the particles *ne(e)* and *na(a)*:

The sentence particle *ne* and its variants, *nee* and *na(a)*, are appended to any sentence type except exclamatory sentences and imply that the option of judgment on the given information is left to the addressee. Thus, these particles give the effect of softening the basic nature of each sentence type. As a result, the appropriate use of these particles reflects the speaker's consideration of the addressee, and the addressee feels more participation in the conversation with mutual understanding. Thus, these particles may be called particles of rapport. (Uyeno 1971, 131–132)

Frequent Use of Particles

To find out how frequently interactional particles are used, I examined their occurrences in the Japanese conversational data I collected. The frequency of representative interactional particles is given in table 3.

A total of 863 interactional particles occurred in sixty minutes of conversation. The sixty minutes included 1,244 sentences and 2,112 phrases bounded by pauses. Given the fact that Japanese interactional particles normally appear at the end of phrases, it turns out that they appear quite frequently, roughly once in every 2.5 phrase-final positions (see table 3).

Particles yo and ne

The two particles *yo* and *ne* can be discussed in broad terms from two aspects of communication—information-oriented and interaction-oriented. I propose that *yo* is used when the speaker assumes that he or she has more access to and/or possession of the information and wants to focus on the information conveyed in the utterance. *Ne* is chosen when the speaker assumes that he or she has less (or about the same amount of) access to and/or possession of the information and wishes to concentrate on feelings and attitude more than on information.

TABLE 3.   Frequency of Interactional Particles in Three-Minute Segments of Conversation among Twenty Pairs

Interactional particle	Number	%
ne	364	42.18
sa	148	17.15
no	138	15.99
yo	128	14.83
na	49	5.68
Other	36	4.17
Total	863	100.00

The choice of *yo* and *ne* can reveal the speaker's assumption of the level of the addressee's knowledge. Consequently, it can communicate important interpersonal meaning. For example, a teacher visiting his or her student's father may express his or her thought as in [5a] or [5b], depending on how the teacher views the student-father relationship.

[5] Ojoosan wa Tookyoo no daigaku e
    daughter T   Tokyo   LK university to

    ikitagatteimasu | a. yo |
    want to go | IP |
                    | b. ne |
                    | IP |

Your daughter wants to go to a university in Tokyo.

A teacher who assumes that the father doesn't know his daughter's wish selects *yo* based on the assumption that he or she has more access to and/or possession of information than the addressee. If the teacher's assumption is reversed, *ne* is appropriate.

In fact because one's access to and/or possession of information is directly linked to relative social power, indicating possession of information to a social superior may threaten the superior's position. In such situations speakers usually choose *ne* over the predicted *yo*. For example:

[6] Buchoo, ja   kaigi wa sanji   to yuu koto
    manager then meeting T three o'clock QT say fact

    desu ne
    BE   IP

Manager, so the meeting is at three, isn't it *(ne)?*

Even when one addresses one's boss to remind him or her of the time of the meeting—which means that the speaker assumes that the boss doesn't know or is likely to have forgotten—*ne* is the preferred choice. After all, the information provider gains instant power in the human interaction, and a social subordinate is expected to avoid disrupting the hierarchy.

The discussion of *yo* and *ne* points to a curious complementary phenomenon between information and interaction. When one has the upper hand on information, so to speak, he or she may feature it while deemphasizing the interaction process, including concern for (the feelings of) the partner. But when one has little information and faces a partner assumed to have more access to and possession of information, a speaker is more likely to focus on the possessor of the information, i.e., the partner. Armed with insufficient information, we wish to have our information legitimized by someone who knows more. A casual information exchange can become an emotional negotiation that forces the informationally weak to become interactionally dependent. To me this tendency is the key to understanding the complementary functional relationship between *yo* and *ne*.

The speaker's choice between *yo* and *ne* depends on whether the focus is on information or interaction. When information is stressed, the participants hope to complete the information exchange successfully. *Yo* signals this intention. If the information exchange does not occur as expected, a variety of emotional reactions can be evoked. Such reactions include an impression of self-centeredness and a lack of consideration and cooperation. Instead of achieving emotional resonance, the speaker may encounter a disappointing emotional response. *Ne* is a device that helps avoid or remedy this potential failure in interpersonal emotional involvement. It plays down the information and calls attention instead to interpersonal feelings, in an attempt to assure some level of emotional engagement. Or the speaker may choose not to use *yo* or *ne* at all, or both *yo* and *ne* together. The combination *yo ne* can evoke or communicate information not shared while simultaneously adding information about interpersonal affect. The mechanism for choice operates on both personal and interpersonal levels, for although the particle used expresses the speaker's attitude, it also reflects the partner's attitude, because the choice is based on what the speaker thinks the partner expects.

What is ultimately achieved through the manipulation of *yo* and *ne* is the speaker's personal expression. The speaker manipulates how the communication encounter should be viewed, whether information or interaction is in primary focus. The speaker shifts the focus between these two essential but different aspects of communication by the appropriate use of *yo* and *ne* in relation to the addressee's level of knowledge.

English "You Know" and the Like

In English, what we might call "attitudinal phrases" function like Japanese interactional particles. These attitudinal phrases normally carry minimal referential meanings; they are primarily used to appeal to interpersonal rapport and emotion. Beyond intonation, which plays a major part in English when expressing attitude, English speakers use the following strategies.

1. Vocatives (name, nickname, or phrases such as "honey," "my friend," and so on)
2. Tag questions ("don't you?")
3. Insertion phrases ("you know," "right," "like," and so on)
4. Connectives, as when ending an utterance by saying "but uh . . ."
5. Sentential attitudinal phrases ("I mean," "I think," "I don't know," "frankly," "honestly," and so on)

If we examine American casual conversation (taken from the conversational data mentioned earlier) these phrases appear quite frequently. For example:

About Rick

(7.1) *B:*   Rick would not like the idea/
(7.2)   if anyone looked at you in a bathing suit/
(7.3)   on the beach/
                    (*A:* You got it.)
(7.4)   *I mean*/
(7.5)   *you know*/
(7.6)   he's *like*/
(7.7) *A:*   He's a very fragile type./
                    (*B:* Yeah.)
(7.8)   But he's so tall how can you tell when he's looking at you/
             (*A:* laugh)
(7.9) *B:*   He's tall but *I mean*/
(7.10)   I'm getting used to that *you know*/
(7.11)   *like* it doesn't bother me at all./

In this conversation portion speaker B uses "I mean," "you know," and "like." These are used to manage the flow of conversation and convey personal attitude. In the American casual conversational data, "you know" appeared quite frequently; there were sixty occurrences in the data sample. Seventy-five percent of female speakers and forty-five percent of male speakers used "you know" at least once in the three-minute segment.

In examining "you know" in American English, I consider two primary uses: (1) with falling intonation and (2) with rising intonation. Here are more examples.

About new restaurants

(8.1) *A:*   Yeah I wondered that place is any good and I also wondered about/

(8.2)   *you know* where they used to have/Allen's?/

(8.3) *B:*   Yeah┌—there was./

(8.4) *A:*   └—They opened something new there./ ─┐

                                            (*B:* └─Yeah.)

(8.5) *B:*   Ronda or something./

(8.6)   I walked inside was kind of interesting./

(8.7)   Didn't look very crowded though I hope it/

(8.8)   *you know* catches on./

About escargot

(9.1) *A:*   Oh I like escargot./

(9.2) *B:*   I don't./

(9.3)   I just keep on thinking slime/

(9.4)   sludge/

(9.5)   sea bottoms *you know*./

"You know" in (8.2) marks the expression as a question about the identification of the restaurant. The fact that speaker B answers the question supports this interpretation. "You know" in (8.8), however, acts as a filler, occupying the pause between "it" and "catches on." The fact that this "you know" is pronounced quickly and softly supports this interpretation. Now in (9), speaker B, after expressing her opinion about escargot, ends her turn with "you know." In this way B, who thinks her image of escargot is common, encourages A to recall that common knowledge. "You know" is said with the falling intonation that marks the end of one's speaking turn.

English "you know" is used in the following situations:

1. To inquire about or confirm a piece of information that is shared with the addressee
2. To inquire about or confirm common knowledge in the society
3. To fill in a pause
4. To mark the end of utterance and/or speaking turn

"You know," ne, *and* yo *in Contrast*

Let us return to the Japanese sentence [5] and contrast it with its English counterpart.

- [5] Ojoosan wa Tookyoo no daigaku   e
      daughter T Tokyo LK university to

```
ikitagatteimasu |  a. yo  |
want to go      |    IP   |
                |  b. ne  |
                |    IP   |
```

Your daughter wants to go to a university in Tokyo.

[10] Your daughter wants to go to Japan, | a. you know? |
                                         | b. you know. |

Example [10a] asks whether the partner knows that his or her daughter wants to go to Japan, while example [10b] presumes that the parent already knows this and seeks confirmation.

The functions of "you know" in [10], when compared with the functions of *yo* and *ne* in Japanese, are significantly different. In Japanese the speaker decides the use of *yo* and *ne* based on his or her judgment of relative information access and/or possession, and the purpose of these particles' use is not limited to inquiring about or confirming the information itself. Choice of Japanese *yo* and *ne* also depends on whether the speaker chooses to feature the informational or the interactional aspects of communication. In English, as is made evident by the word "know," the expression "you know" is most directly concerned with informational content. Although there are functions common to *yo/ne* and "you know" (marking the end of an utterance, for example), there is also a clear difference. In English, although "you know" may act as a conversational filler, its primary use is to offer or elicit information. Japanese particles concern themselves with the speaker's assessment of the situation of talk—especially in its relational understanding of the partner's information access and possession. This distinction again points to the different role of relationality in Japanese and American speech communities. In Japan assessing the partner's knowledge level and behaving accordingly are the norm; in English, more importance is likely to be placed on information.

Words Dear to the Japanese Heart

One way to peek directly into the thoughts and feelings of the Japanese people is to look at the words they cherish. I have chosen some aphoristic expressions and favorite words to popular songs for this purpose.

Japanese people are often encouraged to have a few favorite mottoes. Elementary and junior high school classrooms often have an inspirational motto posted above the blackboard so that every student can see it and work hard to live up to it. Such phrases and rallying expressions appear even in factories and corporate offices, where they may be written in black ink with a brush, framed, and hung on the wall.

According to Yoshihiko Inagaki (1989), the ten most popular word categories, in descending order, are: (1) effort words, (2) sincerity words, (3) perseverance words, (4) thank-you words, (5) determination words, (6) thoughtfulness words, (7) greeting words, (8) harmony words, (9) love words, and (10) friendship words.

This list is based on a nationwide survey on attitudes toward language conducted by NHK (Japan Broadcasting Corporation). The survey was administered on September 8 and 9, 1979, in six hundred locations throughout Japan. The subjects were 3,600 Japanese people aged sixteen or over, of whom 2,639 responded.

The degree of consistency in choice of favorite words is surprising. I am not aware of any survey of this kind in the United States. The consensus on favorite words may have resulted from the common educational experience of the Japanese people. Admittedly survey research sometimes intimidates, so that respondents, in striving to be socially acceptable, may have overrepresented their love for virtuous-sounding words. Even so, the ten favorite themes can be interpreted as indicative of Japanese people's aspirations and moral values. The actual Japanese words selected are words that are somewhat abstract, yet subjective and emotional in nature. The phrase *doryoku* 'effort,' which is the favorite, seems to appeal most to people's emotional aspirations.

Another example of Japanese cultural texts is Japanese popular song lyrics. Traditional Japanese popular songs called *kayookyoku* (or *enka*), in contrast to mottoes, seem to favor sentimental words. According to Tadao Kabashima (1979), between the 1930s and the 1960s, the most frequently used words in traditional Japanese popular songs were "love affair," "heart," "dream," "to cry," "tears," and "flower."

More recently, Shigeo Hinata (1996) examined the initial word in popular song titles. Based on 2,700 titles appearing in a *kayookyoku* collection featuring popular songs between 1945 and 1995,

Hinata lists the following ten words as occurring most often in the initial position: *koi* 'love affair,' *kimi* 'you,' *ai* 'love,' *ame* 'rain,' *natsu* 'summer,' *hana* 'flower,' *anata* 'you,' *sayoonara* 'good-bye,' *Tookyoo* 'Tokyo,' and *akai* 'red.' Given that *koi* and *ai*, as well as *kimi* and *anata*, are synonyms, their prominence is even more impressive. The next most frequently occurring initial words are *otoko* 'man,' *yoru* 'night', *namida* 'tears,' *ano* 'that,' *aoi* 'blue,' *kaze* 'wind,' and *yume* 'dream.' Apparently sentimentalism continues to be of significant appeal in Japanese popular songs.

This sentimental tone carries through even when English words are used. According to Etsuko O. Reiman (1996), Japanese popular songs are incorporating more English words and sentences. For example, as recently as 1988, 577 of 704 (78.6 percent) of songs popular among youth contained English phrases. Such insertion phrases as "oh," "wow," and "hey" often accompany "you," "I," "my," and "me." In addition to such frequently appearing prepositions as "on," "up," and "in," English content words ranking among the top fifty are: "love," "baby," "night," "heart," "kiss," "dance," "blue," "tonight," "cry," "boys," "know," "dream," "chance," and "lonely." Although in general one expects popular songs to appeal to the emotions, it is no exaggeration to say that Japanese songs are overwhelmingly sentimental.

In contemporary Japan, popular *kayookyoku* or *enka* continue to spin heart-wrenching love stories and woeful tales of broken dreams. To give readers an idea of the kind of words favored, here is a translation of a song that was very popular in the 1980s. The title of the song is *Yagiri no Watashi* ('Ferry port of Yagiri'). (The transcription of the Japanese text appears in the appendix.)

Ferry Port of Yagiri

"Please take me and run."
"Come with me, my love."
Evening rain is falling
At the ferry port of Yagiri.
My parents' will, even that I have disobeyed.
Want to live for love, the two of us we do.

"Please don't leave me."
"No, I won't, my love."
The north wind is wailing
At the ferry port of Yagiri.

Wounded by vicious rumors, the town of Shibamata we are leaving.
Wherever the boat takes us, our destiny it is.

"Where are we going?"
"To some place where nobody knows us, my love."
The boat swaying, the oar creaking,
Off the ferry port of Yagiri,
Holding our breath, huddling gently together,
Rowing the boat into tomorrow, our parting this is. (Gotooshoin
1992, 195; my translation)

In many ways, Japanese people are, to overstate it, addicted to
emotional portrayals of human relations. Tear-jerking songs such as
Yagiri no Watashi are popular at karaoke bars. Wherever karaoke,
what Narumi Kunihiro (1994) calls "the electric geisha" machine, is
set up, even in the smallest towns in the Japanese countryside, these
emotion-laden stories are sung repeatedly night after night. Just as
Americans prize stories in which the underdog comes out on top,
Japanese people consider sincerity and devotion precious. On a
personal level, the Japanese hold these mottoes and sentimental
phrases close to their hearts.

The Japanese communicational style, which is brimming with
emotion, allows the Japanese speaker, within certain genre and
social situations, to express individuality freely. Far from being hesitant, submissive, and inexpressive, the Japanese express themselves
eloquently—often uninhibitedly, given the right circumstances.

According to Hazel Rose Markus and Shinobu Kitayama, different societies give focus to different kinds of emotions, depending on whether an interdependent or independent view of the self
is endorsed. In societies where the interdependent self is promoted, "emotions, such as sympathy, feelings of interpersonal
communication and shame, which have another person, rather
than one's internal attributes, as the primary referent are prevalent" (Markus and Kitayama 1991, 235). The kinds of emotions
packed into Japanese words are often other-focused, or at least
directly associated with the feelings of others. Even when ego-
focused emotions are prevalent, interpersonal and situational
circumstances must be right for their expression. Japanese
emotional expressions, although individual-based, respond to
relationality cues.

Swearing and Expressions of Ridicule

The reader may have the impression that Japanese people are thoughtful and considerate, always accommodating, or very emotional and sentimental. But the Japanese are no exception when it comes to such emotions as anger and hate. It is human nature to get upset, angry, and infuriated from time to time. Japanese use swear words, express anger, and ridicule others pointedly.

In the *uchi* context, Japanese people express frustration, anger, hostility, and fury with candor. Among friends, family members, even between teachers and students, where strong personal relationships exist, venting anger and frustration is expected. Because of the strong *amae* relationship, sooner or later the negative feelings will be assuaged. Most blunt verb endings are used with strong phonological emphasis. Swear words, such as *bakkayaroo* 'you idiot' and *chikushoo* 'damn (you)' are primarily used by male speakers. Here are a few examples taken from comics (see figs. 4–6).

(11) *Mr. Gori (teacher):*

Omaera zen'in hoshuu   da   hoshuu!
you   all   extra study BE extra study

Nigakki   mo sangakki   mo doyoo   mo
second semester also third semester also Saturday also

nichiyoo mo   zuu-u-tto hoshuu   da-a!!
Sunday   also forever   extra study BE

All of you, after-school study, I'm ordering you to do it!! (blunt ending)

(11)

Figure 4. Examples of blunt language (Mizusawa 1992, p. 52)

The second semester, the third semester, Saturdays, Sundays, forever . . . you are going to do after-school study!! (blunt ending)
(Mizusawa 1992, 52)

(12) *Editor-in-chief:*

Sassato shigoto shiro-o, kono noonashi kisha!!
quickly work   do   this   lousy   reporter

boonasu yaran   zo.
bonus   give-NEG IP

Get your work done, this (you) lousy reporter! There will be no
bonus for you!!

Reporter Taniguchi:

Hai-i!! Kuso.
yes   shit

Yes, sir!! Shit! *(kuso)* (Mizusawa 1992, 24)

(13) *Koota:*

. . . na wake nee   daro. Bakkayaroo.
     fact BE-NEG BE   idiot

That can't be! Idiot! *(bakkayaroo)* (Ikeno 1992, 191)

(14) *Reiichi:*

Kono onna ga kono onna ga oreno kao o
this girl S this girl S my   face O

dainashi ni shita n   da-a. Chikushoo.
useless as did   NOM BE   damn

This girl, this girl, she scarred (*lit.*, made useless) my face!

Damn! *(chikushoo)* (Ikeno 1992, 152)

Female speakers also use blunt endings, although the female use of
swear words is somewhat limited. A female may shout *baka* 'fool,
idiot' as shown below.

(15) *Nanami:*

Koota no baka!! Daikkirai!!
Koota LK fool   hate

Koota, such an idiot! *(baka)* I hate him!! (Orihara 1992, 130)

Interestingly, when girls become members of delinquent female
cliques (or behave like "bad" girls), they take on a male blunt
speech style. Speaker A in (16) offers one example of a typical
speech style of high school girls involved in threatening acts.

Figure 5. Examples of swearing (Mizusawa 1992, p. 24; Ikeno 1992, pp. 191 and 152; Orihara 1992, p. 130)

(16) *A:*   Ichinen   no kuseni taido   dekai   n
            first-year student BE despite behavior arrogant NOM

            da yo. Daitai nee nan   na no   yo kono chairoi
            BE IP anyway IP what BE NOM IP this brown

            kami. Dasshoku shite n   janai   no-o?
            hair bleach   do   NOM BE-NEG IP

            You are only a first-year student, but you're behaving like
            seniors. (blunt ending followed by *yo*)
            Anyway, what is this brown-colored hair of yours? *(yo)*
            Bleaching your hair, huh? *(no)*

Kaho: Kore wa umaretsuki de . . .
            this T natural   BE

            This is the natural color . . .

A: Umaretsuki demo nan   demo mezawari na n
            natural   or   what or   bothering BE NOM

            da yo ne.
            BE IP IP

            Whatever it is, it bothers me (blunt ending followed by *yo
            ne*). (Orihara 1992, 18)

When people in the *soto* relationship are involved in conflicting
positions, the formal speech style is maintained, but the tone
becomes critical, contemptuous, ridiculing, and often threatening.
The following segment is taken from a late-night television debate.
The television debate offers a public forum where people legiti-
mately engage in argument. In fact the participants are expected
(and are perhaps under some pressure) to express opposing views.
The participants were debating the animal-rights movement. Mr.
Kawai, representing the group that feels the animal-rights movement is too radical and has gone too far, talks fast, in an angry and
excited tone. The transcription of the Japanese text appears in the
appendix.

(17)

Well, I think animal-rights people are hypocrites. The reason is *(desu
ne)* that when they are asked what they would do in concrete terms,
they never give an answer *(yo)*. For example, Mr. Hirose *(desu ne)*, let's
assume that there is a lion right in front of you, let's hypothesize that.
At that moment *(desu ne)*, what are you *(anata)* going to do? Huh?
There may be some cases you must kill the animal; it may attack you

Figure 6. Use of blunt language by girls (Orihara 1992, p. 18)

and you might be killed, right *(desho)?* But you just say that the situation like that doesn't exist today or something *(desu ne)*. That's nothing but an excuse, isn't it *(janai desu ka)?* If you *(anata)* are serious about the animal-rights movement, I think you should give concrete answers to the questions right here and now *(desu yo)*. That's all.

(Transcribed from the Asahi television program *Pre-stage*, September 24, 1992; my translation)

Mr. Kawai maintains the *desu/masu* style, and yet the delivery of these endings is emphatic and accusatory. The particles *yo* and *ne* follow *desu*, signaling interpersonal and informational attitude to the statement. He uses *desho* 'isn't it' and *janai desu ka* 'isn't it the case' with emphatic stress to express accusation. The pronoun *anata* 'you,' which is not normally used to address one's interlocutor, is used to express an antagonistic attitude.

Expressions of fury and ridicule, then, are as much a part of Japanese as accommodating, considerate expressions. When a Japanese speaker is excited, personal emotion as an expression of the individual dominates the discourse. In comparison to the United States, though, such individualistic expressions are likely to be used only in a limited number of situations. In the contexts of the *uchi* relationship, or where conflict is expected, as in the television debate, Japanese people directly express anger and fury. But when they are aware that the situation calls for avoiding disagreement, they rarely show anger and fury. Instead they initiate tireless behind-the-scenes negotiations, searching for compromises that will minimize unexpected conflicts. Japanese emotional expressions are, although self-revealing, still responsive to relationality cues.

8 Japanese Sentence Structure:
Grammar in Context

Japanese sentences differ from English in word order and in structural axis. The subject-object-verb word order and the prominence of the topic-comment relation are two obvious ways in which Japanese speakers organize information differently from speakers of English. The Japanese preference for nominal predicates, which is related to the topic-comment structure, is significant. Another noteworthy point is that the Japanese speaker frequently adds, especially at the end of an utterance, a variety of "extras," manipulative devices that qualify an utterance by responding to needs arising from the conversational context. Although American English also uses extras, they are more restricted.

The use of the Japanese verbs of giving and receiving also exemplify the society-relational orientation of Japanese communication. Discussion of these verbs illustrates that an identical phenomenon—of giving and receiving objects or doing things for someone—is described in different ways across languages. The Japanese are more compelled than are Americans to describe the dynamics of human relationships when giving and receiving occur.

There is also a fundamental difference between Japanese and English sentence structures in the way they express passivity. When viewing and describing an event, it is possible to take either (1) agent-causes/does-something-to-someone and (2) something-happens, or something-is-caused-by-someone. The Japanese language, compared with English, is skewed toward the second type of description. This tendency is supported by how Japanese passive sentences function.

Constructing a Sentence

The Japanese concept of the sentence differs from that of English in two important aspects. First, although a subject and a verb are required in an English sentence, in Japanese both are not necessarily required. Second, the basic English word order is subject-verb-object, while in Japanese it is subject-object-verb.

Generally speaking, in Japanese any and all elements are left unsaid as long as what is unsaid is assumed to be understood or unnecessary. Nouns, verbs, and particles are frequently omitted, especially in speech. This tendency is closely associated with relationality cues; expressions are tailored to the specific information required. The subject-object-verb pattern is not rigid. Instead, the minimum that needs to be mentioned is included, followed by the verbal element, which is placed at the end of the sentence. Giving unnecessary information is a sign of clumsiness in Japanese, as it indicates a lack of the expected language skills.

In the absence of a noun referent, English demands the pronoun "it" or "they." One usually says something like "It's five o'clock." (What does "it" refer to?) The Japanese counterpart would be *Go-ji* 'Five o'clock' or *Go-ji desu* 'Five o'clock (it) is.' Of course an English speaker may also say "Five o'clock" in answer to the question, "What time is it?" The point is, however, that there is no Japanese sentence equivalent to "It's five o'clock." The fairly rigid grammatical requirement of a subject in English is absent in Japanese.

Closely related to our discussion is the lack of a Japanese pronominal system. Although some phrases correspond to English pronouns, their use is highly restricted—particularly the second person *anata*, whose use is normally avoided. More frequently used referential terms are names and other descriptive phrases describing relationships. For example, the Japanese use family terms extensively—mother, father, aunt, uncle, and so on—for self-reference. The use of these terms also extends to fictive circumstances—what Takao Suzuki (1978) calls "other-oriented self-designation." For example, a husband may be called *otoosan* 'father' by his wife. Here the wife views her husband as a "father" from the child's point of view. Obviously the wife is not the husband's biological daughter. In fact the husband calls himself "father" when facing a child, another case of other-oriented self-designation—identifying self in relation to the weaker or the weakest among relevant members. This also occurs among Americans, but on a much more limited basis. Multiple self-referencing terms such as *watashi* 'I,' *watakushi* 'I-polite,' *boku* 'I-male self-reference,' *ore* 'I-blunt male self-reference,' and so on are also available in Japanese; appropriate use (or deletion) depends on context.

Japanese word order allows for greater maneuverability, since not all elements are required in a sentence. The most important element in the Japanese sentence is the verb, which normally appears at the end of the sentence. Although the word order is relatively free, there is a preferred order of elements within the sentence. First, topics, if they appear, come in the initial position. By identifying a topic, both speaker and listener align themselves to acknowledge a common starting point. Like English ("white house"), and unlike Spanish *(casa blanca)*, Japanese modifiers precede the modified (*shiroi* 'white' *uchi* 'house').

This word order in Japanese may play a part in making (or changing) one's commitment to a statement toward the end of the utterance. This point has been made in the past more than a few times, but Yoshiyuki Morita gives a good example: *yame-sase-rare-taku-nakatta-rashii-wa-yo* 'it seems that he didn't want to be forced to resign' (Morita 1995, 62). The speaker's intention—that it seems that he didn't—appears toward the end of the utterance.

Since all the elements related to the verb—negation, question, speculation, affirmation, and so on—follow the verb stem, it has been said that Japanese allows the speaker to adjust the statement type to a kind more easily accepted by the partner. By observing the partner's response, one may make the statement less or more assertive, for example. In English, the speaker is forced to reveal his or her position earlier in the sentence, when the predicating verb is selected. Syntactic fluidity and flexibility make it possible for speakers of Japanese to respond to the ongoing needs of communication and to take the forms most appropriate in the context.

Subject-Predicate and Topic-Comment

One of the essential grammatical elements of an English sentence is the subject. In English the grammatical relation of the subject and the predicate plays a major role in sentence construction. Since Western linguistics traditionally emphasizes the subject-predicate as the basic, universal grammatical relation, linguists tend to assume that sentences are naturally structured in terms of subject and predicate. In Japanese, however, there is another important construct, the topic-comment connection.

What Is Topic?

Topic is the element in a sentence that is talked about. Picture a situation where a newly released movie is mentioned in conversation. As your friend mentions the movie, you might respond by saying [1].

[1]   I saw that movie already.

In the situation described, this is perhaps the expression most expected. But it is also possible to say something like [2].

[2]   That movie, I saw (it) already.

This sentence has a noun phrase, "that movie," moved to the beginning of the sentence. Its position identifies "that movie" as the topic of the sentence, something the rest of the sentence talks about.

Along the same lines, M. A. K. Halliday (1967, 212) claims that the underlined phrases in the following sentences are topics (although he uses the term "themes").

[3]   *John* saw the play yesterday.
[4]   *Yesterday* John saw the play.
[5]   *The play* John saw yesterday.

In each example the underlined words identify what is being talked about in the rest of the sentence. Halliday goes even further and points out that "who," in a sentence like "Who saw the play?" is also topic. He reasons that elements appearing at the beginning of the sentence are topics, and they are followed by comments. In general we understand the topic as "what is being talked about" and "the point of departure for the clause as a message" (Halliday 1967, 212). As an English speaker, one notices that sentences [2] and [5] have limited use. English seems to prefer sentence structures like [1], [3], and [4], where an agent (preferably human) occupies the position of the grammatical subject, followed by the verb and the object.

The Topic Marker wa

Unlike English, which makes an element the topic by putting it in initial position, Japanese provides particles, among which *wa* is the most common, to mark a topic overtly. The expression most likely to be used in talking about a new movie would be something like this:

> [6] Sono eiga   wa moo   mita.
>   that   movie T   already saw
>
> That movie *(wa)* I already saw (it).

Although it is normal for the topic—*sono eiga wa*—to appear at the beginning of the sentence, the topic may appear elsewhere. Compare the example below, where *sono eiga wa* is also the topic.

> [7] Moo   sono eiga   wa mita.
>   already that movie T   saw
>
> I already saw that movie *(wa)*.

A nominal phrase followed by a short pause, but no particle, may be a topic as well. For example, *Sono eiga, moo mita* 'That movie (pause), I already saw (it)' is possible.

There is a striking difference between Japanese and English here. Neither Japanese sentence contains an explicit grammatical subject, corresponding to English "I." The English expression, "I saw that movie already," and its Japanese counterpart, *Moo sono eiga wa mita*, show obvious structural differences. Expression of topic, as in example [2], is possible in English, but it is unusual. Topic is not strictly a grammatical concept. A topic represents no grammatical case such as subject or object. Instead it marks a piece of information that is being talked about in the sentence. What does this observation mean? How should we understand the differences we witness here in Japanese "topic" sentence versus the limited use of such sentences in English?

According to Charles Li and Sandra Thompson (1976), languages can be categorized according to whether they favor subject-predicate or topic-comment. English is a subject-predicate language; Japanese is a language in which both subject-predicate and topic-comment are prominent. According to a more radical view held by Akira Mikami (1960), the only connection in Japanese sentence construction is the topic-comment relationship. Mikami proposes that there is no need to recognize the so-called grammatical subject in Japanese. He points out that the idea that a sentence consists of two parts, subject and predicate, is a phenomenon peculiar to European languages and does not apply to the Japanese language. "Grammar that distributes the same syntactic role to the powerful expression 'X *wa*' and to the weak expression 'X *ga*'—which in fact are the case in almost all of the current textbooks and reference books—cannot be recognized as a grammar of the Japanese language. Such a grammar ignores the form of the Japanese language itself. And naturally as a consequence such a grammar totally fails to explain the syntax of the Japanese language" (Mikami 1960, 25; my translation).

This poses a challenge to a fundamental grammatical rule. The grammatical thread of subject and predicate is not so universal as one might think. The fact that Japanese highlights both the topic-comment and the subject-predicate relationships although English focuses on the subject-predicate relationship alone, has a profound influence on how information is structured and expressed in these two languages.

Wa *in Discourse*

The difference between Japanese and English becomes even sharper when we look at topic-comment structure in Japanese discourse (the level beyond a single sentence). In earlier studies (Maynard 1980, 1987b) I argued that the topic marker *wa* in Japanese has a "staging" function in narrative discourse—it presents the narrator's different perspective or point of view.

To find out how the topic marker *wa* does and does not appear in certain contexts, I looked at two Japanese folktales narrated by Jooji Tsubota; the first story is titled *A Peach Boy* and the second *A Cucumber Princess*. Note how the expressions "the old man" and "the old woman" are marked by particles—with the topic marker *wa* or the subject marker *ga*. The data are given in English; parenthetical phrases are followed by *ga*, italicized phrases by *wa*. (Transcriptions of the Japanese texts appear in the appendix.)

A Peach Boy
(8.1) Once upon a time there lived (an old man and an old woman) (*ga*).
(8.2) Now, it happened one summer day.

(8.3) *The old man (wa)* went to the mountain to collect firewood.

(8.4) "See you later."

(8.5) *The old woman (wa)* saw the old man off,

(8.6) and said, "Well, I'll go to the river to get some washing done,"

(8.7) and went out to the river carrying a washing tub.

(8.8) Scrub, scrub, scrub.

(8.9) *The old woman (wa)* worked hard washing clothes.

(8.10) After a while, something came floating down the stream. (Tsubota 1975, 24)

A Cucumber Princess

(9.1) Once upon a time there lived (an old man and an old woman) *(ga)*.

(9.2) One day (the woman) *(ga)* went to the river to do the washing.

(9.3) From upstream, two boxes came floating down the stream.

(9.4) They came bobbing down the river.

(9.5) Seeing this, (the old woman) *(ga)* called out,

(9.6) "Hey, box filled with things, come this way! Empty box, go away from me!"

(9.7) The box with content approached her.

(9.8) So she picked it up and returned home.

(9.9) That evening when she opened the box with the old man, a cucumber came out of the box. (Tsubota 1975, 18)

Since the topic is something that is being talked about, it must be something that the reader can identify. When a participant appears for the first time (new information in a discourse), it is marked in English by the indefinite article—"an old man" and "an old woman"—as shown in (8.1). When they appear the second time (given information), English uses the definite article—"the old man"—as shown in (8.3). Looking at how Japanese distinguishes these two types of information, one may conclude that new information is marked by *ga* and old information by *wa*. To some extent this is true. In both stories, "an old man" and "an old woman" make their first appearance in the narrative world with *ga*. In both cases, the story develops with an episode about the old woman. In lines (8.5) and (8.9) of *A Peach Boy*, "the old woman" is marked by *wa*, while in line (9.2) and (9.5) of *A Cucumber Princess*, "the old woman" continues to be marked by *ga*. This poses the question: Why does a participant who has been introduced earlier in discourse continue to be marked by *ga?*

Topicalization as a Staging Device

The *wa/ga* marking strategy, although often coinciding with the given/new distinction, should be treated differently. It is a device available to the storyteller for "staging." "Staging" is how the narrator manipulates the marking of topics (and deemphasizes nontopics) when telling a story. Through staging strategy, the narrator organizes information according to his or her perspective, placing participants at different spots on the narrative stage for different lengths of time in the consciousness of both the narrator and the reader.

Participants marked as topics are expected to remain on stage longer, providing points of reference for the development of the topical flow. What the narrator wishes to accomplish through staging is to discriminate those who are topics from those who are not in such a way that characters marked as topics remain activated, evoked, and stored in the reader's consciousness.

For new and unexpected information, the avoidance of *wa* marking—the strategy of nontopicalizing—is practiced. Non-topics usually continue to be marked by *ga* even though they represent given information. *Ga* is attached to indicate new information not in the sense that it cannot have been previously mentioned, although that is often the case, but in the sense that the speaker presents it as not being currently activated in the reader's or listener's consciousness. A direct reference point for non-topics' integration into the topical line is missing. In this sense, participants who have not been made topics provide subordinate and secondary information within the structure of the narrative. These participants do not stay on the stage for long; instead they appear, disappear, and reappear at various points in the plot. Non-topics often become the focus of attention when their actions and descriptions are introduced as if constituting new information from the point of view of characters who are topics. Because of its dramatic impact, the nontopicalized participant's action is described vividly, and his or her movement is often more likely to receive close attention.

Above and beyond plot development, staging strategy can be used to manipulate participant description. Descriptions of characters who are topics is state-oriented. Events are viewed as a chain of changing states associated with those characters. This is because topicalized participants serve as constant reference points, and events in the narrative are integrated as changes happening to them. But the actions of nontopicalized participants are described not as changes of states, but as active events, and with vivid imagery. The narrator focuses on the participants as if they are new. Descriptions of such characters are action-oriented, as opposed to the state-oriented descriptions of topic characters.

Staging strategy, linguistically manipulated by the use of *wa* and other topic markers, plays an important role in the manifestation of the speaker's point of view. Discerning topic is vital in organizing and representing information in Japanese.

It is possible to achieve an effect similar to Japanese topicalization in English (Maynard 1982). English uses combinations of various devices and strategies, such as definite articles and pronouns, to mark given information. The speaker's viewing position is manifested through choice of verbs and assignment of grammatical cases as well as through syntax (e.g., active versus passive). But a fundamental difference persists between Japanese and English ways of presenting the organization of information. The frequent use of *wa* and the deletion of topics in Japanese offer evidence that the topic-comment relation—and therefore, the organization of information according to the speaker's point of view—is one of the two basic (if not the primary) constructs of sentence and discourse in Japanese.

The difference between Japanese and English is not that English cannot mark topic, since moving an expression to the beginning of the sentence does this. The difference is that the topic structure plays a more dominant role in Japanese than in English. (This point is elaborated in Maynard 1994a.) Japanese people are often more interested in offering commentary on a set topic than in describing the world in subject-predicate terms. The topic is identified relationally with the knowledge of the addressee and in the context of the situation, offering another example of the society-relational orientation of the Japanese language.

Nominal Expressions

The Japanese language frequently uses nominalization, the process of changing a clause into a noun (or nominal clause) by using nominalizers like *koto* and *no*. A similar grammatical process is available in English; that-clauses, if-clauses, "to" plus infinitive ("to buy"), and gerunds ("buying") are nominalization strategies in English.

Below is a case of *koto* nominalization.

[10] Kinoo   katta   koto   wa   tashika   da.
     yesterday bought NOM   T   certain   BE

It is certain that (I) bought (it) yesterday (*lit.*, That (I) bought (it) yesterday is certain).

What is the difference between this and a sentence without nominalization, such as *Kinoo tashikani katta* 'I certainly bought it yesterday'?

When a speaker chooses to express thoughts and emotions using nouns instead of verbs, what are the semantic consequences? According to Ronald W. Langacker, the verb "explode" and the noun "explosion," though both may describe the same event, differ significantly in semantic (and cognitive) terms. Langacker says: "*Explode* imposes a processual construal on the profiled event, while *explosion* portrays it as an abstract region. . . . Nominalizing a verb necessarily endows it with the conceptual properties characteristic of nouns" (1987, 90). The distinction Langacker draws between the process (of what happens) and an abstract region (of a conceptual unit) is useful for understanding Japanese nominalization as well.

When a clause is changed into a nominal, as in a nominal predicate, the event described is treated as a thing or a fact, rather than as an active event. In a clause, the semantic content often defines an agent who initiates an action, and the event is captured as it is caused by the agent. In a nominalized expression, the event is no longer described as an active one, but becomes a state. The nominalized event is like a still picture, while the event described in the verbal predicate is like a movie.

Yoshihiko Ikegami's (1991) thesis that the Japanese language prefers *koto* 'thing, affair, event' over *mono* 'thing, object' is significant for understanding Japanese nominalization. Ikegami illustrates the difference between the two concepts by citing M. A. K. Halliday and Ruqaiya Hasan's (1976) example. In the example "One of the jurors had a pencil that squeaked. This, of course, Alice could not stand," the demonstrative "this" refers either to "a pencil that squeaked" or "the squeaking pencil." "A pencil that squeaked" refers to *mono* (as an object), while "the squeaking pencil" refers to *koto* (as an event). In fact, "this" could refer to "that the pencil squeaked," which seems to be a more accurate way of capturing the *koto*-ness of the second interpretation. Ikegami contends that "Japanese has a predilection for the *koto* type of expressions rather than ... the *mono* type" (1991, 295).

The following pair of Japanese sentences adapted from Ikegami (1991, 296) illustrates a similar difference.

(11) Michi de naiteita   kodomo o tasukete-yatta.
     street on was crying child   O helped

(12) Michi de kodomo ga naiteita no   o
     street on child   S crying NOM O

     tasukete-yatta.
     helped.

Ikegami continues that (11) is roughly equivalent to "I helped a child who was crying in the street" while (12) translates literally as "I helped that a child was crying in the street." Structurally, (11) displays noun modification, *michi de naiteita* modifying the noun *kodomo* 'child,' which functions as the object of the verb *tasukete-yatta* 'helped.' In contrast to this, in (12), *that a child was crying in the street* is the content of the fact—*koto*—which in turn functions as the grammatical object of the verb *tasukete-yatta* 'helped.' This expression captures the event as a whole in a nominal clause rather than focusing on the agent of the action. The speaker in (12), unlike that in (11), does not describe the event as agent-does-something (the child was such that he or she was crying), but takes a stance as an observer who reports the incident as a "thing."

Semantically, nominalization signals some distance between the event and the speaker. The event becomes objectified and abstract (cf. Brown and Levinson 1987). In conceptual terms, the event is conceived as a "region." Nominalization seems to provide an environment conducive to expressing the perspective of an observer or a commentator in relation to that "region."

There is a distinct preference for nominalized expressions, at least in some Japanese discourse. When original Japanese and English translations of novels are compared, there are many cases where the Japanese writer uses nominal clauses, but the English translator does not. One such example is given in the two sentences below, taken from novelistic discourse.

(13) === hi   ga nagaku natta koto wa kakushi yoo
         daytime S long   became NOM T hide

```
mo   naku,   = = =
also  BE-NEG (Abe 1968, 6)
```

(14) = = = but the days had obviously grown longer. (Saunders
      1966, 4)

The Japanese has *koto*, which changes the clause *hi ga nagaku natta*
into a nominal. In English, however, there is no nominalization.
The distinction between *mono* and *koto* explicated by Ikegami is
apparent. Note that in the Japanese, the nominal clause *hi ga
nagaku natta koto* refers to *koto* as an event, while in English translation "the days had obviously grown longer" concentrates on "the
days," *mono*, as an object.

Verbal and Nominal Predicates

Two types of predicates in Japanese are the verbal, which takes the
regular verb as the main predicate, and the nominal, which uses the
copulative "be" (*da/desu* and variants) as the main predicate. The
two sentences below represent these two types.

[15] Kinoo   tashikani katta.
     yesterday certainly bought
     Yesterday (I) certainly bought (it).

[16] Kinoo   tashikani katta   no da.
     yesterday certainly bought NOM T certain BE
     It is that yesterday (I) certainly bought (it).

In the first example the verb *katta* 'bought' is the predicate associated with "I," while in the second example the copulative *da* con-
cerns itself with the fact that I bought it yesterday. Although both
Japanese and English can express a similar thought either with or
without nominal predicates, in Japanese nominal predicates are
more useful rhetorically.

Nominal Predicates in Japanese

My examination of Japanese nominal predicates is confined to
those that take the nominalizers *no*, *koto*, and *mono* (in *no da*, *koto da*,
and *mono da*), although there are other ways to form a nominal
predicate in Japanese. For example, in *Amerika no eikyoo o uketeiru
kanji desu ne* 'I have (*lit.*, it is) the feeling/impression that it is influenced by America,' *kanji* 'feeling/impression' nominalizes the preceding clause and is followed by the copula. An array of modal

usages of nominal predicates in Japanese, for example, *wake da* 'that's why,' *hazu da* 'it should,' and *tsumori da* 'intend to' function in a similar manner. (See Kitagawa 1995 for an analysis of *wake* in Japanese discourse.) Nominal predicates in Japanese, especially *n(o) da*, have been studied extensively in Japan and elsewhere. They have been referred to by a variety of names including "extended predicate" (Jorden 1963; Noda 1992), "*n(o) da*" or its formal counterpart "*n(o) desu*" (Kuno 1973; McGloin 1983, 1984), and "*no dearu*" (Mikami 1972, Shimozaki 1981).

By choosing the nominal predicate, one chooses a mode of predication qualitatively different from utterances without it. In Maynard (1992) I argued that the sources of this difference lie in the cognitive process of (1) objectifying and stativizing the event through nominalization, (2) personalizing the utterance by the predicate *da*, and (3) organizing information as is situationally and interpersonally appropriate by using the topic structure *n(o) da*. It is generally agreed that *n(o) da* functions, as Tadaharu Tanomura (1990) characterizes it, to provide background information relevant to a statement, especially, as Keizoo Saji (1991) suggests, interpretative, explanatory, and persuasive information.

When the nominal predicate is used, the rhetorical effect changes. The nonprocessual, stative nature of the *n(o) da* expression aligns with the tendency of the nominal clause to be marked by a topic marker. Nominal predicates, coupled with the topic-comment organization, work together in framing a conceptual "region" followed by personal commentary. This strategic combination propels the Japanese language toward a state-oriented, comment-centered mode of communication, a preference for the rhetoric of commentation.

"Rhetoric of commentation" refers to a preference for personal commentary, over propositional information (who-does-what-to-whom). The nominalization-commentation combination "wraps" propositional information by conceiving of it as a "region" and emphasizes the addition of the speaker's attitude toward that information. Joy Hendry (1990) uses the term "wrapping" in a broad cultural sense that includes honorific language, and I think the term can be extended to many other aspects of the language as well.

In earlier work I introduced a similar term, "social packaging" (Maynard 1989, 31), referring to "a socially motivated act to construct the content of utterance in such a way as to achieve maximum agreeableness to the recipient." There I was discussing the

"social packaging" achieved by conversational strategies (final particles, fillers, and so on), but the term can also apply to sentence
structure. Many grammatical devices and structures of Japanese
enhance the rhetoric of commentation, among them nominal predicates, adverbs of emotional attitude, and topic-comment structure.

Contrasting Verbal and Nominal Predicates in Japanese and English

A contrastive analysis of Japanese and English novelistic discourse
demonstrates the importance of nominal predicates (cf. Maynard
1995, 1996a). I have chosen two modern novels, one Japanese and
the other American: Kooboo Abe's *Tanin no Kao* and Saul Bellow's
Dangling Man, along with E. Dale Saunders' English translation
The Face of Another and Minoru Oota's Japanese translation
Chuuburarin no Otoko. It is essential to incorporate translations in
both directions, because if only a Japanese original and its English
translation are examined, we fail to observe how English (when not
used for translation purposes) uses nominalization. For statistical
purposes, I have examined the first two hundred sentences in the
original Japanese and English novels and their translations.

English expressions that are considered comparable to Japanese
nominal predicates include clauses marked by "that," "if," infini-
tives, and gerunds. The use of these forms in nominal predicates is
rather limited in English. And although we can find sentences with
forms of "be" followed by "that" or "if," they often appear in translations corresponding to limited cases of Japanese nominal predicates, if at all. In our data there are no cases where the *no* nominal
predicate, the most prevalent kind in Japanese, is translated into a
"be" plus "that" or "if" construction in English. The most striking
discrepancy between nominal predicates in Japanese and English
novelistic discourse is how the *no da* predicate is handled in English.
In the following examples, although *no da* occurs in Japanese, no
nominalizing expression appears in the English translation.

(17)... kono ame ga agareba   moo   sugu natsu
      this rain S let up-COND already soon summer

  na no   daroo. (Abe 1968, 6)
  BE NOM BE

(18) Soon, when the rains let up, it would be summer. (Saunders
1966, 4)

(19) Nanibun, mondai no choosho wa gorannotoori ooban no
anyway   question LK statement T as you see   large LK

nooto   sansatsu ni gisshiri   kakikomareta
notebook three   in completely filled was written

ichinenkan ni wataru kiroku na no   dearu. (Abe 1968, 61)
one year   to extend record BE NOM BE

(20) For as you can see, the statement is a record stretching over a
whole year and filling three notebooks the size of folios. (Saunders 1966, 4)

A similar phenomenon is observed in translation of English into
Japanese. In the English original, there are no nominal predicates,
but in its corresponding Japanese translation, nominal predicates
appear:

(21) Books do not hold me. (Bellow 1944, 10)

(22) Shomotsu ga boku o toraete-kurenai no   da. (Oota 1971, 6)
books   S I   O hold-NEG   NOM BE

The difference in rhetorical effect between Japanese and
English is sharply contrasted in these examples. In (21) the main
predicate takes the verb "hold," and we find no nominal predicate
wrapping the event and transforming it into a state-oriented, com-
menting mode of expression. In the translation, however, the event
is presented as being state-oriented, and the *da*-predicate conveys a
personal judgment of the nominal clause.

Given this significant difference in rhetorical effects, the use of
nominalization (or its absence) will influence the overall effect of
the discourse. The conceptual "regions" associated with nominalization seem to be universal, but the preference for or against use of
nominalization differs among languages. In my data, only a few
cases of nominalization occur in English, and cases of nominal
predicates are even rarer. Statistics for the initial two hundred sentences of *Tanin no Kao* and *Dangling Man* and their translations
appear in table 4.

The nominal predicates (*n[o] da, koto da,* and *mono da*) occur
with much greater frequency both in the Japanese original and in
the translation into Japanese. *N(o) da* is by far the most common (51
of 61 nominal predicates in *Tanin no Kao* and 20 of 24 in
Chuuburarin no Otoko). This is not an isolated phenomenon. For
example, in Japanese casual conversation, I found that 25.48 per-

TABLE 4.   Nominal predicates in the first 200 sentences of *Tanin no Kao* and *Dangling Man* and their translations

Title	Number of nominal predicates	% nominal predicates	Number of sentences
Tanin no Kao	61	30.5	200
The Face of Another	9	4.23	213
Dangling Man	5	2.5	200
Chuuburarin no Otoko	24	11.32	212

cent of all sentence-final positions (317 of 1,244) were marked by *n(o) da* (Maynard 1992). Likewise, in Maynard 1993b I reported that in ten *taidan* (published interview) dialogues, 25.82 percent (520 of 2,014) sentence-final positions were marked by *n(o) da* nominal predicates. Of course it is possible to express one's thoughts and feelings in Japanese by using expressions other than nominal predicates or the topic-comment organization. Still, the Japanese preference toward a focus on the whole event is more readily described in the state-oriented nominal structure.

The nominal predicate does not occur with such frequency across all types of discourse. In straight news reports, nominal predicates occur less frequently (Maynard 1997a). This phenomenon is evident in Japanese television news programs. When anchors comment on news items—to the audience as well as among themselves—nominal predicates occur much more often than when they report straight news (Maynard 1997b). This is because the straight news report centers on what happened—who did what to whom, what resulted, and so on. The kind of novels I have examined, however, fall into a genre whose text is often self-reflective, commentative, and rich in personal thoughts and reflections. But even when this language-internal variability is taken into consideration, where the speaker's or writer's personal view is expressed in Japanese discourse, nominal predicates are significantly frequent.

Sentence-final Manipulation

Verbs are primary and are placed at the end in Japanese syntax. In spoken Japanese, however, verbs seldom appear alone at the end of a sentence. In conversational data, I have found that sentence-final expressions are rarely simple verb forms. Rather, they are accompanied by such extras as auxiliary forms and particles. This strategy of ending sentences with elements other than verbs helps make the sentence less final, implying that it remains open for interpersonal negotiation. Table 5 lists the frequencies of eleven different types of expressions observed in sentence-final position.

As shown in table 5, in the conversational data 35.05% of sentential units were accompanied by interactional particles. Sentence-final verbs are often accompanied by tag question-like auxiliary forms in Japanese which overtly solicit listener responses and rapport, such as *janai* 'isn't it?' or *deshoo* 'isn't that right?' These expressions amounted to 9.73% of all sentence-final forms. Nominal endings were also frequent, partly due to ellipsis and postposing, and their rate was 16.40% of all sentence-final forms. Other endings include gerund ending (7.48%), conjunctions (5.63%), adverbial phrases (5.55%), grammatical particles (3.78%), fillers (3.38%) and nominalization (1.05%). Out of all the sentence-final forms, only 11.98% (the total of 8.28% plus 3.70%) showed simple verb endings.

Simple Abrupt Verb Forms

Simple verb forms occur in sentence-final position very infrequently among our sentences, although they are much more common in written Japanese. Let us examine the context for simple verb forms in the conversational data. In these data the normal speech style is abrupt. (Formal styles occur, but only when a specific need arises,

TABLE 5.   Frequency of Sentence-Final Forms in Three-Minute Segments of Conversation among Twenty Japanese Pairs

Type	Number	%
Final particles	436	35.05
Nominals	204	16.40
Taglike auxiliary forms	121	9.73
Verb (simple nonpast)	103	8.28
Verb (gerund)	93	7.48
Conjunctions	70	5.63
Adverbial phrases	69	5.55
Grammatical particles	47	3.78
Verb (simple past)	46	3.70
Fillers	42	3.38
Nominalization	13	1.05
Total	1,244	100.03

for example, when reconstructing a dialogue in which the formal style was used.) When and why do speakers end sentences with simple abrupt forms, without any extras?

There are two obvious reasons for this choice. In the first, the speaker expresses surprise, an abrupt remembrance, or a sudden emotional surge. In the second, the speaker is in the narrative setting, taking a point of view internal to the world under discussion. The following samples exemplify these two cases.

About teaching

(23.1) Doo shiyoo./ Kimichantachi   nani hanashita
      what do   Kimi and others what talked

      n   da./
      NOM BE

      What should we do, what did Kimi talk about? (abrupt)

(23.2) Aa wakatta./   Kyooshoku no hanashi da./
      oh understood teaching   LK talk   BE

      Oh, I got it. (abrupt) It's about teaching. (abrupt)

About a train ride

(24.1) Uchi no   chichioya soo da yo./
      my   LK father   so   BE IP

      My dad is like that, you know.

(24.2) Soide norikomu to   nee/ kutsu o   nuide
      then get on   when IP   shoes O   take off

      nee/
      IP

      (Un)
        yeah

(24.3) biiru o   katte nomi hajimeru./
      beer O buy   begin to drink

      When he gets on (the train), he takes off his shoes, he buys beer, and begins to drink. (abrupt)

(24.4) Shinbunshi shiku   no./
      newspaper spread IP

      He spreads the newspaper.

In data set (23), the speaker wonders about her friend's topic of conversation, then suddenly recalls it and reports that it was about teaching. The speaker does not design the utterance in an interactionally sensitive manner, for example, by adding interpersonal particles. In data set (24), the speaker talks about her father's buying and drinking beer in the simple abrupt form. The Japanese verb used here is *nomi hajimeru* 'begins to drink.' The present tense of this verb shows that the speaker is taking a point of view internal to the setting where the incident takes place. It is as if she were seeing her father drink beer, and she describes the action dramatically and vividly. The choice of the simple abrupt style achieves (1) immediacy and directness in expression, and (2) an internal narrative perspective. Simple abrupt endings also occur in verbatim repetitions of the partner's immediately preceding speech.

There are, however, other reasons for a speaker to use simple abrupt forms. The next example is part of a dialogue taken from fiction. The sentence-final verb form is explained in parentheses.

(25.1) Kore to   itte gen'in ni   naru   yoona   dekigoto
       this QT   say cause IO   become such as incident

       ga atta   wake   dewanai to   omoimasu ne.
       S   there was reason BE-NEG QT   think   IP

       I don't think there was a specific reason that caused the incident. (formal)

(25.2) Moshi omotedatta kenka demo   shiteireba,
       if   apparent   fight such as   do-COND

       kitto   Harue no kuchi kara kinjo
       certainly Harue LK mouth from neighbor

       ni hiromatteiru hazu desu kara.
       IO spread   should BE   since

       If they actually had a fight, the neighbors would know, since Harue is certain to have spread that. (formal)

(25.3) Tabun,   Harue nishitemireba, jibun to doonenpai
       perhaps Harue for   self as same age

       no onna   ga hitoride shareta uchi ni sunde
       LK woman S alone   stylish house in live

       akanuketa   minari   de tsuukinshiteiru.
       fashionable clothes in commute

       Perhaps for Harue, (it was upsetting to see that) a woman about the same age as herself lives by herself in a stylish house and goes to work wearing fashionable clothes. (abrupt)

(25.4) Tokitama   gaisha   de okurarete kaettekuru.
       sometimes foreign car by drive-PASS return

And sometimes the woman is driven back home in a foreign car. (abrupt)

(25.5) Soo yuu hade na kurashi ga netamashikatta to
       such   showy   life style O   was jealous   QT

yuu koto janai   n   deshoo ka.
say NOM BE-NEG NOM BE   Q

Isn't it that she was jealous of such a showy lifestyle? (formal) (Natsuki 1981, 75)

In this segment, Yazu, a secretary at the public prosecutor's office, reports to Akiko, a district public prosecutor, how Harue, a neighbor of a crime suspect, commented about the suspect. The discussion centers on why Harue maintains an unfriendly attitude toward the suspect. The utterances (25.3) and (25.4), unlike (25.1), (25.2), and (25.5), take simple abrupt endings and describe the kind of life the suspect leads, as if they were from a list. In fact "such" in the last sentence triggers a case of sentence anaphora (reference to a sentence identified earlier in the discourse) and refers to the two sentences (25.3) and (25.4). In this discourse segment, those two sentences provide information that modifies "such a showy life-style." Because of this, there is no need to make them conform to the expected speech style, in this case formal. Nor is it necessary to add extras, since neither sentence is directly addressed to the listener. This is parallel to the phenomenon that subordinate clauses normally do not carry interpersonal features; main clauses do.

Sentence-Final Manipulations in English

Now let us take a look at how sentences end in the American conversational data. A quick glance reveals that most sentences end without attitudinal phrases (extras). In our data the following forms appeared as extras in sentence-final position.

1. Insertion phrases including "you know," "right," "O.K."
2. Tag questions
3. Calling the listener by his or her first name
4. Adding phrases to express hesitation and ambiguity such as "or something," "like"
5. Ending the utterance with conjunctions like "though" and "but"

Some examples follow.

About a basketball game

(26.1) Oh, we saw that thing in the pub, *Tom.*/
(26.2) 1978 they won twenty-six in a row./

About restaurants

(27.1) *A:* They opened something new there./

                                      (*B:* ‾Yeah)

(27.2) B: Ronda *or something.*/

About vacation

(28.1) *B:* We can't go to Florida though, can we/ can we now?/
(28.2) *A:* No not/ not if you go there./ I'll explain to my grandma she won't be thrilled *but.*/

Sentence-final forms with and without extras occur as shown in table 6. In Japanese and English the proportion of simple abrupt forms to expressions with extras is almost completely reversed. Most (88.02 percent) sentence-final Japanese expressions are accompanied by extras, but only a fraction (10.07 percent) of English expressions include them.

How to End a Sentence in Japanese

Beyond the points already discussed, Japanese people often end sentences with phrases like those below.

    na yoo desu 'It seems that'

    da to omoimasu 'I think that'

    da to omowaremasu 'It is thought that'

    na no dewanai deshoo ka 'I wonder if it is not the case that'

All these sentence-final manipulations package the content of information. By personalizing the information and signaling that it

TABLE 6. Frequency of Sentence-Final Forms in Three-Minute Segments of Conversation among Twenty American Pairs

Forms	Number	%
Without extras	1,152	89.93
With extras	129	10.07
Total	1,281	100.00

is only the speaker's judgment or speculation, the speaker softens the impact of the message. This leaves space for negotiation, the preferred situation for Japanese people. Leaving room to negotiate is especially important when the speaker expresses an opinion to someone expecting to receive respect and deference.

Japanese speakers learning English may overuse, in both speaking and writing, the English phrase "I think." "I think that's right," "I think I will conclude that," "I think I can't do that," "I think I will go," "I think yes," and so on. This style often gives Americans the impression that Japanese people are (1) repetitive or (2) opinionated. Some Americans also use "I think" quite frequently. The speech style is a marked one in American English and makes the speaker seem repetitive. When hesitantly added, "I think" may express lack of confidence; when stressed, it conveys the impression that the speaker is opinionated.

Japanese people using "I think" are probably trying to be cooperative, accommodating, and friendly by translating the strategies they know. Americans, however, show cooperation, accommodation, and friendliness by making precise, straightforward statements, sometimes accompanied by softening devices. The intention is the same, the strategies are very different. When Americans end sentences without extras, especially in conflict discourse, Japanese people are likely to feel threatened, hurt, or angry. The Japanese may feel Americans are not considerate enough. But there is no malice involved here on either side—only stylistic differences.

Giving, Receiving, and Doing

Verbs of Giving and Receiving

Japanese verbs of giving and receiving involve elements not explicitly coded in English. First, depending on who receives, two different types of verbs of giving are used. If you or someone close to you (*uchi* member) is the receiver, the verb chosen for expressing giving is *kureru*; someone *kureru* 'gives' something to oneself or the *uchi* member. On the other hand, if someone other than you or your *uchi* member is the receiver, the verb *ageru* 'give' is used instead. For receiving, *morau* 'receive' is used regardless of whether you or someone else receives. The difference between the two Japanese verbs for "give" lies in the empathy one is expected to feel toward the people involved in giving and receiving. When you or someone close to you is involved in the giving and receiving, empathy is stronger toward the receiver, even when the verb still describes giving; the verb expresses the feeling "someone-gives-to-me."

Social status markers also affect verbs of giving and receiving. Depending on the relative social status of the people involved, different forms of the verbs *kureru*, *ageru* and *morau* are chosen. The figure below, adapted from Keiichiroo Okutsu (1983, 26) illustrates the choice of appropriate donatory verbs in Japanese and English.

English has two verbs to choose from, "give" and "receive." In Japanese, in addition to this basic distinction, even when the giver is the speaker, if the receiver is the self or the *uchi* member, *kudasaru* or *kureru* 'give to me' must be chosen. (See Maynard 1990, entries 71 and 73.)

The seemingly simple acts of giving and receiving involve understanding of one's place in relation to the event. Japanese donatory verbs are explicitly responsive to the web of human relations.

Choice of Japanese and English Donatory Verbs*

giver	receiver/giver	receiver
give (to me) *kudasaru*		give (to someone) *sashiageru*
receive (from someone) *itadaku*		give (to someone) *ageru*
	speaker *uchi* member	
give (to me) *kureru*		
receive (from someone) *morau*		give (to someone) *yaru*

*The domain above the dotted line refers to people higher in social status than the speaker; below the dotted line, people of lower status.

Giving/Receiving and Doing

The system of donatory verbs illustrates clearly the relevance of context when applied to the exchange of favorable actions. In Japanese, when acts are performed for the benefit of others (and occasionally to their detriment), a matrix of appropriate language cues come into play.

Imagine that a friend taught you how to play chess. In English one may describe the situation by saying something like "My friend taught me." But in Japanese the literal counterpart to this expression, *tomodachi ga oshieta* '(my) friend taught (me)' is inappropriate. Instead, an expression using "give-to-me" must be added to the verb meaning "teach," as shown below.

[29] Tomodachi ga   oshiete-kureta.
     friend   S   taught

   My friend (kindly) taught-*kureta* me (for my benefit).

Compare [29] with its English counterpart.

[30] My friend taught me.

The Japanese language requires describing the benefit of being taught. In the Japanese sentence, although the speaker does not appear in the expression, the identity of the recipient is clear. The speaker's personal involvement is indirectly expressed through choice of donatory verb. Japanese speakers must make this relationship clear; statements carrying only neutral information convey an overwhelming tone of inappropriateness. But in English the neutral statement is expected.

Similar empathy requirements apply when the speaker teaches someone else. One cannot use the neutral form [31] to describe the act of teaching someone; instead, [32] must be used.

[31] Imooto   ni   tenisu o   oshieta.
     younger sister IO   tennis O   taught

   (I) taught (my) younger sister (how to play) tennis.

[32] Imooto   ni   tenisu o   oshiete-yatta.
     younger sister IO   tennis O   taught

   I taught-*yatta* (my) younger sister (how to play) tennis (for the benefit to her).

The speaker can also describe being taught by using the verb expressing *morau* 'receive.'

[33] Ane   ni   oshiete-moratta.
     my elder sister   by   taught

(My elder sister was kind enough and) I was taught-*moratta* by her.

Compare a similar expression in English.

[34] I had my sister teach me.

Although this sentence implies that the speaker, "I," initiated the sister's action, the Japanese expression with *morau* does not. It simply states, "I received the benefit of my elder sister's action of teaching me."

When giving and receiving verbs accompany other verbs, the combination implies that the transaction is in some way related to the recipient's interest. In asking the question "Who did this?" if no personal interest is involved, a speaker would ask *kore dare ga shita?* If a positive (or sometimes a negative) influence is assumed, *kore dare ga shite-kureta?* is preferred. Depending on the context this expression can imply gratitude or reprimand.

Because of the implication of personal interest, special care is required when using the verb of giving. A question like *kore katte-agemashoo ka?* 'shall I buy this for you?' implies that the listener is helpless, perhaps incapable, and in need of charity. It also says that the speaker is conscious of doing a favor, which in itself is offensive. Polite Japanese encourages, instead, the use of *kore kaimashoo ka?* 'shall I buy this?'

In Japanese, the combination of "do-*kureru*," "do-*yaru/ageru*," or "do-*morau*" must be chosen, while in English, simple "do" suffices. English uses other linguistic strategies to express benefit or loss from a transaction. For example, one hears such expressions as "he did it for me," "she bought this for me," and so on. The difference is that in Japanese, specification of the donatory relation is strongly expected.

The Donatory Relationship in Translation

To illustrate the pervasive use of donatory verb forms, let me compare an excerpt from the English translation of Kooboo Abe's novel *Tanin no Kao* 'The face of another' (1968) once again

with the Japanese original. In the following, the English parts
that correspond to Japanese original phrases containing donatory
verb forms are italicized. The Japanese expressions are given in
brackets. (The transcription of the Japanese text appears in the
appendix.)

(35)

> Well, let's drop it for now and wind things up. It serves no purpose
> to pile justifications on justifications. It is more important that *you
> should go on reading* [yomi tsuzuketeite-*kureru* koto na no da] the let-
> ter—my time quite *overlaps with* [kasanariatteite-*kureru* koto na no da]
> your present—that *you should keep on reading* [yomi susunde-*kureru*
> koto] the notebooks . . . without giving up . . . to the last page, when I
> will catch up with your time.
>
> (Now *you're relaxed* [kutsuroide-*kureteiru* daroo ka], aren't you?
> Yes, yes. The tea's in the squat green can. The water's already boiled
> and now in the thermos jug, so *go ahead and use* [tsukatte-*moraitai*] it.)
> (Saunders 1966, 5–6)

This excerpt is from the novel's introductory section, which
takes the format of a letter addressed to "you." The author unfolds
the entire novel as a record kept in three different notebooks. The
paragraph cited here precedes the introduction to the first notebook, the black notebook. Here the "I" asks the favor of "you" to
read the letter as well as the entire novel. In the original Japanese,
"do-*kureru*" appears four times and "do-*morau*" once. The feeling
expressed here is that "you" will kindly continue reading the book
for "me," making the expression "do-*kureru*" (do-give-to-me)
obligatory. One case of "do-*morau*" appears in the expression of
request, *tsukatte-moraitai* 'I would like you to use (that).' Here
"your" action is something that "I" "receive"; because it is "I" that
requests, if you agree, I "receive" the benefit (of fulfilling my wish)
from you. Japanese expressions of request usually take the donatory
verb form, as in *tsukatte-kudasai* 'please use.'

The donatory relation is by no means evident in the English
translation. Although the use of the modal "should" conveys indirectness, it does not carry the meaning of "you" reading for "me."
The notion "do-*morau*" seems to be ignored totally; the translation
does not convey at all the benefit the "I" "receives."

In describing events and actions, Japanese speakers cannot help
but make the donatory relationships explicit. English generally lacks

explicit markers for donatory transactions. Gauging who receives what from whom for whose benefit (or loss) presupposes, in the Japanese language, an awareness and understanding of relationality. I am not saying that Americans are unaware of these relationships. The difference lies in the Japanese obligation to express the relationality, an obligation that is absent in the American context.

Expressions of Passivity

Transitive and Intransitive Verbs

The first of two basic ways of describing an event is the transitive, "agent-operates-on-another-entity," as in *John eats an apple*. The second is the intransitive, "agent-conducts-itself," as in *John sleeps*.

The Japanese tend to view and describe events as occurring by themselves. The language, which is equipped with a sentence pattern that identifies the source of such intransitive activity, is skewed toward intransitive descriptions. Let us call the person directly experiencing an act and immediately reporting this occurrence the experiencer-speaker. The experiencer-speaker responds to an experience as an intransitive act. For example:

> [36] Umi   ga   *mieru.*
>   ocean S   can be seen
>
>   I can see the ocean.

Unlike its English counterpart, in which the seeing of the ocean is attributed to an agent, who appears as the grammatical subject, the Japanese sentence makes *umi* 'ocean' the source that evokes the experiencer-speaker's response. Critically, *mieru* 'can be seen' expresses the observer's passive reaction to the ocean; *mieru* does not presuppose the experiencer-speaker's intention of seeing. *Umi ga mieru* states that the ocean came into the speaker's view. This is a passivity that is not often expressed in English. Although it is possible to say *an ocean came into my view* or *the ocean was viewed by me* in English, few would choose to express it this way regularly. Yet this kind of passive construction is so pervasive in Japanese that it generally passes as the Japanese equivalent of the English active expression *I can see the ocean*, or *I see the ocean*.

The characterization above does not mean that Japanese speakers do not use transitive expressions. When a transitive verb is appropriate, the Japanese will, of course, use it. There is a widely told tale related to the choice of transitive versus intransitive verbs in Japanese (cf. Kindaichi 1985). A foreign maid explained to her Japanese employer, *koppu ga kowaremashita* 'the glass broke' by using the intransitive verb. This expression does not imply that the maid broke the glass. Had she said *koppu o kowashimashita* 'I broke the glass,' she would have assumed blame. This shift in perspective results from the choice of the verb *kowasu* instead of the intransitive verb *kowareru*. The glass might have been old and possibly cracked, so perhaps the maid did not cause the break. Still, Japanese people would prefer to hear *koppu o kowashite shimaimashita*, an expression that assigns responsibility and willingly accepts blame. This expression, normally coupled with apologetic phrases, is the expected strategy for apology in Japan. In this case, the grammatical choice between the transitive and the intransitive verb is made not on the basis of who-does-what but on how one decides to identify with or distance oneself from trouble.

The Japanese Passive

The frequent absence of agent in Japanese expressions noted earlier influences how so-called passive sentences function. In English we can find the active and its passive counterpart in a pair of sentences.

[37] The teacher praised the boys.
[38] The boys were praised by the teacher.

Not all active and passive counterparts make sense in English, and these two sentences demonstrate the relationship of English active and passive as simply as possible. Some Japanese passive sentences are, however, distinctively different from any English equivalents. Examples:

[39] Ame ni   furareta.
    rain by   fall-PASS

    (*lit.*, I was rained on.) I was caught in the rain.

[40] Sono otoko wa gonen   mae tsuma ni   shinareta.
    that man   T   five years ago wife by   die-PASS

    (*lit.*, The man was died by his wife five years ago.) That man's wife unfortunately died five years ago.

Although the literal English translation of *furareta*, a past tense passive form of *furu* 'fall,' is given in the passive expression, *ame ni furareta* is not a passive sentence in the strict sense, because the verb *furu* is intransitive and does not have a transitive counterpart. Likewise, *shinareta* is a past tense passive form of *shinu* 'die,' another intransitive verb. Although the passive form is used, it does not create a passive sentence.

What are these sentences, then? Why are passive forms used in Japanese in these situations where no passive meaning is possible? The answer lies in a different interpretation of passivity. In English, making a sentence passive transforms the object of the transitive verb into the grammatical subject, which changes the focus. In Japanese, passive sentences express emotional or material influences related to an observation, feeling, or event. The passive describes the speaker's reaction to the source. Influence may be positive or negative, although it is more frequently negative. Choice of the passive form of an intransitive verb, as exemplified above, implies that the influence is negative, often to the point of psychological or physical injury. The event is a source of annoyance and suffering. Passive forms in Japanese suggest a sense of inevitability, a lack of control, an inability to prevent something from happening or to cause something to happen.

There are passives in Japanese that correspond to English passives. Examples:

[41] Otokonokotachi wa sensei   ni   homerareta.
 boys   T   teacher by praise-PASS

The boys were praised by the teacher.

[42] Kono hon wa takusan no hito   ni   yomareteiru.
 this book T many   LK people by is read

This book is read by many people.

Although passives like these are used in contemporary Japanese and function similarly to English passives, use of the passive form to express emotional and material influence is central in Japanese, but peripheral in English.

Other syntactic features marked by the Japanese suffix -*(ra)reru* share similar effects of passivity in a broad sense. As Yoshiyuki Morita (1995, 147) points out, all -*(ra)reru* forms (passive, respectful, and potential), involve an incident or a situation beyond a person's control. Such incidents or situations influence the person who experiences their consequences.

In interpreting the characteristics of Japanese sentence structure, let us return once again to the concept of relationality. The Japanese preference for structuring information according to topic implies that speakers of Japanese will describe the world accordingly. Rather than automatically assigning agency status to the most prominent human candidate and building the sentence with a subject and predicate, a Japanese speaker organizes information along a topic-comment axis.

Through the use of nominalization and nominal predicates, an event is captured as a "region" to which the speaker adds comments. In general, Japanese subscribes to a rhetoric of commentation, which places priority on personal attitude at least as much as, if not more than, the propositional information. Japanese verbs of giving and receiving have implications far beyond the act of exchange, as they explicitly indicate how the transaction influences each person's interest in the web of interpersonal relationships. Japanese passive sentences also point to the experiencer-speaker, who describes the world as it influences his or her interest.

The Japanese mode of linguistic expression requires that the speaker (1) place himself or herself as an observer of the event and (2) assume the role of conveying his or her response to the event. In ordinary language use, Japanese speakers cannot escape from identifying themselves in relation to their context. This contrasts with American English, which encourages the speaker to (1) identify himself or herself as a human agent and (2) express himself or herself as one who constructs a propositional structure.

Although American speakers can and do respond to relationality cues, Japanese speakers often step back from the scene and relate to it differently. In Japanese the information is viewed through the eyes of the experiencer-speaker more extensively than it is in English. The process of interpreting and packaging, or wrapping, information versus expressing it explicitly, draws a significant distinction between Japanese and English ways of communication.

9 Japanese Communication Strategies: Collaboration toward Persuasion

Six different strategies show how the Japanese work toward collaboration in communication. Negotiating with someone across cultures raises a question as to the effectiveness of one's strategies. It has been suggested that Japanese and American negotiating styles differ, and it is worth dicussing these differences. Conversation cannot take place without listener participation. Listener behavior in Japanese casual conversation contrasts with that in American conversation. A nonverbal sign pervasive in Japanese talk, that is, head movement, is one example of the contrast. Head movement performs what I call an "interactional dance." Both listener response and head movement in Japanese conversation illustrate the close coordination between participants.

Americans and Japanese collaborate, but certain strategies found in Japanese are significantly absent in English. Critics of *nihonjinron* 'discussions of the Japanese' may find the characterization of these differences disturbing, but empirically supported differences in communication strategies do exist, and I find it important to focus on these phenomena.

Another characteristic strategy observed in Japanese communication is silence. Although silence is communicative in all cultures, the Japanese are said to tolerate silence more readily than Americans. Silence in Japan functions in several different, even opposing, ways.

Japanese speakers place importance on cooperation and collaboration in face-to-face encounters, but Japanese people find themselves in situations of conflict as well. Conflicts, in fact, occur more pervasively than usually presumed. The Japanese work to avoid the occurrence of emotionally upsetting situations in a number of ways. Considering the increase in global communication—and in the number of potential conflicts between Japan and other cultures and nations—an understanding of how the Japanese deal with conflict has practical importance.

The last part of this chapter shifts its focus to another communication strategy, rhetorical structures. Beyond the use of western rhetoric, certain Japanese genres follow the principle of *ki-shoo-ten-ketsu*, which once again demonstrates the Japanese preference for a rhetoric of commentation.

Negotiating and Persuading

Japanese and American Business Negotiation Practices

According to John L. Graham and Yoshihiro Sano (1984, 1986), Japanese and Americans use different rhetorical strategies and show different behavioral patterns in a typical business negotiation. Graham and Sano call American negotiation "the John Wayne style" (1984, 8–9). An American negotiator believes that he can handle any negotiation situation alone, just like the independent and self-realizing lone gunman in the western myth. The negotiator insists on being called by given name (emphasizing equality), even when this may make the Japanese negotiator uncomfortable. And the American negotiator—secure in the ability to deal with any situation singlehandedly—has no need to "check with the home office" unlike the Japanese counterpart. The American wants to "get to the point" as quickly and precisely as possible, expects the other party to "lay his cards on the table," expects the other party to speak up, is not likely to take no for an answer, and so on.

The John Wayne behavioral paradigm often works well between Americans. But with a Japanese negotiating team, its effectiveness is questionable, since it may lead to disengaged interaction. Once the negotiation process starts, additional problems arise because the importance placed on the various steps of the negotiation process differ. Graham and Sano (1986, 59) offer a list (a simplified version follows) summarizing the behavior of Japanese and American business negotiators at four stages during negotiation.

TABLE 7.   Stages in Negotiations

Japan

1. *Nontask sounding.* Considerable time and expense
2. *Task-related exchange of information.* The most important step: first offers (usually highly priced) with long explanations and in-depth clarification
3. *Persuasion.* Primarily behind the scenes; vertical status relations dictate bargaining outcomes
4. *Concessions and agreement.* Concessions made only toward the end of negotiations—a holistic approach to decision making; progress difficult to measure for Americans.

The United States

1. *Nontask sounding.* Relatively shorter periods
2. *Task-related exchange of information.* Information given briefly and directly; first offers (usually with "fair" price)
3. *Persuasion.* The most important step; minds changed at the negotiation table and aggressive persuasive tactics used
4. *Concessions and agreement.* Concessions and commitments made throughout—a sequential approach to decision making.

The differences are striking. Japanese take much more time in nontask sounding and exchanging personal information, which is used to judge the trustworthiness of the negotiators. While Americans spend more time and effort in attempting to persuade the Japanese negotiators by using aggressive tactics and arguing for their declared position, the Japanese tend to offer only a wild ballpark figure, "listen," and then ask questions during the persuasion stage. For Americans, reaching a final agreement step-by-step (linear progression) is more comfortable, while for the Japanese, a holistic approach is preferable. Japanese and American negotiators may find themselves trapped in the middle of negotiations if they both behave in accordance with their normal rhetorical and behavioral patterns.

Are You Ready to Argue?

Part of the reason Japanese and American negotiators are sometimes unable to engage in satisfying and fruitful interaction lies in the fact that Japanese people tend to dislike arguing unless the situation is one in which arguing is encouraged or expected. Alicia M.

Prundy, Donald W. Klopf, and Satoshi Ishii (1990) conducted a psychological survey that measured the approach and avoidance tendencies of argumentativeness of 168 Japanese and 153 American college students. The results found that (1) the Japanese subjects were not inclined to argue, but the Americans were prone to do so, (2) Japanese were more intuitive and nonargumentative, (3) confronting differences was a serious blunder in Japan, and (4) Americans viewed argument as a positive communication exchange. These tendencies come through in the analysis of business negotiations as well.

Of course, as has been pointed out by many researchers repeatedly, and as Graham and Sano (1984) carefully note, we must be aware of the danger involved in stereotyping Japanese and American businesspeople. Not every Japanese or American person behaves in the ways described above. There are argumentative Japanese and nonargumentative Americans. The personality of the negotiator influences the negotiation style used at the real-life Japan–U.S. negotiation table. Other factors—age, gender, relative rank of the negotiator, and relationship between the companies the negotiators represent—play a role in determining negotiation style, whether Japanese or American.

In this regard, Graham (1981) makes an interesting point about America's trade friction with Japan. In Japan, negotiating parties feel more comfortable if status distinctions exist and are understood, and buyers always hold a higher social status than sellers. Americans go out of their way to establish equality between buyers and sellers. In the United States, aggressive persuasive tactics— threats, warnings, and the like—are used by both parties in a business transaction. In Japan, however, although aggressive tactics are used, they tend to be reserved for the buyer, in the later stages of negotiation (when all else fails). While bargaining between Americans is an exchange between brothers, bargaining in Japan is more an exchange between father (buyer) and son (seller). The two are not equal partners; the seller must be more open to accept the buyer's decision, because refusing it or engaging in open argument will jeopardize the relationship.

Graham concludes that "a Japanese seller and an American buyer will get along fine, while the American seller and the Japanese buyer will have great problems" (1981, 9). He is not suggesting that a change in negotiation style would, by itself, solve international trade friction, but it is useful to understand the different sociocultural expectations and to appreciate the hidden messages that a choice of persuasive style conveys in an already difficult intercultural discourse.

Communication Strategies in Negotiation

Haru Yamada (1990) reports that in cross-cultural business communication, Japanese and Americans optimize different cultural strengths. The Japanese strength is shown in the group and the American strength in the individual. After examining Japanese, American, and Japanese-American intercultural business meetings, Yamada notes, "American participants take long monologic turns, distribute their turns unevenly among participants, and take the highest proportion of turns in the topics they initiate; Japanese participants take short turns, distribute their turns relatively evenly among participants, and continue to distribute their turns evenly regardless of who initiates a topic" (1990, 271).

Overt responses to relationality cues are clearer in the Japanese interactional style than in its American counterpart. The Japanese often remain vulnerable, frustrated, and hurt because their negotiation style does not allow them to express their disagreement, resentment, or anger as explicitly as their American counterparts do. The rhetorical style that postpones the conclusion to the end of the sentence and the discourse also agrees with the sense of relationality. The conclusion is reached only after a long prelude—after gauging the other's responses, expressing abundant warning, and seeking assurances of the other's sympathy.

Serious consequences can result from misunderstandings about negotiation style. According to the August 1983 issue of *Time*, "At one top-level conference, for example, President Nixon asked for a cut in Japanese textile exports, and Prime Minister Sato answered, '*Zensho shimasu,*' which was translated literally as 'I'll handle it as well as I can.' Nixon thought that meant 'I'll take care of it,' but the Japanese understood it to mean something like 'Let's talk about something else'" (40).

Although these incidents are frequently cited in the Western press to ridicule the indirect and confusing ways in which the Japanese people negotiate, misunderstandings are never caused by one party. The true meaning of the expression *zensho shimasu*, for example, must be interpreted in the context of the Japanese negotiation style. To interpret otherwise and blame the misunderstanding on one party does little to improve mutual understanding.

Inviting and Being Invited

Other situations of negotiation and persuasion that differ cross-culturally are occasions of inviting and being invited. Not knowing how to negotiate such situations can result in traumatic experiences. This is because inviting, being invited, and responding to that invitation are closely associated with the human feelings of being accepted or refused, being courteous or rude, and so on.

Polly Szatrowski (1992) points out two aspects that characterize Japanese invitation and refusal interaction. First, Japanese participants rely more on their coparticipants in the conversation, which results in coproduced stages. Second, Japanese speakers develop the invitation process by (1) showing "sensitivity for the invitee," and (2) showing compassion or sympathy. For example, Szatrowski provides an interaction example in which an invitee, whose goal may be to refuse, leaves open the possibility of accepting while developing the conversation toward a refusal.

Szatrowski cites Judy Davidson's (1984) work in discussing English invitation strategies. Although Davidson's work is based on British English interaction, American discourse seems to be similar. Davidson demonstrates that when there is potential for refusal, the inviter proceeds in such a way as to make the invitation more acceptable to the invitee. The inviter provides subsequent versions of the invitation by adding components, inducements, reasons for acceptance, and alternatives. So, for example, if an inviter senses that the invitee may not be expressly interested in accepting the invitation, he or she adds something like, "Well, we've got wonderful entertainment planned for the evening."

According to Szatrowski, a Japanese inviter will go through several "invitation stages"; he or she shows sympathy for the invitee by always leaving some option for a refusal. In the invitee's "answer stages," he or she gradually develops a story, always gauging the inviter's response, trying to convince the inviter that he or she cannot accept the invitation after all. Through this prolonged give-and-take negotiation process, both participants successfully avoid losing face.

Responding to an invitation with a flat no almost always causes awkwardness both in Japan and in the United States. We all thank the inviter. And we all tell lies and make excuses when we cannot accept invitations from others. The real reason for your refusal could be that you know from past experience that the party you are being invited to will be unbearably boring. But we cannot voice such a response to a friend's face. Japanese and American invitation-refusal interaction processes differ in the kind of strategies used and the level of negotiation processes involved. Here again, Japanese speakers behave depending on relationality cues, adjusting spontaneously to the interactional exchange (which they themselves help create), and continuously decide on a course of action based, in part, on the other's response.

Listener Responses

In observing conversation we usually notice the speaker's actions more than the listener's. It is obvious, however, that conversation cannot go on without a listener. The brief comments and utterances offered by a listener are called "back channels." These expressions, since they often do not have an easily identifiable meaning, have sometimes been considered marginal and insignificant semantically, but they are quite meaningful in conversational interaction. What, then, are the characteristics of listener responses in Japanese casual conversation? What are their types, frequencies, and functions? How do they compare with listener responses in American conversation? (See Maynard 1987a, 1989 for further discussion.)

By back channel I mean: (1) short messages the listener sends during the partner's speaking turn; (2) short messages the listener sends immediately following the speaker's turn (without a pause); and (3) short messages that include (a) brief utterances, (b) laughs, chuckles, and so on, and (c) clearly visible head movements. Brief utterances are phrases such as "uh-huh," "hmm," and "yeah." Another type of utterance frequently observed in conversation is laughing. As for clearly visible head movement, I have limited my discussion to vertical head movement (nods) and horizontal head movement (headshakes).

Having identified specific types of conversational behavior to focus on, let us look at a segment of Japanese conversation taken from the data collected.

About becoming a Japanese-language teacher

Back-channel expressions as well as head movements (H) occurring as back channels are placed near the words they respond to. Japanese particles and auxiliary expressions are given in parentheses. (The transcription appears in the appendix.)

(1.1)   *A:*   But

(1.2)   there's great pressure

(1.3)   'cause (I'm graduating from) law school.

                              H   H   H
                        (*B1:* Oh, I see, I see.)

(1.4)   So

(1.5)   I'm told that it's not good enough for me *(sa)*.

(1.6)   *B:*   You mean (you hear that) from people around you *(ne)*.

                              (*A1:* H)

(1.7)   From your parents' view, if the child does.

                              H   H   H
                        (*A2:* Yeah, yeah, yeah, yeah)

(1.8)   *A:*   But nowadays parents don't,

                        (*B2:* I see.)

(1.9)   say those things.

                  (*B3:* HH)

(1.10)   The way my friends look at it, they say things like, "It's not good enough for you" *(sa)*.

                  (*B4:* Uh huh.)

(1.11)   You see, we're all together

(1.12)   in the same Japanese-language teacher training class *(sa)*

                              (*B5:* Yeah.)

(1.13)   and although we aren't exactly friends, there are people who are taking the class together *(no)*.

                        (*B6:* Uh huh.)

(1.14)   There are nine or ten students in the class and

                              (*B7:* Uh huh.)

(1.15)   we've become friendly with each other.

                        (*B8:* H)

(1.16)   Most of them are older *(sa)*

                        (*B9:* Uh huh.)

(1.17)   women, many of them are.

                              H
                        (*B10:* Uh huh.)

(1.18)   They wish to become teachers after leaving clerical positions at companies *(ne)*.

                        (*B11:* Hmm.)

(1.19)   And those people *(sa)*
                (*B12*: Hmm.)
(1.20)   say to me, "The job isn't good enough for you" *(yo)*.
(1.21) *B:* Oh, I see, they say (something like) you're graduating
            from D University's law school.
                (*A3*: Yeah, yeah.)
(1.22) *A:* "I graduated from C University you know," they say *(yo)*.
(1.23) *B:* So although we are talking about D University *(ne)*
(1.24)   more than the way those of us on the inside can see it
                (*A4*: Uh huh.)
(1.25)   as you know what I mean by the expression I just used
                (*A5*: Yeah.)
(1.26)   when seen from the outside
                (*A6*: H)
(1.27)   the Law School at D University is still good and is first-
            rate, I should say *(ka)*.
                H   H   H
                (*A7*: Yeah, yeah, yeah.)

In this conversation segment, twelve cases of B's back channel and seven cases of A's back channel are found. Some back-channel devices are strictly verbal, as in the case of B's back channel (B2); some are strictly nonverbal, as in A's back channel (A1). Some listener back-channel behavior combines verbal and nonverbal, as in B's short utterance (B1). During this segment, which lasted forty-seven seconds, listener back channels occurred nineteen times, at least once every 2.47 seconds.

The total number of back-channel expressions in our conversational data was 871. The most frequently occurring types among all back-channel expressions were brief utterances such as *un* 'uh huh,' *hontoo* 'really,' and *soo* 'I see,' which totaled 614 (70.49 percent) of all back channels. Head movement accompanied these brief utterances 62.87 percent of the time (386 out of 614). The second most frequent category, head movement independent of verbal cues, occurred 164 times (18.83 percent). Head movement occurred either independently or with verbal back-channel expressions 63.15 percent (550 out of 871) of the time. Except for one horizontal headshake, the head movement was all vertical. Laughs occurred 93 times.

Back channels in Japanese conversation appear only in certain contexts. Most often, they respond to a speaker's use of interactional particles immediately followed by a pause, as shown in (1.6), (1.10), (1.12), (1.13), (1.16), (1.18), (1.19), and (1.27). In our data there were 688 contexts followed by back channels. Because more than one back channel can occur in a single context, the number of contexts is smaller than the number of back channels. Particle endings marked 40.84 percent (281 out of 688) of contexts. Auxiliary verb endings can function like final particles. Such endings as *deshoo* 'isn't that right?' and *janai* 'isn't it?' marked 54 contexts with back channels. Speaker overtly solicited listener response by using final particles or auxiliary verb forms in 48.69 percent (355 out of 688) of contexts.

Of the 688 contexts where back channels occurred, 352 (51.02 percent) came at major grammatical junctures. Some were accompanied by particles and/or head movements. Speaker's head movements appeared in 38.08 percent (262 out of 688) of contexts. Use of particles in non-sentence-final position increased the opportunities for back-channel expressions. This linguistic property of Japanese suits the way the language is used in interaction.

Back channels apply to a broader range of behavior, including at least the following six functions:

1. continuer (a signal sent by the listener to the speaker to continue the talk)
2. displaying of understanding of content
3. giving emotional support for the speaker's judgment
4. agreeing
5. strong emotional response
6. minor additions, corrections, or requests for information

Listener Responses in American Conversation

I also analyzed back-channel behavior (specifically "uh huhs" and the like, brief comments, head movements, and laughter) among Americans. Segment 2, given below, a forty-seven-second segment taken from our data, has four cases of back channel, two each by speakers A and B.

About a restaurant named K. Miller

(2.1) *A:* I ordered some escargots/
(2.2) and got me a Coke./
(2.3) I was like/
(2.4) *B:* I have never been to K. Miller./
(2.5) *A:* I don't know just like/
(2.6) strikes me as being very pseudointellectual./

(2.7)   Don and I were walking past (?) going to that little shop/

(2.8)   past it's open only three days or something./⌐
                                    (B1∠Um hmm)

(2.9)   you know the one I bought my uh/

(2.10) dice bag./

(2.11) B: Yeah I think I know what you mean./⌐
                                    (A1∠Yeah)

(2.12) A: And we were going there and this guy came out of K. Miller because he notices us looking at the menu and he goes/

(2.13) "Hey, Babe, want a drink? Come on inside, I'll pay for you."/
        (B2 Laugh)

(2.14) And we were like "Oh, go away."/

(2.15) B: Weird./⌐
              (A2∠Yeah)

(2.16) No, I heard the food's actually good, though./

(2.17) A: All I know is Polly offered me a slimy little escargot and I said "Thank you but no." Laugh/

(2.18) B: Oh, I like escargot./

(2.19) A: I don't./

(2.20) I just keep on thinking slime/

(2.21) sludge/

(2.22) sea bottoms, you know./

After examining the American conversational data, I found a total of 428 cases of back channels, 373 near or at an identifiable pause.

The most common American back-channel strategies were brief utterances like "uh huh," "yeah," and "right," which accounted for 50.23 percent of the total. Head movement accompanied these brief utterables 50.70 percent of the time, somewhat less frequently than in the Japanese data (62.87 percent). American pairs engaged in head movement without verbal cues 150 times (35.05 percent), while the Japanese pairs did so 164 times (18.83 percent). The Americans laughed 63 times (14.72 percent), as compared with 93 times (10.68 percent) for the Japanese.

In looking at back-channel contexts in American English, I focused on devices similar to those in Japanese, namely, (1) grammatical junctures, (2) sympathetic circularity sequences ("you know"), and tag questions (as in "aren't you?" in "You're going, aren't you?"), and (3) head movement. In the American data, 82.84 percent of back channels occurred at the point of grammatical completion. Sympathetic circularity sequences were the context only 6.97 percent of the time; head movement, only 7.78 percent. In American conversation, the grammatical completion point is clearly the single most powerful context for back channel.

Muttering versus Silent Listener

The continuous flow of back channels sent by the Japanese listener and the speaker's ready acceptance of such frequent feedback suggest that Japanese speakers have a strong inclination toward mutual monitoring and cooperation. While in English, other speaker behaviors and listener back-channel strategies that I have not investigated (such as eye gaze, as suggested by Adam Kendon 1967, 1977) are used for similar purposes, back-channel monitoring through brief utterances and head movements is characteristically Japanese.

The difference in back-channel behavior is partly a function of the language itself, as certain devices are available only in Japanese. Some have suggested that Japanese interactional particles function like English tag questions. But in Japanese, such particles can be placed in the middle of the sentence, while in English the tag question is used only at the end of the full sentence—and that usage is much more restricted.

English and Japanese offer different contexts for back channels. The Japanese language provides a comfortable environment for more frequent back channels, which suggests that merely stating that Japanese speakers resort to frequent back channels tells only part of the story. The language and the manner in which people use it are conducive to the production of a back-channel filled text.

The typical Japanese listener seems to be muttering as he or she listens to the speaker. Muttering indicates listening. Back channels are almost like background music accompanying the speaker's utterance. American listeners are more silent while listening to the speaker. Being attentive here means listening silently, inserting back channels mostly at grammatical junctures. Grammatical completion points provide coherent semantic units, and back channels send the message that the meaning has been understood, and there is no need to relinquish a speaking turn. Both Japanese and American listeners are attentive, but how they express their goodwill differs. Unless one understands this, the difference in conversation management style will leave a sense of disengagement—however successfully and naturally other aspects of the conversation may be performed.

Misinterpretation of Conversation Management

If Japanese and American ways of managing conversation are so different, what happens when a Japanese speaker talks with an American speaker? Even when either or both speakers know the other's native language, difficulties may arise. A Japanese speaker may use both verbal and nonverbal back-channel devices frequently in a very short span, creating in the American speaker a feeling of mindless agreement or inappropriate rushing. Such difficulties are caused in part by different values and social meanings associated with similar signs.

Different values attached to specific behavior in a given context often become sources of misunderstanding in intercultural communication. The more the behavior resembles one's own mannerism, as in the case of back channels and head movements, the more difficult it is fully to appreciate cross-cultural differences. Whether participants interact in English or Japanese, Japanese speakers are more likely to engage in frequent vertical head movement. The Japanese listener may look for signals to send back channels, such as the speaker's head movement, but without success. Conversely, an American speaker may wonder why Japanese speakers send frequent back channels where there is no need for them. Differences in listener responses can become a source of irritation and frustration.

Head Movement as Interactional Dance

Despite considerable interest in nonverbal communication in recent years, few empirical studies have examined specific body movements in Japanese discourse. I focus here on the vertical and horizontal head movement already identified. Head movement is both pervasive and obvious in Japanese conversation. Since it is observable in American conversation as well, the contrast should reveal useful similarities and differences in one aspect of Japanese and American nonverbal communication.

One may argue that head movement is not a significant communication sign but rather a purely stylistic device peculiar to each individual. Head movement, however, occurred frequently in all the subjects I examined in a manner that can be predicted and interpreted. While head movement often occurs with other verbal and nonverbal signs and may have only a secondary and sometimes

redundant role in communication, its pervasiveness and prominence deserve our close attention.

Based on observations of the Japanese conversational data, I
maintain that head movement is multifunctional. At the phonological level, head movement occurring with phonologically prominent
segments may mark emphasis or a request for clarification. At the
syntactic level, it functions as a clause boundary marker. And at the
interactional level, head movement serves as (1) affirmation, (2) a
claim for the end of the speaking turn and turn transition, (3) pre-
turn and turn claim, (4) turn-transition period filler, (5) back channel, and (6) rhythm. All these functions work together to manage
the conversation appropriately.

Head movement occurs in the context of conversational interaction. Paying close attention to the turn-taking environment, let us
now examine segment (3), taken from my Japanese casual conversational data. An English translation follows. Note that H (the underlined H) shows that both participants are nodding at the same time.

About the city of Narashino

                                                      a:H
(3.1)   *A:*   Nani Kimitsu ni onsen   ga ann   no?/
               what Kimitsu in hot spring S   there is IP

(3.2)   *B:*   Aa nani geetobooru taikai datta kamo-
               oh what croquet   match BE   may
               shinkattari-shite./(laugh)

                                             b:H   ┌─H-H
(3.3)   Yoku Chiba iku n   da yo ano hito./ │
               often Chiba go NOM BE IP that person ┘

(3.4)   *A:*   c:└─H Aa
                                                  ah

                                   d:H
               ima wa Chiba ni sunderu n   janai   no   ka./
               now T Chiba in live   NOM BE-NEG NOM Q

(3.5)   *B:*   Iya dakara uchi to   ato   Chiba ni Narashino
               no so   home and other Chiba in Narashino
               tte   tokoro ga atte/─┐
               QT   place S   there is
                                    │
                                   / e:H
                        (*A:*└─Un aru)
                              yes there is

```
                                            f:H-H-H
(3.6)      Soko ni itoko   ga sunden no    ne./
           there in cousin S  live    COM IP

                                       g:H
                                     (A: Hun)
                                       uh huh

(3.7)      de   nanka Chiba ni  geetobooru tomodachi ga
           and like   Chiba in  croquet    friend    S

                  h:H̲  i:H
           iru    ka ┌─ra/
           there is because
                 (A: └─j:H̲)

(3.8)      Tenki  no ii ┌─ hi  wa/ (laugh)
           weather S  good day  T

                        │  k:H
                    (A: └─ Ten laugh)
                          wea . . .

           l:H
(3.9)      Soo tenki   no ii    hi  wa taitei  dakara itoko  n
           yes weather S  good day T mostly  so    cousin LK

           chi  itte/ ─┐
           home go     │
                 (A: └─m:H)

(3.10)     asonde te/ ┌─ n:H̲-H
           play       │
                 (A: └─ o:H̲)

(3.11) A:  Soo ka uun Narashino tte    ano yakyuu no
           so  Q  uh  Narashino QT     that baseball LK

                                    p:H
           Narashino kookoo      ga aru    toko?/
           Narashino high school S  there is place

           q:H
(3.12) B:  Un anmari chikaku janai      no ┌─ kamoshirenai kedo/
           yeah not so near   BE-NEG    may │
                                            │
                                            │  r:H      s:H
(3.13) A:                                   └─ chikaku janai
                                               near    BE-NEG

               t:H
           no    ka./
           NOM Q
```

u:H
(3.14) *B:* Un demo ano ichioo   kihontekini wa Narashino
       yeah but   well more or less basically   T   Narashino

       de./   ┌─v:<u>H</u>
       BE   │
              │
(3.15) *A:*   └─w:<u>H</u>-HAa demo moo   Narashino to   ka ittara
                     ah but   already Narashino QT Q say

       sokono hen machi shika nai   n
       there   area town   only BE-NEG   NOM

       ┌─ ja-nai   ka tte./   ┌─(laugh)
       │ BE-NEG Q QT   │
       │   x:H   │   y:H-H
       │   │
       (*B:* └─ Machi shika nai)   (*B:* └─laugh)
          town   only BE-NEG

(3.16)   Ikenai wa/
          wrong IP

             (*B:*z:H-H)

                        aa:H
(3.17)   Konna koto itcha ikenai no   ka./
          such   thing say   wrong NOM Q

(3.18) *B:* Sokorahen ni Narashino pureeto   toka miru
          around here in Narashino license plate or   see

          to   sa/ (laugh)
          when IP

          Hoo   to   ka omotchatte./
          oh well QT Q   think

(3.1) *A:* You mean there are hot springs in Kimitsu?
(3.2) *B:* Well, I hear there are Japanese croquet meets or something
             there.
(3.3)   She goes to Chiba often.
(3.4) *A:* Oh, doesn't she live in Chiba now?
(3.5) *B:* No, she's at our house, and there's a place called Narashino
             in Chiba,
                   (*A1:* Yeah, there is.)
(3.6)   and that's where my cousin lives.
                   (*A2:* Uh huh)
(3.7)   And she has some friends to play Japanese croquet with in
             Chiba, so . . .
(3.8)   on the days when the weather is good,
                   (*A3:* Weath[er] . . .)

(3.9)   right, when the weather's good, most of the time she goes
             to my cousin's place
(3.10)   and plays there
(3.11) *A:* I see ... Narashino ... You mean Narashino where that
             Narashino High School, which is famous for their baseball
             team, is located?
(3.12) *B:* Yeah, but (the school) may not be really that close.
(3.13) *A:* Oh, it's not nearby.
(3.14) *B:* But basically it is in Narashino City.
(3.15) *A:* Oh, well, when you mention Narashino, there must be
             nothing but just a small downtown.
                  (*B1:* [only] downtown)
(3.16)   It's wrong,
(3.17)   I really shouldn't say such a thing.
(3.18) *B:* When I see a Narashino license plate, I think, "Oh,
             well ..."

In segment (3), which is forty-eight seconds long, there are
twenty-seven occurrences of head movement, fifteen by speaker A
and twelve by speaker B. A makes seven head movements—a, d, p, r,
s, t, and aa—during A's turn, and five—e, g, j, k, and m—during B's
turn, while B makes six head movements—f, h, i, l, q, and u—during
B's turn, and three—x, y, and z—during A's turn. A makes three—c,
o, and w—and B makes two—n and v—head movements during the
turn-transition period. There is also one case, b, where the head
movement spans B's turn and the transition period.

Head Movement in American Conversation
American head movement is indicated in the following segment of
conversation, also forty-eight seconds long.

About a basketball game

                a:H
(4.1) *A:* You think that/
(4.2)   I think/
                (*B:* Yeah b:H)
                c:H
(4.3)   I think they have a tournament at the RAC/ ⌐
                                         (*B:* ∠ At the
                                                 RAC d:H)
(4.4)   in March./ ⌐
                (*B:* ∠Right)

(4.5)   I think they advertised it the last game I went to./
(4.6)   B: Because we were in it not too long ago you know./
(4.7)   Rutgers was a contender/
(4.8)   one of my/ earlier years here./

                                                          e:H   f:H
(4.9)   My freshman or sophomore years they went/ up there./
(4.10) A: Oh, we saw that thing in the pub, Tom./
(4.11)   1978 they won ┌─twenty-six in a row./
                     g:H   h:S
(4.12) B: └─Yeah, but I wasn't here then./
(4.13)   Yeah, I know that./
(4.14) A: But I'm saying/
(4.15)   probably that was the last year they really did that
             well./ ─┐
                (B: └─Uh huh)

                                           i:H
(4.16) B: Probably we lack in that we have lost Joe./
(4.17) A: Yeah, Joe/
(4.18)   Joe Johnson, 195 pounds draft./ (laugh)
(4.19) B: He's got cut out all those articles of the paper./
(4.20)   I mean I can't/ (laugh)
(4.21)   I can't I'm surprised that he's not/
(4.22)   like you know/
(4.23)   all ah all/
(4.24)   what's that word I'm looking for?/
(4.25) A: All-American.
             j:S
(4.26) B: Oh no no no what would you get/
                   k:H   l:H   m:H
(4.27)   when people keep praising you and stuff./

In this segment there are eleven cases of vertical head movement, two by speaker A and nine by speaker B. A makes all the head
movements during his own turn, while B makes six head movements in his turn and two in A's. There is one instance of head
movement by B, head movement f, during the turn-transition
period. There are also two headshakes, h and j.

The Japanese conversational data yielded 1,372 occurrences of
head movement; the American, 452. The primary function of head
movement in American casual conversation is as a back channel followed by emphasis, although it was considerably less common than
in the Japanese counterparts.

We can draw the following conclusions from comparing head movement in Japanese and American conversation.

1. Japanese speakers use head movement much more than Americans do.
2. Head movement in both Japanese and American conversation signals the listener's response.
3. Japanese speakers often nod during their speaking turns (458 times, or 33.38 percent of occurrences). Americans are much less likely to do this (37 times, or 8.19 percent of occurrences). Japanese speakers use head movements to punctuate the flow of discourse much more frequently than Americans.
4. The second most frequent use of American head movements is the vertical head movement that occurs with phonological prominence with the emphatic function (15.71 percent of all occurrences). In Japanese the emphatic use is uncommon (1.24 percent).
5. American speakers use the headshake more often (7.74 percent) than Japanese (1.24 percent).

Interactional Dance and Empathy

Head movements in Japanese conversation often occur in pairs, triplets, or even quadruplets. Such examples are found in head movements b, f, n, w, y, and z in the first example, about becoming a Japanese-language teacher. The reason for this phenomenon is unclear, but it may be interpreted that head movement fills in and reinforces the "rhythmic ensemble" (Ron Scollon's term [1982]) of conversation. Repetitious head movement contributes to the rhythm by beating the tempo of the conversation. In the data examined, the speed of each head movement seems to match the overall speed of conversation: fast-paced conversation is accompanied by fast head movement, slower conversation by slower head movement. When head movements appear in groups, they do not occur randomly, but are distributed in such a way as to be synchronized with the tempo of the talk.

The rhythmic synchrony of head movement made by both participants occurs four times in the first Japanese data set—in head movements b/c, h/j, n/o, and v/w. The speaker-listener synchrony of head movements h and j shows how completely they are "in sync" in maintaining a flow of conversation. As speaker B marks the clause boundary, speaker A responds to it with a continuer, as if she had predicted B's head movement. Likewise, the synchrony of head movements n and o demonstrates the smooth coordination participants achieve when filling the turn transition. It seems reasonable to interpret this phenomenon as an example of rhythmic ensemble on the part of two speakers. These synchronized head movements are like dances the participants perform as a demonstration of empathy. They both express mutual cooperation and acknowledgment. The participants are conversing at the same tempo, making the identical movement in synchrony, and staying on the beat even during turn transition. Such rhythmic ensemble, along with various functional aspects realized by head movement and other strategies, helps interactants feel comfortable with each other as they make their way through the complex social and verbal entanglement of face-to-face encounters.

Head movement helps manage conversation in Japanese. Face-to-face conversational interaction without head movement would most likely make the participants feel awkward, as if something was missing. This sense of awkwardness is found not in the language per se, but in the strategies of conversation management.

Although plural head movements occur in American conversation for rhythm taking, I found no case of rhythmic ensemble—no dance of synchronized head movements—performed by both participants. This lack of synchronized head bobbing is the most striking difference between Japanese and American head movement. Although Americans may use other signs to communicate similar messages, they do not tend to achieve coordination in discourse through head movement. In Japanese, head movement plays important communicational roles in segmenting discourse, for example, notifying participants of the clause-final position and the turn-final position. The synchrony of head movement between the speaker and the listener also functions as a sign of constant and consistent empathy-building on the part of both participants.

The Eloquence of Silence

Silence is not an empty space, failed to be filled with words. It is meaningful. As William J. Samarin (1965, 115) aptly puts it, "Silence can have meaning," and "Like the zero in mathematics, it is an absence with a function." In both Japanese and American culture, silence plays an important social role. In America, for example, some institutional settings—houses of worship, libraries, and hospitals, for example—require silence. Such is the case in Japan as well.

Daniel N. Maltz (1985) presents an interesting case of silence (and noise) related to styles of worship in England and America. Many Americans think of a moment of silent prayer as an expression of religiosity, and the constitutionality of such activity at public schools is a politically sensitive issue. According to Maltz (1985), Puritans in the sixteenth century, Quakers in the seventeenth century, and Pentecostals in the twentieth century responded differently to criticism, and each protested the dominant religious assumptions of their time. Puritans stressed inspired preaching in response to ritualistic reading and recitation. Quakers stressed the silence of inner religious experience in response to the superficiality of talk. And Pentecostals advocate the making of a joyful noise. The use of silence by the Quakers and noise by the Pentecostals show that both silence and noise have important social connotations.

Silence or pauses within speech, however, have different cultural values. Ron Scollon (1985) proposes that American speech is a kind of perpetual-motion machine. "If one assumes the engine should be running, the silences will indicate failures. Smooth talk is taken as the natural state of the smoothly running cognitive and interactional machine" (1985, 26). It is difficult for people and researchers alike to give up the idea that we are a "humming conversational machine" (Scollon 1985, 26). Silences during conversation are viewed negatively in America.

If we were to place cultures along a silence-noise continuum, Japanese culture is skewed toward silence. Satoshi Ishii and Tom Bruneau (1988, 311) state, "The Western tradition is relatively negative in its attitude toward silence and ambiguity, especially in social and public relations." They remind us that silence is not the empty absence of speech sound: "Silence creates speech, and speech creates silence" (1988, 312). Following Ishii and Bruneau, we may consider that silence and speech "function as the 'figure' and the 'ground,' one being possible because of the other's existence, but dynamically so. Generally, silence is regarded as the ground against which the figures of speech are perceived and valued. The two should sometimes be perceived in the reverse way; silence should be treated as the figure against which the ground of speech functions. Most people, especially in Western cultures, are unconscious of this interdependence between speech and silence" (1988, 312).

Takie Sugiyama Lebra (1989) cites the significance of silence among Japanese by listing four dimensions of silence that she regards as culturally salient and mutually contradictory: truthfulness, social discretion, embarrassment, and defiance. First, the Japanese view a person as split into inner and outer parts; truth resides in the inner part. Spoken words form outer parts and therefore cannot be completely trusted. Truthfulness is found in silence. Second, Japanese people may choose silence in order to win social acceptance or to avoid social rejection. Lebra's first and second dimensions of silence function in opposite ways. While the first dimension attaches truthfulness to silence, the second often functions to hide truthfulness. Not saying certain things and keeping silent can be socially beneficial, but not being completely frank may give others an impression of concealment and disguise.

Third, silence helps people avoid embarrassment. For example, a husband and wife may be too embarrassed to express their love in words, so they remain silent. Fourth, silence may express hostility or defiance. The defiant silence, unlike the silence of social discretion, is openly expressive and self-assertive. Silence for Japanese, then, is a communicative device that can express many intentions and feelings.

Silence across Cultures

The different values and interpretations silence sustains in Japan and in the United States can cause problems in intercultural discourse. The following negotiation exchanges are taken from Don R. McCreary (1986, 36). Speakers E, G, and H are American negotiators; J and K are Japanese.

H: We don't really want to have to absorb the uh the costs on this

E: I just think it's only fair that you do absorb a certain amount of those costs

G: We wanna know if you're gonna give us a small break on the unit cost

E: I don't understand why we just can't get a—a general idea of your feelings about that

G: Do you understand that?

J: (30-second silence, downturned face.)

In this negotiation, repeated complaints from American negotiators were met with silence or evasions because the Japanese team had not reached a consensus on any discount and so was unprepared to give an answer. But the need to appear favorably disposed to the general process of negotiation was finally reflected by a yes in English from the assistant manager, K.

G: Can I assume then that we have reached some tentative agreement on . . . the cost factor per unit . . . ?

K: Uhh . . . yes.

G: Good!

Speaker K, in this case, is only maintaining the interactional relationship with his interlocutor. He is *not* agreeing to the terms, but is saying, "Uh-huh, I am listening to you, the information has reached me, and I am paying attention to you." In this situation, silence was not returned by silence, but by continuous speech on the part of three members of the American negotiating team.

Not being able to maintain silence or to respond in silence to another's silence can be quite costly. According to McCreary (1986, 53), western negotiators' inability to refrain from speaking in response to silence caused the following incident. Howard Van Zandt, who spent seventeen years as ITT's top manager in Japan, recalls an occasion when the head of a Japanese firm, presented with a contract to sign, did nothing. Van Zandt's ITT boss hastily sweetened the deal by $250,000, which made Van Zandt gasp: "If he had waited a few more minutes, he would have saved the company a quarter of a million dollars" (Greenwald 1983, 42).

McCreary (1986, 54) explains that this was just a case of *haragei* 'nonverbal communication; negotiating without the use of direct words.' The Japanese negotiator's silence was more likely to have been directed at the Japanese behind him, "those lower-level managers who had negotiated the deal and settled for something less than what their superior believed was the optimum position." If U.S. negotiators are not amenable to changes that their counterpart's silence may require, they may become angry, impatient, or both, and their reaction may surprise or confuse the Japanese.

Conflict and the Myth of Harmony

Japanese communication strategies place importance on cooperation and collaboration, but this does not mean that Japanese people
do not engage in conflict. The idea that Japanese people never disagree is as much of a myth as the notion that Americans always
speak their minds and often become argumentative. Japanese society has plenty of conflict—witness the frequent spats and domestic
fights featured in Japanese television dramas. Television series without a high incidence of conflict are virtually nonexistent. Of course,
conflict is an important feature of drama. Still, a desire for—if not a
preoccupation with—maintaining nonabrasive human relationships
is strong in Japanese discourse. Given the Japanese desire for cooperation and collaboration, or what Kimberly Jones (1990, 1992)
calls the "myth of harmony," an examination of how Japanese people handle conflict linguistically should once again reveal the society-relational nature of the Japanese language.

Everyday conflicts are mostly among *uchi* members. Blatant and
blunt confrontations often occur among close friends, where the
amae relationship is well established. Here the raw emotions and
hard feelings that may result from confrontation and conflict are
usually assured of being mended. The *amae* relationship is expected
to survive day-to-day emotional skirmishes among its members.

Conflicts between people who do not share the *amae* relationship, however, can be potentially harmful, even destructive.
Strongly voiced disagreements with people to whom one is
expected to show deference are considered especially damaging. In
some situations, however, as Jones (1992) explains, conflicts are
"ratified"—considered appropriate—in Japan. The television
debate where participants argue about issues is a good example. In
televised debates, participants are expected to disagree on political
or economic issues, and they can do so with abandon. The main
concern is not conflict avoidance but "focusing on issues, keeping
the talk on the subject, choosing controversial topics to discuss,
establishing individual positions, and arguing without compromis-
ing" (Jones 1992).

When the conflict is not socially ratified, participants must
work hard to ratify it. Jones discusses a case where coworkers were
involved in a rather tense conflict. After a few minutes of strained
conversation, the participants reached an impasse. They abruptly

stopped talking, turned away from each other, and returned to their desks without having resolved anything. Even in these circumstances, however, there was a concern for ratification. For example, one sign Jones (1992) observed was a concerted effort to make light of the situation; coworkers strove for a playful tone, introducing laughter and jokes during the confrontation. They attempted to put the conflict situation into a framework of play. Every ratification of conflict Jones found in her data involved some sort of reframing of the conflict as play. Defusing the conflict through play dissipates the threat of a troublesome encounter.

I suspect that this reframing strategy of "play" is fairly common in communication across cultures. Certainly Americans use it, too. The differences between American and Japanese reframings lie in their explicit and inexplicit strategies. Jones (1990, 305) notes that in the coworkers' conflict, in addition to explicit opposition moves, participants used inexplicit strategies of conflict reframing, including style-switching, repetition, parallelism, and laughter.

If, after all reframing strategies are exhausted, the conflict is still not ratified, Jones (1990, 306) concludes, "It seems . . . impossible for the participants to dispute with each other comfortably." Even the Japanese may have bought into the myth of harmony—good Japanese should not and do not quarrel in public. Japanese people are discouraged from engaging in conflict unless the situation is ratified, either socially or interpersonally; Americans seem less threatened or hurt when they find themselves in conflict discourse. Americans may not always need to reconcile themselves in conversation. Differences of opinion are not felt to harm the relationship.

Speakers of Japanese, however, are likely to feel that achieving reconciliation or agreement in conversation is important and that unresolved differences of opinion may threaten the future relationship. Situations where anger and antagonism can be appropriately expressed without damage are rarer in Japan than in the United States. Among Americans, open, frank, and fair conflicts do not necessarily cause lasting ill-will. A certain level of opposition is even expected from each individual, since everyone is encouraged to behave on his or her own. But Japanese people remain relationally vulnerable, and unplanned conflicts in the *soto* relationship normally result in psychological and emotional stress. The bitter aftertaste of an unexpected verbal spat in Japanese discourse can linger on in the hearts of the participants for a very long time.

Rhetorical Structures

Communication involves more than managing interactional strategies. Discourse, composed of units larger than the individual sentence, is exceedingly important. How sentences are put together in Japanese, some have claimed, differs from the rules governing western rhetoric. What are the characteristics of Japanese rhetorical structures, the organizational principles of Japanese discourse?

Although the organization of discourse has much in common across languages, some differences exist. What is cohesive in meaning in one culture may not hold in another. Although the premise of cohesiveness is its logical property—it makes sense—sociologists and anthropologists have long known that logic, like language, is culturally bound.

Both the Japanese and other peoples have criticized the Japanese language's lack of a "logical" foundation. The language has been called "illogical" or "alogical." This view is misleading, however, because the so-called logical foundation normally refers to the logical syllogism, which occurs only in limited cases in everyday rhetoric. In the traditional model of western rhetoric (for example, Aristotle's), what is advocated is the rhetorical syllogism (or enthymeme) whose premises and conclusion are probable. They need not be logically valid. Not all English statements come with supporting reasons introduced by "for," "because," "since," or an "if . . . then" clause.

Logic-based rhetoric is suitable only for certain types of discourse, both in the West and in Japan. Japanese writers use logical progressions, although to a more limited extent than English writers do. Depending on the genre, Japanese texts employ mixtures of rhetorical structures, including—and going beyond—deductions (enthymemes) and inductions (use of examples). English texts do, too, but Japanese writers seem to have more freedom. Some methods of creating connected discourse are effective and ideal in Japanese, but do not work in English. This often creates the impression that Japanese texts are difficult to understand, too subjective, and lacking in cogent arguments—and that the writer's intention is ambiguous, at best.

Robert B. Kaplan (1972) describes rhetorical patterns across cultures in a bold and controversial way. According to him, five different types of rhetorical movements (that is, from the introduction of a topic to its conclusion) are found in expository writings: (1) circular (Oriental), (2) straight linear (English), (3) zigzag (Romance), (4) broken zigzag (Russian), and (5) broken parallel linear (Semitic). English argumentation is characterized as a straight line running directly from topic to conclusion. Orientals (presumably including the Japanese) go in circles before reaching a conclusion. Kaplan uses a diagram of a line spiraling inward (explanation) toward the center (conclusion). Obviously, his characterization is oversimplified. But it raises an important point about the nature of so-called logical cohesiveness.

Japanese discourse organization shows multiple types of cohesiveness, and often mechanisms are mixed in real-life discourse. For example, the basic discourse structure is tripartite, consisting of initial, middle, and final parts. As in English, this simplest organization reveals itself in brief expository discourse. Beyond this are other organizations. A five-part organization rules Japanese traditional (Buddhist) rhetoric. Its elements are: *okori* 'beginning,' *uke* 'leading,' *hari* 'main point,' *soe* 'supplement,' and *musubi* 'conclusion.' Another organization, *ki-shoo-ten-ketsu*, has four parts.

Ki-shoo-ten-ketsu

Ki-shoo-ten-ketsu has its origin in the structure of four-line Chinese poetry and is frequently referred to in Japanese as a model organizational structure for expository (and other) writing. The four elements are: (1) *ki*, presenting a topic at the beginning of one's argument, (2) *shoo*, following *ki* and developing the topic further, (3) *ten*, introducing a relevant idea not directly related to or connected with *ki*, and (4) *ketsu*, bringing all the elements together and reaching a conclusion.

A classic example of this four-part organization is a story about the daughters of Itoya.

(5.1) *Ki* (topic presentation)

Daughters of Itoya (the thread shop) in the Motomachi of Osaka.

Oosaka Motomachi Itoya no musume.
Osaka   Motomachi Itoya LK daughter

(5.2) *Shoo* (topic development)

The elder daughter is sixteen, and the younger one is fifteen.

Ane   wa juuroku, imooto   wa juugo.
elder daughterT   sixteen   younger daughterT   fifteen

(5.3) *Ten* (surprise turn)

Feudal Lords kill (the enemy) with bows and arrows.

Shokoku daimyoo   wa yumiya   de   korosu.
provinces feudal lord T   bows and arrows with kill

(5.4) *Ketsu* (conclusion)

The daughters of Itoya "kill" (the men) with their eyes.

Itoya no musume wa me de   korosu. (Nagano 1986, 102)
Itoya LK daughter T   eye with kill

Note the pun on the word *korosu* 'to kill,' which is achieved by *ten*, a diversionary train of thought. All of a sudden the story line switches to the "killing" of feudal lords, which is reconnected to the girls' "killing" (attracting) men through their devastatingly attractive glances.

The point of the discourse reveals itself only at the *ketsu* stage. Comprehending *ketsu* in relation to the preceding parts becomes crucial, because the beginning gives no clues about where the discourse is headed. To complicate matters, *ten* leads the discourse astray by adding an unexpected thought. Unlike some writings in English in which conclusions are stated at the beginning of the paragraph or the discourse (topic sentence), in certain Japanese discourse, the conclusion may not be revealed until the very last sentence of the essay. This often gives the impression that Japanese discourse is difficult to comprehend.

The prevalence of the *ki-shoo-ten-ketsu* principle in Japanese discourse may give the impression that somehow Japanese people fail to create or appreciate logically cohesive discourse (or worse, that they are incapable of logical, rational thinking). Nothing could be further from the truth. In straight news reports, Japanese writing is more "objective" (in the sense of being based on facts) than English writing. According to Suzuko Nishihara and Tomoyo Shibahara (1995), an examination of eighty articles of identical length reporting on identical topics in the Japanese *Asahi Shimbun* and the *International Herald Tribune* yielded the following interesting information. Japanese articles contained primarily factual information (such as factual occurrence, background information, and reference). English articles contained, in addition to factual information, more speculative statements (conjecture, implication, citation, and prediction).

Rhetorical structures in Japanese are multiple. Depending on the purpose of communication, different (combinations of) organizational principles are chosen. In line with the spirit of collaborating toward persuasion, Japanese writers present conclusions gradually (sometimes indirectly), often after giving extensive background information. (Similar strategies are used by Japanese business negotiators as discussed earlier.) The tendency to place the conclusion toward the end of the text is evident in Japanese newspaper columns as well. I examined thirty-eight newspaper opinion columns called *Koramu Watashi no Mikata* 'Column, my view,' all written by different reporters, appearing in the *Asahi Shimbun* International Satellite Edition distributed through its New York facilities for the months of January through April, 1994. Given that in "Column, My View" the reporter's conclusion is summarized in the headline, I located the position in the text where the headline paraphrase appeared. The earliest headline paraphrase appeared, on average, at a point 86.73 percent into the column, corroborating the tendency to put the conclusion toward the end.

I also investigated where in the column the writer's comments appear. Commentary sentences are marked by linguistic devices directly conveying the writer's personal views (nominal predicates, verbs referring to the writer's act of writing, speculative modal expressions, and so on). These commentary sentences constitute 20.06 percent of all sentences (excluding direct quotation), but their appearance in the column-initial paragraph is limited to 12.24 percent. Paragraph-initial sentences are predominantly noncommentary (87.16 percent of the time). Sentences within each paragraph follow a noncommentary to commentary pattern 81.5 percent of the time. Writers clearly delay offering personal commentary in newspaper columns.

I must mention that the *ki-shoo-ten-ketsu* organization has come under fire in Japan. For example, Takeshi Shibata (1992) suggests that the information age requires discourse in which the conclusions appear at the beginning, especially in practical genres. But the Japanese continue to use various rhetorical structures, and *ki-shoo-ten-ketsu* is expected to play a significant role in literary and other genres.

The *ki-shoo-ten-ketsu* mode of rhetorical progression matches Japanese sentence structure, which places the verb at the end. Additionally, other structural features of the Japanese language—extras, attitudinal adverbs, topic-comment structure, nominal predicates, and so on—all work to create a specific kind of discourse. Rather than giving priority to the propositional information (who-does-what-to-whom) in sentence and discourse, wrapping the referential information becomes important. The wrapping process prioritizes the rhetoric of commentation in Japanese.

Japanese communication strategies offer varied ways of responding to relationality cues. Rather than thriving in confrontational discourse, the Japanese tend to collaborate toward persuasion. Belief in the myth of harmony may restrain people from exploring their anger except under appropriate conditions. The muted confrontational business style of the Japanese people seeks collaboration from the other party. One's action is constantly evaluated and aligned, it seems, in its relation to the addressee and to the context. Context is actively manipulated and created by extensive listener response and a nonverbal interactional dance, both of which require active participation from a partner. The multiple functions of silence in Japanese discourse also help accommodate the need to show sensitivity toward a society-relational orientation. When a conflict situation occurs in Japan, participants work to ratify it by turning it into play.

In contrast to the Japanese preference for avoiding unexpected confrontation and conflict, Americans show their respect and concern for a partner by being open, straightforward, and, if necessary, by expressing the confrontation explicitly, not in silence. Americans' collaboration is based on these sincere actions, and they seek solutions not by avoiding them but by negotiating through them.

I am not saying that the Japanese people are collaborative while Americans are not. Rather, I am pointing out that how people confront each other and how they collaborate to reach solutions differ. More specifically the communication strategies used in conflict situations show marked differences.

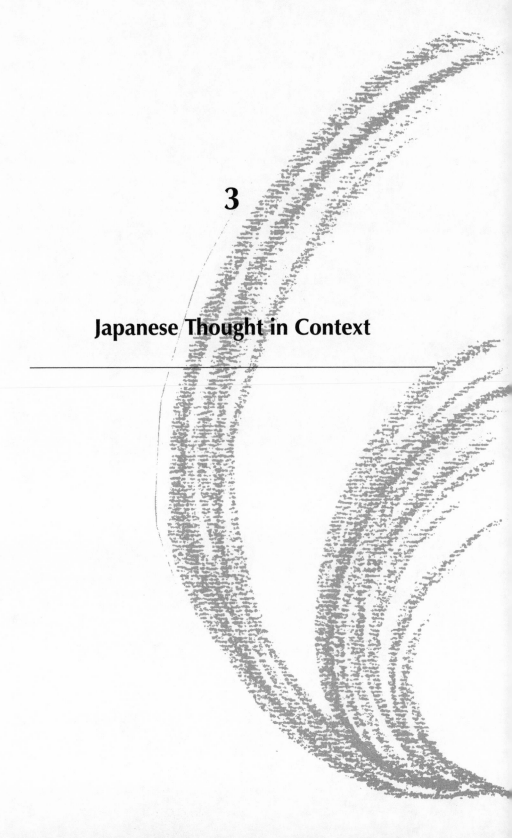

3

Japanese Thought in Context

10 Relationality and
Language-Associated Thought

The characteristics of the Japanese language depicted in part 2 point to the importance of the underlying dynamic of relationality proposed in part 1 and mentioned repeatedly. Although it is natural to assume that individual differences exist in interpretation of and response to relationality cues, broad cross-cultural differences in understanding relationality also exist. Japan tends to be society-relational; America, self-relational. The Japanese language contains many built-in mechanisms for expressing messages cued by relationality.

Japanese as a Society-Relational Language: A Summary
Every language operates on the basis of some kind of relationality, and within the boundaries of a single language, different degrees of importance are placed on relationality. For example, formal written communication (official documents, scientific reports, and so on), although essentially relational, maintains a relatively rigid form and is only slightly expressive in response to contextual relationality cues. Casual face-to-face conversation, which includes extensive verbal and nonverbal information, responds more fully to varied contextual and social relationality cues. Even given this intracultural variability, however, it is possible to identify a characteristically Japanese variety of relationality.

Part 2 examined items selected from contemporary Japanese language, each reflecting, to varying degrees, the Japanese society-

relational orientation. A summary of how Japanese reflects relationality follows.

1. Styles change depending on interpersonal, social, and situational context. This shows the language's overt response to the
   relation it holds to context, for example, politeness, honorifics,
   masculine/feminine speech, and so on.
2. Certain phrases express the speaker's personal and often emotional attitude toward the information and the addressee. These
   phrases reveal meaning that is motivated and/or encouraged by
   interpersonal relationality cues, for example, adverbs, interactional particles, sentimental words, and swear words.
3. Rather than prioritizing information only, the speaker's perspective toward that information is overtly expressed, always
   taking the addressee's point of view into account. Examples
   include topic-comment structure, sentence-final manipulation,
   verbs of giving and receiving, and passive sentences.
4. Rather than prioritizing the specification of who-does-what-to-
   whom, the event as a whole is presented first in a nominal
   clause; then personal attitudes are added. This structural preference contributes to the rhetoric of commentation shown by
   topic-comment structure, nominalization and nominal predicates, and rhetorical structures.
5. Strategies abound to avoid unratified confrontation, and verbal
   expressions are constrained by interpersonal relationality cues,
   which the speaker recognizes. Speech styles that encourage
   interpersonal rapport reveal the importance of monitoring and
   collaboratively responding to others, for example, collaborative
   strategies, listener responses, joint head movement, silence, and
   ratified conflicts.

Between Language and Thought

How are modes of Japanese communication associated with the
ways people think and feel in Japanese? Recall that the nature of the
relationship between language and thought—whether language
controls or influences a speaker's thought, and how this process is
related to culture—remains controversial. I believe that the way a
language is coded encourages speakers to engage in those kinds of
thinking and feeling that the codes of the language readily express.
But the structure of language alone does not form one's expressive

range. How one uses that language also encourages particular kinds of thinking and feeling.

The relationship between language and thought can be understood as follows. If we accept John R. Searle's (1995) view that language is essentially constitutive of a society's institutional reality, we can posit that language is indispensable for establishing, understanding, and engaging in social realities. Social phenomena are simply too complex to be described or referred to without using language. Although some aspects of reality are language-independent, many others require language, which is capable of representing things beyond itself. Our conditioned social perceptions and conventionalized social rules skew our understanding of the world.

It is uncertain whether we follow social rules consciously or unconsciously. According to Searle (1995, 145), social rules play a crucial role in explaining the behavior of a society's members, because those members acquire the "disposition" associated with the rules. Social facts, which in part are built of language, influence members of a society to be disposed to understand, to behave, and to think in certain ways.

Within a single language, though, we find expressions that point to contradictory orientations of thought, so the relationship of language and thought is far from simple. Words and structures that describe an identical event from opposing points of view are useful and necessary ingredients of language. But it is still possible to draw a general outline of a particular language and its profiles of thought.

In discussing language-associated thought, I have concentrated on language in its most ordinary form, everyday conversation. Such language inevitably influences, although indirectly and diffusely, a person's view of the world.

As we reinforce our worldview through language by (re)interpreting and acting out a specific kind of relationality in our daily lives, we continually attest to the importance of the relationship between language and thought. Language offers a mediatory device for an individual's socialization and self-identification in a given culture, and Japanese modes of communication profoundly influence some of the ways Japanese people think and feel. But relationality has a fluid quality: Not every aspect of contemporary Japanese society and culture—and consequently its language and thought—can be explained as being society-relational.

Changes in the Orientation of Relationality

Urbanized Japanese society in the 1990s seems to be becoming increasingly alienated. The traditional sense of community is losing ground because of the spread of apathy among the populace. This tendency is documented by Sooichiroo Tawara (1993), particularly in relation to the Japanese police. When the ineffectiveness of the police was pointed out to the chief of the criminal investigation section of the Tokyo Metropolitan Police Board, Tawara reports, the chief replied that city dwellers in Japan are not interested in each other, or more accurately, they avoid being involved with each other. Residents rarely open their doors even to detectives investigating a case affecting the neighborhood. When detectives *are* invited in, residents seem indifferent to what is happening around them. What little spark of interest a detective's questioning may arouse quickly fizzles, since city dwellers have isolated themselves and are not personally connected to others in their community.

Given this transformation from interconnectivity to alienation, the traditional society-relational orientation is no longer the single most fitting description of some social aspects of urban Japan. Things have become far more complex. The global creeping of convergent material values has blurred some of the formerly clear boundaries around cultures. Japanese people undoubtedly desire individuality and freedom. Stories depicting a lone samurai, whether old or new, have enjoyed and continue to enjoy a broad-based popularity. Although the direction in which Japanese society is heading challenges tradition, in general terms, the Japan of the 1990s remains more society-relational and more preoccupied with relationality than the United States.

Changing Language

With societal change comes linguistic change. In contemporary Japan, the media exert a major influence on the Japanese language and its use. Although the Japanese are expected to show restraint in voicing opinions or offering frank observations, a popular cartoon character does just the opposite. Shinchan, a very outspoken and often offensive preschooler, has attracted attention in Japanese children's culture. According to the *Wall Street Journal* (February 11, 1994), Shinchan, the protagonist of six volumes (and twenty million copies) of "Crayon" comic books, a weekly television cartoon, and a movie, comes right out and says what he is thinking. In one of the recent *Kureyon Shinchan* 'Crayon Shinchan,' for example, the comic book writer Yoshito Usui (1994, 20) has Shinchan yell out to his mother, *"Deta na, kaijuu shiwakuchan"* 'Here comes the monster, the Wrinkled.'

The language of this rude, lewd little boy is said to influence Japanese four- to twelve-year-olds. Whether such straightforward talk—a speech style ignoring conventional relationality cues—will continue as the children mature remains to be seen. Likewise, whether this manner of communication influences how children think and feel in Japanese is unclear. The society-relational orientation of the Japanese language is likely to hold for the foreseeable future, and Japanese ways of communication will persist. But a loosening of traditional restraints on the language, however exaggerated, may well shift traditional orientations of Japanese thought.

11 Centrality of Scene:
The World as a Relational Place

Same Scene, Different Expressions

In Japanese the scene often assumes primacy when describing an encounter, event, or phenomenon. This contrasts with English, where the focus is on an agent, an actor or doer who initiates some action within the scene. In order to explore this line of thinking further, let us try an example.

Picture the plains of Nebraska, where a farmer hears a distant cry of birds and looks up to the sky. He or she notices sandhill cranes flying in formation over the gray autumnal prairie. How will he or she express this scene? For Yamabe no Akahito in eighth-century Japan, the image of the crying cranes flying over the water is etched in his waka appearing in *Man'yooshuu*, a waka anthology.

> *Wakanoura ni shio michi kureba*
> *Kata o nami*
> *Ashibe o sashite tazu naki wataru.*
> As the tide flows into Wakano Bay
> The cranes, with the lagoons lost in flood,
> Go crying toward the reedy shore.

The critical part of the poem is *tazu* 'crane(s)' *naki* 'crying' *wataru* 'go across.' Yoshihiko Ikegami (1981, 1988, 1991) explains the difference between what is expressed in the original and in its English translation: "Faced with a scene in which a crane (or group of cranes) is (are) flying from one side of the scene to the other, we can either concentrate on the moving object(s) in the foreground (i.e., the crane[s]) and see the situation in terms of the *change in locus* of this "individuum," or we can concentrate on the whole scene and see the situation in terms of the *change in state* brought about as the flying crane(s) shift position in the whole scene" (1988, 2; italics in original). The Japanese expression *tazu naki wataru* creates the image that the scene as a whole changes rather than stressing the movement of the crane(s) itself (themselves). Ikegami (1991, 287) summarizes this interpretation by the expression "focus on the whole event" in contrast with "focus on the individuum." The shifting state of the scene portrayed in the Japanese poem does not quite survive in the English translation "The cranes, . . . go crying. . . ." The English translation portrays the cranes as agents, and their movements become the focus of attention. These differing ways of describing an event represent the figure-ground dichotomy in human perception. As Ikegami (1988, 2) states, we "can see a situation in such a way as to let a figure emerge from the background or in such a way that the figure merges with, or is submerged in, the background." In the poetics of Yamabe no Akahito, the figure merges with the background.

Ikegami (1988, 9) goes a step further and states that in Japanese texts "an individuum is not seen in isolation; it is not clearly separated from what it stands contiguous with. It is merely a part of a larger whole, with which it may become merged to the extent of losing its identity." This statement echoes many rhetorical and philosophical statements made about Japanese literature and culture. And in the example of classical waka poetry we see a similar effect—the event is interpreted as a change in state, rather than as a sequence of actions. Tetsuo Anzai (1983), following Ikegami's discussion, states: "In English, when interpreting a situation, there is a strong tendency to focus on the agent of the *mono* 'object,' analyze the event in terms of a cause-and-effect relationship, and conceptualize it as such. On the other hand, the strong tendency in Japanese is to interpret the whole situation as a *koto* 'event' and capture the relationship between that event and the human beings from the point of view of the observer/speaker" (1983, 105; my translation).

Following Ikegami and Anzai, I refer to the difference between Japanese and English as scene-orientation versus agent-orientation. For Japanese people, the scene of an event as a whole assumes the primary focus of attention (in comparison to English, where the agent is the primary focus). Nominalization and nominal predicates function in a similar way: Clausal information is captured by a region, which often coincides with the scene. Viewing reality as scene-oriented promotes the worldview that the scene holds various contextual and interpersonal relations in balance. This tendency to see the world as a relational place is one profile of Japanese thought.

Often a natural or human act stirs different emotions in people. The appearance of a flock of birds in the sky may trigger different reactions. Although expressions of what is being observed differ individually in eloquence, one cannot deny differences based on culture. Here linguistic expression and thought are descriptively linked, and those who share a similar linguistic culture are likely to see things in a similar way. The primacy of scene, in contrast to agent, offers an insight into how the Japanese perceive and understand a segment of the world.

12 Nonagent Orientation:
The World as "Becoming"

Closely related to the Japanese sense of "scene" is the Japanese language's preference for using verbs equivalent to English "be" and "become." While English prefers to express an agent, Japanese has several strategies for suppressing the notion of agency. One strategy privileges locative expressions over agents. Verbs like *aru* 'there is/are' and *naru* 'become' are preferred. Observe the following expressions.

[1] Sano-san ni wa musuko ga futari *aru*.
   Mr. Sano at T son S two there are

   (*lit.*, There are two sons at Mr. Sano's.) Mr. Sano has two sons.

[2] Watashitachi wa kono tabi kekkonsuru koto ni *narimashita*.
   we   T this time marry   fact to become

   (It has become that) we will be getting married soon.

In Japanese sentences a locative expression or a topic appears where the agent would be in English; "Mr. Sano" and "we" specify agents in the English translation, but in Japanese they do not. Accordingly, Ikegami (1981, 1988) typologically identifies Japanese as "Be-language" versus English "Have-language" as well as Japanese "Become-language" versus English "Do-language." In Japanese "Be-" and "Become-" language, reality is interpreted in a way quite different from English. The agent becomes less prominent and more diffused, and the context in which the agent appears assumes greater significance.

175

Look for a moment at how the English language encourages its users to perceive and describe events. Heinz Werner and Bernard Kaplan's characterization of Indo-European languages is relevant here. Werner and Kaplan explore the relationship between (linguistic) symbol and reference. They suggest that correspondence, "a mutual process of convergence," must occur between the meaning and the form of representation. Maintaining that language uses certain models to that end, they state: "In Indo-European languages, the model used for connoting states of affairs and articulating them linguistically is the human action model. A total event is basically articulated into agent, action, and object; the relationships between these are portrayed in sentences in which the vehicles for the referents are related to each other through a 'syntax of action'" (1963, 57).

The power of this Indo-European action model with the human-as-agent becomes evident when one considers its broad-based application. Two of Werner and Kaplan's English examples are: (1) we say "X kills a dog" as well as "X feels pain," as if the state of feeling is an action and pain an object acted upon; (2) we say "X has dark skin" or "A equals B" to express attributes and conceptual relations in terms of this action model.

In contrast, Japanese tends to frame the event as (1) something existing rather than someone possessing something, and (2) something becoming or happening, often beyond the agent's control, and not as something that an agent who has full control "initiates and causes to happen." The Japanese are more likely to interpret an event as a situation that becomes and comes to be on its own, while Americans tend to perceive an event resulting from an agent doing something and causing things to happen.

Incorporating the concept of the centrality of scene, we can conclude that one of the ways the Japanese are characteristically encouraged to see things is as the scene becoming, whereas from the American perspective it is the agent doing. The world that becomes is also a world where elements are held in balance, located in mutual interrelation. Here, instead of recognizing an agent acting on an object, multiple elements constructing the entire scene find themselves in a relational balance. The nonagent orientation of the Japanese language is also clear from the discussion of Japanese passives, nominalization, and nominal predicates.

I caution the reader that Japanese discourse does not completely lack humans as agents, nor is it devoid of the human element. Although the person as agent plays a smaller grammatical role in Japanese than in English, the human element certainly appears in Japanese expressions. The human factor in English is a person who is the agent of an action, whereas in Japanese it is a person who responds to an event as a whole and who describes the scene with his or her personal view, including a marked preference for seeing a scene that becomes.

13 More than Words:
A World beyond Description

Communication in any society transcends the exchange of verbal expression, but in Japanese, there is a marked tendency to mistrust the persuasive potential of words. According to Dean C. Barnlund:

> To the Western argument the self-expression is valuable, the Japanese might reply that this is true only if there is first sufficient inner reflection: The quality of outer dialogue can rise no higher than the quality of an inner monologue.... The introspectionist emphasis found in Eastern religions is more highly regarded by and seems more congenial to the Japanese than the expressionist emphasis found in Western religions and philosophy.... Linked to this elevation of inner dialogue is the lower status accorded to words. There is a sense that reality cannot be captured in words, that any statement about one's inner experience inevitably will distort and oversimplify it. (1989, 116–117)

In general, American society attributes a higher status to words and to an individual's verbal ability. Verbal skill is a survival skill in American society, where upward mobility depends on it. In a court of law, a lack of verbal skill may actually be a matter of life or death. The American philosophy of "getting it in writing" and trusting written contracts, which makes words paramount, contrasts with Japan, where written documents are often important when they are supported by both parties' goodwill and sincerity. Given a choice between a person and his word, Americans give the impression that they are more likely to trust his word. For the Japanese people this does not necessarily hold.

The idea that language, especially written language, does not sustain a central authority in Japan is aptly described by Mara Miller as "non-logocentrism." In Miller's words, "logocentrism refers to an insistence on the centrality of words, or logos, usually with connotations of rationality or logical argument in addition to language per se" (1993, 482). The absence in Japan of logocentrism is expressed, among other things, by a preference for silence over speech, for the oral over the written word, for visual or kinesthetic communication over the verbal, and so on.

Language as Event and Language as Manifestation of a Sincere Heart

Historically the Japanese have revered *kotodama* 'spirit/soul of words' and believed that a living entity, a spirit, if you will, dwells within language. As Roy Andrew Miller (1977) explains, it is possible to comprehend the meaning of *kotodama* by the way it was written in Old Japanese. Two different Chinese characters were assigned for *koto; koto* for 'words' and *koto* for 'affair, matter.' According to Roy Miller, the source for this orthographic variation is found in the *kotodama* concept itself, "where the idea that the 'thing' referred to by a given word is coeval as well as coextensive with the 'word' that refers to it" (Miller 1977, 264). The close association between the "word" and the "affair, matter" referred to is indicative of the Japanese people's view of language. Language is not *mono* 'object,' but *koto* 'affair, matter,' an event where a spirit resides. Yet words themselves construct only a portion of social interaction, since they "live" when one speaks from the heart and infuses them with spirit. Consequently, words form only a part of sincere communication.

Language as Object and Conduit

The English language tends to employ words as tools of communication, devices for expressing oneself logically, cohesively, and as clearly and convincingly as possible. Communication is a conduit, as argued by Michael J. Reddy (1979). Reddy enumerates the "conduit metaphor" in English language by referring to English sentences, including the following:

(1) You have to put each concept into words very carefully.
(2) Try to pack more thoughts into fewer words.

(3) Try to get your thoughts across better.
(4) None of Mary's feelings came through to me with any clarity.

Reddy states that English treats thoughts and ideas as things contained in words—as seen in (1) and (2). They are delivered through a conduit from the originator of the message to its receiver, as in (3) and (4). This understanding of language, evidenced in English usage, skews the view of communication toward the conduit process. According to Reddy, English shows a tendency to treat language as an object that can be transmitted from one place to another, to give a false impression that communication is a "success without effort" system rather than an "energy must be expended" system (1979, 308), and to emphasize the effort made by the speaker or writer while trivializing the function of the reader or listener.

In the American view, words are compact, useful, and manageable—almost tangible objects that can be transported from one person to another. This contrasts with the Japanese view that words are meaningful only in the context of the communication event. As Motoki Tokieda (1941) maintains, language is not an objective entity; it is a subjective experience.

More than What Words Express

The American view of language contrasts with the Japanese view that communication involves far more than words. For the Japanese, social, situational, psychological, and emotional factors must be incorporated before understanding (the spirit of) words. The more modern Japanese view of language is not unlike Reddy's, but the traditional Japanese view of language still resides in contemporary Japanese thought. Looking at language as event rather than object infuses many aspects of Japanese thinking. For Japanese speakers, language is ultimately a subjective experience that comes to life in context, when one finds oneself connected with others in society.

14 Echoing "Voices from the Heart":
A World of Things and Emotions

The language-as-event view is attested to by the traditional scholar's understanding of the Japanese language. The historical background of language studies again shows that the Japanese language places importance on emotional expression and personal attitude, and that these are related to a preoccupation with society-based relationality. The thought processes associated with this view include the assumption that much of what constitutes the reality of everyday life comes into focus only when placed in the context of human subjectivity. That is, many things in the world do not exist in and of themselves; the subjective human experience is what gives them meaning.

This view of the subjectivity of the Japanese language is not new. Traditionally language scholars in Japan have treated the emotional and expressive aspects of language—let us call these "modal" aspects—much more seriously than have scholars in the West. Unlike western tradition, which emphasizes information or propositional meaning, Japanese scholarship has a long and thriving tradition of viewing language as an expression of the speaker's subjective and expressive voice. Although many aspects of traditional Japanese language studies have contributed to this view of the language, the category of *te-ni-o-ha* (or *te-ni-ha*) particles has consistently served as a starting point. An awareness of the qualitative differences between the *te-ni-o-ha* category and other parts of speech sheds light on the dual structural forces of Japanese.

In his *Gengyo Shishuron* ([1824] 1979), Akira Suzuki, a scholar of the Japanese language during the Edo period, described four categories of words: nominals, adjectives, verbs, and *te-ni-o-ha* particles. Suzuki grouped the first three into one large category, *shi* 'referential words,' and put *te-ni-o-ha* in an opposing category. According to Suzuki, referential words are like containers. They cannot open without *te-ni-o-ha*. *Te-ni-o-ha* particles represent "voices from the heart" and are like hands that manipulate the containers. Suzuki concludes that the voices of *te-ni-o-ha* distinguish and express states of one's heart, *kokoro*, and the expressions of *shi* distinguish and describe objects ([1824] 1979, 23–24).

Suzuki's work was resurrected by Motoki Tokieda, who in 1941 introduced his theory of language, *gengo kateisetsu* 'theory of language as process.' Tokieda (1941, 1950) views language as the process by which the speaker expresses ideas through linguistic sounds. Language is not a product (or an object) with a rigid internal structure, Tokieda insisted, but a *shinteki katei* 'psychological process' (1941, 86). Based on this theory of language as process, Tokieda identifies two categories, *shi* and *ji*—corresponding to the traditional categories of *shi* and *te-ni-o-ha*—and claims that all Japanese lexical items are either *shi* 'referential words' or *ji* 'nonreferential, functional words.' Tokieda defines *shi* as an expression that has undergone the objectifying process. *Shi* represents an objective and conceptualized notion of referents, which includes grammatical categories of nouns, verbs, adjectives, and adverbs. *Ji*, on the other hand, is an expression that has not gone through the objectifying process. It represents the speaker's subjective perspective toward the referent, and it includes conjunctions, exclamatory expressions, particles, and auxiliary verbs.

While the distinction between *shi* and *ji* is applicable to other languages, analysis of Japanese using the two categories is particularly productive. The abundance of *ji*—language-explicit means of expressing personal emotions and attitudes—can again be traced to the sociocultural characteristics of Japan. (In part 2 we observed an array of examples of the Japanese language and its use that demonstrate the centrality of modal aspects.) Ultimately, viewing the language not only as a conveyer of information but also as the expression of the speaker's perspective leads to a worldview that places importance on subjective interpretation.

15 Manipulation of Textual Voices: A World of Shifting Points of View

The world created in part by linguistic expressions reflecting multiple voices is a relational place defined by fluid and shifting points of view. Quotation is a device through which one expresses multiple voices. In self-quotation, where the quoter and the quotee are the same person, one would not expect to find such multiple voices. Partly because it is unexpected, however, the phenomenon of multiple textual voices reveals itself in its most crystallized form in self-quotation.

Although it is ordinary for a speaker to quote him or herself in conversation in what Deborah Tannen (1991) calls "constructed dialogue," in Japanese, self-quotation takes on greater variability and is used more extensively. In former Prime Minister Noboru Takeshita's speech (recorded from his testimony before the Diet, December 7, 1992) for example, we find the following. (The transcription of the Japanese text appears in the appendix.)

(1)

(1.1) Uh, this, as you know Mr. Ikeda, I am sure that you, too, know a lot about the Diet.

(1.2) Well, until now I have also known about your relationship with Mr. Eiichi Takahashi, and I want to exchange greetings with you by saying, "It's been a long time," but [I shouldn't].

(1.3) Please, about that point, it is because I trusted Mr. Aoki all the more; I hope you would understand it as I stated.

In the second sentence Takeshita says that he wanted to offer a friendly greeting such as *Ohisashiburi desu* 'It's been a long time.'

Although Takeshita deliberately calls attention to the inappropriateness (given the serious situation of the Diet hearing) of offering such a friendly greeting, his words, after all, do offer such a friendly greeting, and he achieves this by framing the greeting as a quotation. The formulaic greeting *ohisashiburi desu* carries a distinct flavor of actual talk addressed to Ikeda. It is replete with the phonological features (such as tone of voice and speed) typical of actual greeting. Through self-quotation, Takeshita addresses Ikeda not as an official questioner but as a colleague.

Here one can identify two different textual voices reflecting two "subject positions" (Talbot 1992)—that of speaker-as-witness and that of speaker-as-friendly-colleague. This sort of direct quotation, though camouflaged, allows the speaker to animate his or her talk without divagating from the larger framework of the interaction-in-progress. One can breach the rules of appropriate speech behavior by placing the unexpected behavior in a rule-satisfying frame.

The effects of self-quotation observed here include (1) facilitation of the presentation of multiple textual voices that transmit information on different levels of discourse; (2) a more vivid dramatization of the speaker's voice; and (3) distancing—a device for separating the speaker from the quoting situation. The potential for combining these voices gives self-quotation flexibility and usefulness.

Traditionally, the question of textual voices has been the province of narrative or novelistic discourse. Literary discourse presupposes a concept of voice expressed through the author's choice of viewpoint, whether that is the viewpoint of the author, the narrator, or a character. In this context, the appreciation of "multivoicedness" (or polyphony) in language is important. Of particular interest is M. M. Bakhtin's view. Bakhtin (1971, 1981, 1986) insists that the reality of language/speech does not lie in an abstract system of language, but originates in the social event of verbal interaction. The notion that language is inseparable from society encourages the thought that language reflects multiple voices. According to this view, language originates, and is given life, only in the dialogic relation with the voice of the other. Bakhtin's (1986) words are relevant here:

> Utterances are not indifferent to one another, and are not self-sufficient; they are aware of and mutually reflect one another. These mutual reflections determine their character. Each utterance is filled with echoes and reverberations of other utterances to which it is related by the communality of the sphere of speech communication.

Every utterance must be regarded primarily as a *response* to preceding utterances of the given sphere. . . . Each utterance refutes, affirms, supplements, and relies on the others, presupposes them to be known, and somehow takes them into account. (1986, 91; italics in original)

In a sense, every utterance is polyphonic. As James V. Wertsch (1991b, 13) puts it, "Human communicative and psychological processes are characterized by a dialogicality of voices," and they always represent multivoicedness. Although multivoicedness is expected to resonate throughout language, (self-)quotation offers unique instances where the many voices of discourse converge.

Let us observe another example of the self-quotation found in Takeshita's testimony. (The transcription of the Japanese text appears in the appendix.)

(2)

Regarding other things, I do think there is none, but as I stated earlier, about the fact that you demand that I investigate the matter, I will honestly do so—that's what I'm answering.

The words "Regarding other things, I do think there is none, but as I stated earlier, about the fact that you demand that I investigate the matter, I will honestly do so" are framed by the quotative marker *to* and the verb of saying, *kotaeteoru* 'I am answering.' The verb *shimasu*, the formal form of *suru* 'do,' which is not expected normally to occur in indirect quotation, accompanies the quoted portion. Why is self-quotation used here? And more specifically, why does Takeshita find it necessary to frame his answer with *kotaeteoru* 'I am answering'? Given the formal structure of the Diet hearing, Takeshita's words are expected to be interpreted as his answer. After all, Takeshita had been summoned to give testimony by answering the questions raised by the Diet members. Given all this, is it necessary for Takeshita to call his speech act an answer?

One approach to this question is to view language as operating on at least two different levels. The self-quotation presents two distinct voices on two separate discourse levels: (1) Takeshita's direct voice in the quoted portion, reciting an answer, and (2) Takeshita's voice framing the quotation as a proper and formal reply to the query, that is, official testimony offered in the Diet hearing. The discourse maintains a double focus and takes place in two distinct situational contexts.

This double-voicedness, however, does not reside on the speaker's side alone. The double voice addresses two different images of the listener: first, the listener as recipient of the content of the answer; and second, the listener as recipient of a labeled speech act. The multivoicedness observed here involves not only that attributed to the speaker, but that connected to the listener as well.

Speech Act Qualification

Another function of self-quotation is qualifying one's own speech. In an earlier study (Maynard 1996b), I proposed different types of speech act qualification in Japanese self-quotation, including (1) mitigation (selection of words and weakening of an impact), (2) parody, and (3) emphasis. An example of parody taken from our conversational data follows.

(3)   A encourages B to speak louder.

A: Moo sukoshi koe   o   ookikushitara./
    more a bit   voice O   make louder
    Why don't you speak a bit louder?

B: Yappashi./
    as expected
    That's what I thought.
          (A: Un)
              (Yeah.)

    Anoo to   ka itte./ LAUGH/ Dakara./
    uhh QT Q   say   so
    'Uhh . . . (I should say) (LAUGH) So.'

Here B follows A's advice and articulates "Uhh" in a louder voice, but immediately after this performance, he says *to ka itte*, which has the effect of objectifying his own action. B parodies his own performance by choosing the expression *to ka itte* '(*lit.*, saying something like) I should say,' a phrase that suggests self-mockery. The act (of uttering "Uhh") resembles an announcer or a performer's testing the microphone before a performance. B is perhaps self-conscious or embarrassed. By overtly referring to his own act of speech by using the verb of saying in a tone of parody, B controls the effectiveness of his speech. Put another way, through parody, B, the speaker, has license to ridicule or to minimize the speech act of B, the character. Putting one's speech in the frame of saying and placing it in a different context reflects a heightened awareness of the act of speaking.

Self-quotation is used in many languages, including English, but subordinate clauses marked as direct speech appear frequently in Japanese. Self-quotation, by directing attention to the act of saying, offers a chance for the speaker to qualify the speech act in a variety of ways. One reason so many quotative *to* are observed in Japanese spoken discourse may be because of this. By referring to the speech act, which encourages objectification, the speaker can express an evaluation of his or her speech as if it were another's.

The manipulation of multiple voices that Japanese self-quotation facilitates reflects fluid points of view and their shifts. By metalinguistically referring to one's own speech, the speaker successfully distances himself or herself from, and at the same time adds his or her evaluative attitude to, the quotation. This process, resonating with many other elements of Japanese rhetoric discussed so far, paints a picture of the world as a fluid, changing, and relationally connected place where people's shifting points of view proliferate.

16 Speaking as Self-Narrative: The World as a Subjective and Interpersonal Place

Tokieda's theory of language as process emphasizes the speaker's subjectivity. In his theory, Tokieda makes a triangle of the three necessary elements for the existence of language. These are (1) *shutai* 'the speaker, the speaking self,' (2) *bamen* 'place, situation inclusive of the addressee,' and (3) *sozai* 'material.' Tokieda states, "Language exists when someone (speaking self) tells someone (situation) about something (material)" (1941, 40–41).

Speaker Subjectivity

Tokieda's notion of the "speaking self" is the core of his view of language. In a sentence like *Watashi wa yonda* 'I have read,' Tokieda explains, one must recognize that the "I" is not the speaking self. Rather, it is the objectified "I" that is part of the linguistic material. In fact this "I" is, in terms of linguistic material, no different from "cat" in the sentence "The cat ate a mouse." One may refer to this "I" as the grammatical subject, but it is not the speaking self. The speaking self is never expressed in the same way as the linguistic material. Compare the case of a painter who does a self-portrait. The self represented in the portrait is not the actual painter, but an objectified and materialized self. The subject is the painter. To comprehend the subjective voice inherent in linguistic expressions, one must consider the whole of such sentences as "I have read" as

191

shutaiteki hyoogen 'subjective expressions,' created by a separate speaking self.

Tokieda finds the ultimate power of language in this subjective personal expression. A linguistic expression does not simply "refer" to objects; it manifests personal emotion and thought. According to Tokieda:

> The meaning [of language] does not exist as the content or material of language; rather, I think that the meaning is the very way the speaking self grasps [observes, interprets, understands, and expresses] the material. Language does not express the material of language in the way that a photograph reflects objects as they are; rather, language expresses the way the speaking subject grasps the material, and such expression evokes the material in the mind of the listener. This is just like the case of a painter who tries to express, never the material itself, but rather the way he or she grasps [and interprets] the material. The true meaning of language must be the very way that the speaking self grasps the material; that is, it must be the subjective act of giving meaning to the objects. (1941, 404; my translation)

The Importance of Modality in the Japanese Language

This bifurcation of language is equivalent to the two discrete elements in language as given in contemporary terms: objective information (propositional meaning) and subjective expression. Subjective expression encompasses the modal aspects of language. This understanding of language as inclusive of dual and interdependent elements continues to influence language scholars in Japan. For example, Minoru Watanabe (1971), by reexamining the traditional concept of *chinjutsu* 'modality' in Japanese, brings into focus the concept of the modal nature of language. Watanabe (1971) identifies *jojutsu* 'speaker's act of describing facts and things,' and *chinjutsu* 'act of expressing that description toward the addressee.' "*Chinjutsu* refers to the relational function that the speaking self finds existing between himself or herself and the description completed or the description yet to be completed, as well as the relationship the speaker finds toward objects and the addressee. Internal meanings the function of *chinjutsu* creates include the speaker's judgment, questioning, exclamation, appeal, and address" (1971, 106–107; my translation).

Language scholars in Japan traditionally recognize the modal nature of language as a significant—often critically important—

ingredient of language. This contrasts with western language scholars, who view language primarily as a tool for the transfer of propositional information.

This does not mean, however, that modal meaning in language
is totally ignored in western linguistics. The development of pragmatics and discourse analysis in the West over the past two decades
has contributed to the exploration of nonpropositional meanings.
Yet analysis of language with modality and personal "voices from
the heart" as primary focus has never gained enough force to cause
a major shift in thinking about language.

Historically, the West has tended to marginalize the modal view
of language. Language as a device for conveying information that
can be logically characterized seems to have an enduring appeal, as
shown by the force of the paradigm advanced by Noam Chomsky.
In this school of thought, language is often reduced to an abstract
body of linguistic units and rules that can be analyzed by appealing
to the logician's formal semantics. It is an article of faith that language exists apart from the speaker and his or her partner, not to
mention their "voices from the heart." The distinction between
opposing concepts of language in the West and in Japan goes back
to the infancy of modern western linguistics, to the dichotomy of
langue and *parole* introduced by Ferdinand de Saussure ([1915]
1966). Modern western (and western-influenced) linguistics has
principally been concerned with *langue* and only marginally and
hesitantly with *parole*. Until recently linguistics has focused almost
exclusively on information to the detriment of any understanding
of the emotional side of language and communication.

Narrating the Self with Modal Expressions

The Japanese, then, recognize the centrality of language's expres-
siveness—its modality—more than Americans do. Because of the
way the language is coded, Japanese speakers can easily convey
their attitudes language explicitly with varying tones and degrees,
especially in certain genres.

The Japanese language is most Japanese-like when expressions
describing the speaker's attitudes are amply inserted (cf. Watanabe
1985). It is as if the speaker narrates a story about himself or herself
through the manner in which propositional information is
expressed. When emotionally motivated phrases are interposed at
various points in talk, a very personal voice informs the communi-

cation. Sharing emotional vulnerability enhances the sense of involvement in the interaction. The significance of the propositional meaning diminishes; the personal narrative, brimming with personal and interpersonal feelings, gains ascendancy over mere facts. The subjective speaking self, hiding behind a verbal veil, stands at the heart of what is actually being communicated.

Why has this view of language survived in Japan for more than two hundred years? Because the society is preoccupied with societal relationships. In a context where participants' emotions and attitudes strongly color the perspective, participants often predict, respond to, and accommodate others' feelings. Response to others' feelings gains prominence as a mode of culturally defined expression. The behavior encouraged by this subjective and interrelational expressivity fosters a continual response to social, contextual, and interpersonal relational cues.

In Japanese thought, the world is a scene that becomes. The nonagent orientation of the language emphasizes a transitional, fluid state of relationships that transform themselves. The deep-rooted acceptance of the notion of communication involving more than words also reflects the language's structurally induced responsiveness to human relationships.

Emotions of sympathy and sentimentalism, often attributed to the Japanese, tend to derive from being "other focused" rather than "ego focused" (Markus and Kitayama 1991). Reality is defined not merely by material things but also by human emotion. In Japanese reality, many voices speak, and multiple points of view coexist in a fluid and changing state of relationality.

But the Japanese are not trapped in a confining web of relationality. They find resources for self-realization within and beyond their world. Japanese, like Americans, nurture a sense of social and individual will, dependence and independence, and a commitment to self and society. Beyond social context and language, the thought process itself is dynamic, responsive to changing and shifting relationality cues, and is abundant in subjectivity. Seeing the vitality of Japanese ways of communication offers greater understanding in the broader context. As Jerome Bruner (1990) asserts, in the past scholars have viewed language as something that can be formalized, or, more precisely, have directed their attention to phenomena that can be formally modeled. A language like Japanese highlights the aspects of language that cannot be easily formalized. Observing Japanese may lead toward a reevaluation of available theories of self, society, language, and thought.

In a sense, western intellectual thought has come full circle from structuralism to poststructuralism—and to some extent from rigid objectivism to a more tolerant subjectivism. Deconstruction may continue to be fashionable among some western scholars. My view of language and thought, which is in basic agreement with traditional Japanese scholarship, prompts no urge to deconstruct. The recent poststructural intellectual landscape opens a new awareness for viewing modes of Japanese language and thought not as representing the other of the West, but as offering alternative ways of understanding ourselves.

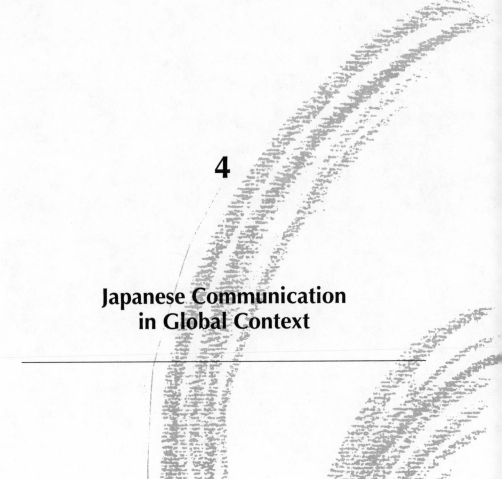

4

Japanese Communication
in Global Context

17 Japanese Text and Talk in Contrast

Social Memory across Cultures

In a 1932 book called *Remembering*, British psychologist Sir Frederick C. Bartlett proposed the idea that remembering is not simply recovering some fixed factual information but is itself a process of constructing knowledge. In one of his psychological experiments, he asked his British subjects to recall a North American folktale called "The War of the Ghosts" at different intervals, from fifteen minutes up to two and a half years later. The story went like this.

The War of the Ghosts

One night two young men from Egulac went down to the river to hunt seals, and while they were there it became foggy and calm. Then they heard war-cries, and they thought: "Maybe this is a war-party." They escaped to the shore, and hid behind a log. Now canoes came up, and they heard the noise of paddles, and saw one canoe coming up to them. There were five men in the canoe, and they said:

"What do you think: We wish to take you along. We are going up the river to make war on the people."

One of the young men said: "I have no arrows."

"Arrows are in the canoe," they said.

"I will not go along. I might be killed. My relatives do not know where I have gone. But you," he said, turning to the other, "may go with them."

So one of the young men went, but the other returned home.

And the warriors went on up the river to a town on the other side of Kalama. The people came down to the water, and they began to fight, and many were killed. But presently the young man heard one

of the warriors say: "Quick, let us go home: that Indian has been hit."
Now he thought: "Oh, they are ghosts." He did not feel sick, but they
said he had been shot.

So the canoes went back to Egulac, and the young man went
ashore to his house, and made a fire. And he told everybody and said:
"Behold I accompanied the ghosts, and we went to fight. Many of our
fellows were killed, and many of those who attacked us were killed.
They said I was hit, and I did not feel sick."

He told it all, and then he became quiet. When the sun rose he fell
down. Something black came out of his mouth. His face became con-
torted. The people jumped up and cried.

He was dead. (Bartlett 1932, 65)

Each subject read through the story twice, and subjects were
asked to recount it as opportunity offered. Bartlett found that subjects interpreted the story according to their own cultural schemata
or their particular social memory. They interpreted the story in the
way they understood things. Subsequent retellings were remarkably
similar in general form and outline to the first. For all subjects,
rationalization—the reduction of material to a form that the subject
could readily and satisfyingly deal with—was very prominent.

We all try to make sense of things, and the way we do this is to
use already existing knowledge. This suggests that knowledge is
interpretable within the cultural discourse that one's own language
allows. Once one has reached a rationalized interpretation, that
understanding continues and is often reinforced by time.

One of the subjects retold the story two and a half years later as
follows: "Some warriors went to wage war against the ghosts. They
fought all day and one of their members was wounded. They
returned home in the evening, bearing their sick comrade. As the
day drew to a close, he became rapidly worse and the villagers came
round him. At sunset he sighed: something black came out of his
mouth. He was dead" (Bartlett 1932, 75). It is true that this short
version seems to make more sense to us—making war against the
ghosts, fighting all day, returning home in the evening, getting
worse at night, having the villagers come around, and dying. Our
attempts at understanding are creative endeavors.

Observing this and other similar cases, Bartlett stated:
"Remembering is not the re-excitation of innumerable fixed, life-
less and fragmentary traces. It is an imaginative reconstruction, or
construction, built out of the relation of our attitude towards a

whole active mass of organized past reactions or experiences, and to a little outstanding detail which commonly appears in image or in language form. . . . The attitude is literally an effect of the organism's capacity to turn round upon its own 'schemata,' and is directly a function of consciousness" (1932, 218).

Fables across Cultures

Some changes have also been made to western fables that were introduced into Japan. According to Yoshihiko Ikegami (1982), Aesop's fable *The Ant and the Cicada* (or *The Ant and the Cricket*) was transposed into Japanese with a minor but significant change. To refresh our memory (which is seldom precise, as Bartlett warns us), let us first see the original, taken from *Aesop's Fables* (1960, 137).

> *The Ant and the Cicada*
>
> In winter time an ant was dragging
> The food he'd stored, across the flagging,
> And cooling what he'd heaped and had
> In summer. A cicada bade
> The ant (for he was starved) to give
> Some food to him that he might live.
> "What did you do," the other cried,
> "Last summer?" "I have nought to hide.
> I hadn't time to work; I passed
> The time in singing." Shutting fast
> His store of wheat, the other laughed,
> And launched at him this parting shaft:
> "Dance in the winter, if you please
> To sing in summer at your ease."

The Japanese version that appeared in a late sixteenth-century translation (based on Ikegami 1982, 284–285; my translation) goes like this.

> In the middle of winter, many ants dragged the crop out of their hole to dry it in the sun and wind. A cicada came by and received a small portion of food. The ant asked, "What did you do last summer and fall?" The cicada answered, "I spent my time singing and had no time to do anything else." The ant laughed at the cicada as he said, "Why don't you sing songs now just like you did last summer and fall?" And the ant gave the cicada a small amount of food.

> Moral of the Story: It is important to fulfill one's duties concerning the future while one still possesses the potential to do so. Those who

indulge in play when they possess strength and time to work will always suffer in the future.

The difference between the original and the Japanese version shows an interesting contrast. Although a similar moral is emphasized, the ant's behavior differs. In the Japanese version, the ant is more forgiving, offering a small amount of food to the cicada. In the original, the cicada must live with the consequences the hard way. As evidence that the Japanese are comparatively more merciful or considerate this is insufficient, but it does demonstrate that a fable can change when transferred across cultures. And more important, the change is what one would expect in a society where the society-relational orientation is primary. Instead of confronting the cicada with a direct refusal, the ant accommodates the cicada's needs. Interpretations of moral teachings and ethics do not necessarily apply universally to all societies. Our understanding is mostly culturally bound; it is often culturally bred, endorsed, and encouraged. Our cultural schema influences our knowledge in such a way that the knowledge fits snugly within it. Our understanding is sometimes so thoroughly steeped in our cultural discourse that we are unaware of the cultural forces defining us. And ironically, even when we criticize this view, we cannot escape from being part of a cultural schema, since criticism itself is a culturally endorsed behavior.

Contemporary Fables

Let me introduce another version of Aesop's fable, this time not from the sixteenth-century collection but from contemporary literature. The story *The Ant and the Cricket* is taken from Shin'ichi Hoshi's book titled *Mirai Isoppu* 'Future Aesops' (1982, 9–11; my translation). It offers a 1980s version. (The transcription of the Japanese text appears in the appendix.)

The Ant and the Cricket

One day toward the end of the fall, when ants were making preparations for the coming winter, a cricket holding a violin came by and said: "Could you spare me some food?"

An elderly ant answered him. "Why didn't you collect a sufficient supply of food during the summer?" "I am an artist. I was engaged in the noble act of playing music. I didn't have time to be bothered by collecting food." "What a terrible sloth! So what if it is an art! Why don't you just continue singing to your heart's content—even in the snow..."

The elderly ant is unsympathetic. But the cricket is not too disappointed. "Oh well, that's O.K. Maybe I should stop by another ant's place..."

As the cricket is about to leave, a young ant calls out. "Please, please wait for a moment."

Turning to the elderly ant, the young ant explains. "Grandfather, please give it some thought. As you know, our colony is packed with food because for generations our ancestors have been the work-loving type. Almost every year we expanded our colony and repeatedly stored additional food; we are at our limit now. When I widened the colony for additional food storage earlier today, the wall collapsed, old food fell down from the other side, and three ants were injured as the food collapsed on them. Unless we ask Mr. Cricket to come in and eat some of our food, no living space will be left for us."

Thus the cricket became the guest of the ant colony. That winter turned out to be an enjoyable one for all the ants. It was as if they had installed a juke box. The cricket plays on his violin whatever music the ants request.

This cricket, being an artist, is also intelligent. As he took an inspection tour of the colony's storage houses, he discovered that some of the old food stored in the back had fermented and turned into sake. The cricket announces to the ants: "Hey, guys, you shouldn't leave it like this. Here, take a sip."

The ants tasted the sake hesitantly, began to feel good, and learned to appreciate alcohol. With sake and songs, they easily learned how to dance. Even when closely compared, these activities are much more fun than working, they found out. During this winter, the traditional values of the ant tribe were totally demolished.

From next spring on, even when the ants came out to the surface, they were unwilling to work; instead, they did nothing but dance to the music of the cricket's violin. Except for... the elderly ant. He was outraged. "What decadence! If we continue like this, soon..."

And in order to convince the young ants logically, the elderly ant began to appraise the food storage and tried to calculate in how many years all the food would be consumed. But the inventory was too massive to handle. It would not run out even if they spent thirty or forty years doing nothing but dancing. So the elderly ant mutters, "Perhaps the world has changed. I don't understand it any more..."

The elderly ant agonized over the incongruity between his belief and reality, and in order to forget this anguish, he drank some sake and ended up dancing with the young ants.

Moral of the Story: Is it permissible to modify, as I did here, a classic story such as this one simply because prosperity has immensely changed society?

This contemporary version seems to cast doubt on the moral values of Japan and the United States, since both tend to monopolize, store, and consume a greater amount of the world's resources than they require to sustain their populations.

Talk across Cultures

Let us move now to spoken discourse across cultures and investigate what we can learn from it. How does the question-answer exchange differ in Japan and America? This exchange is certainly one of the most frequently observed phenomena in human communication. Since a question anticipates and often demands a response, questioning binds two people in reciprocal action. Partly because of its mundaneness, the question-answer interaction often escapes our notice. A closer look at this phenomenon cross-culturally reveals some important differences. Here are two cases, one from Japan and the other from the United States.

In Tokyo, on December 7, 1992, former Prime Minister Noboru Takeshita took the stand as a witness to the so-called Tokyo Sagawa Kyuubin Money and Mobster scandal at the Upper-House Budget Committee of the Japanese Diet. This hearing was widely announced in advance by the media, and public awareness was high. The question-answer exchange between Juuji Inokuma of the Koomeitoo Party and the former prime minister follows. (The transcription of the Japanese text appears in the appendix.)

(1)

Inokuma: But isn't it the case that Mr. Ishii is the boss of the top-ranking organized crime syndicate in Japan? If you heard that such a person was involved (in halting the Nihon Koomintoo's harassment campaign [*homegoroshi*] against Takeshita), I think it is normal [*toozen*] to ask questions about it—who said so, who is directly involved, and what halted the harassment campaign. Please explain more clearly how you understood the circumstances, especially how President Watanabe's mediation played a part.

Takeshita: Well, Mr. Inokuma, you just mentioned that it is normal [*toozen*] that I should ask him that way, but if it is the case, I think I can only say that I did not reach the state of considering it normal [*toozen*]. My intention here is not to be rude. I think I hope that you would kindly understand that I was truly not in an environment where I could ask in concrete ways the very questions (you suggest).

Transcribed from the NHK radio program December 7, 1992; my translation

The question-answer exchange here leaves the impression that it is disengaged, because the answer sought was not given. Mr. Takeshita's response, in his rhetorical style *Takeshita-go* 'Takeshita-speak' (*gengo meiryoo, imi fumei* 'clear-in-language, unclear-in-meaning'), uses several strategies in order to achieve this effect. For example, his use of one specific word, *toozen* 'normal,' in his answer gives the impression that topic continuity is maintained. Yet, by reinterpreting the meaning of the word, Takeshita moves the discussion to a metalinguistic level, effectively avoiding a direct answer. Inokuma does not point out explicitly that the answer is no answer to his question; he continues with a related but separate question. Compare this exchange with the one that follows.

In California, on February 10, 1993, a ninety-minute television interview of entertainer Michael Jackson by talk show host Oprah Winfrey took place, and the program "Michael Talks to Oprah" was aired live. The program was widely announced in advance on ABC; it was viewed by some ninety million people, one of the largest numbers ever recorded in the Nielsen ratings. In the interview we find the following.

(2)

Winfrey: I'm going to ask you this, and it's embarrassing for me to ask this, but I'm going to ask you anyway. Are you a virgin?

Jackson: (inhaling air with surprise) How could you ask me that question?

Winfrey: I'm just, I just want to know.

Jackson: I'm a gentleman.

Winfrey: You're a gentleman.
Jackson: I'm a gentleman. (pause) So I'm a gentleman.
Winfrey: So tha ... O.K. I would interpret that to mean that that means that you believe that the lady is a lady, and therefore ...
Jackson: That's something that is private. You know. Shouldn't be spoken about openly. Call me old-fashioned if you want, but, you know, to me that's very personal. (laugh)
Winfrey: So you're not going to answer it.
Jackson: I'm embarrassed. (laugh)
Winfrey: So you're not going to answer it.

> Transcribed from *Michael Talks to Oprah*, ABC television program, February 10, 1993

Winfrey makes explicit reference to the speech act of questioning and answering several times, framing her activity as that of an interviewer. She is trying to get as much revealing information as possible from Jackson, who had been portrayed by the media as a recluse. She cannot leave Jackson's answer, "I'm a gentleman," which is ambiguous at best, alone. Winfrey starts to rephrase Jackson's expression and attempts to speak for him. Jackson stops her. Realizing that she will not get an answer, Winfrey makes explicit reference to that very fact, repeating twice "So you're not going to answer it."

Although geographically and culturally apart, and although representing different discourse genres, the two examples above present some interesting similarities and differences. In both cases the information sought by the questioner is not revealed. The answering parties use different strategies: Takeshita switches the focus of the testimony by discussing the interpretation of the word *toozen* 'normal'; Jackson makes a self-descriptive statement that leaves the question unanswered. The questioner's response differs sharply in these two situations. In American discourse the lack of an answer is overtly pointed out—twice—where in Japanese discourse it is not mentioned explicitly. The rigor invested in a question-answer exchange, and the way a perceived failure (to produce results) is handled, differ between Japan and the United States.

In the context of the two societies' differing relational axes, this contrast makes sense. In American cultural discourse, it is important to point out what is at issue as accurately (and sometimes as controversially) as possible. This may even involve pointing out a guest's lack of participation. Hence Jackson's less-than-satisfactory behavior (from Winfrey's point of view) is overtly mentioned. In Japanese cultural discourse, although Takeshita's unsatisfactory behavior is acknowledged, there is hesitation to deal with it overtly. Saying something like "So you're not going to answer it" would result in a breach of social convention.

Under certain circumstances, a Japanese interviewer may not be satisfied with an answer, or may take a response as a nonanswer or absence of answer. In such a case, the interviewer may repeat the question, insisting upon and demanding an answer. But such a move, especially when it includes pointing out a guest's unsatisfactory behavior, is often considered rude. The situation is more likely to be handled with more subtlety, for example, by asking a slightly different question. This does not mean that a Japanese interviewer never gets upset or shows frustration over a partner's evasiveness. An interviewer who forces the issue, however, is perceived as threatening and challenging, which often destroys the atmosphere of social comfortableness.

Questions in Contrast

As an example of specific differences observed in the way a question is asked in Japanese and English, I would like to briefly introduce what I call "commentary questions" in Japanese. By commentary questions I refer to the Japanese questions that take a *n(o) da* or *no* ending in the predicate verb. For example, observe the following contrast between an ordinary question (3.1) and a commentary question (3.3) taken from a girls' comic book by Michiko Makino (1992).

Hoshina asks his younger sister Nozomi if what Nozomi has just said is true.

(3.1) *Hoshina:*   Honto ka ima   itta   koto.
                   real Q now said fact
                   Is it true, what you just said?

(3.2) *Nozomi:*   Oniichan.
                  brother
                  (Dear) brother.

(3.3) *Hoshina:*   Honto na no   ka yo!!
                   real   BE NOM Q   IP
                   Is it (really) true?!

(3.4) *Nozomi:*   Un.... demo ...
                   yes   but
                   It is true, but ... (Makino 1992, 68)

Commentary questions emphasize the speaker's modal attitude. They often enhance attitudinal information, for example, emphasis, rhetorical questions, accusatory statements, persistent questions, and exclamatory statements (cf. Maynard 1992, 1994b). The commentary question is also a useful interrogative format for the speaker to maintain varying types and degrees of interpersonal feelings and attitudes.

Commentary questions are quite common in Japanese talk. In my Japanese conversational data, 132 cases of commentary questions, or 36.36 percent, occur out of a total of 363 questions. Other discourse genres also show high frequencies of commentary questions. In *Himechan no Ribon* 'Little Hime's hair ribbon' by Megumi Mizusawa (1992), a girls' comic book, commentary questions account for 43.25 percent of questions. The proportion in *Himawari Nikki* 'The sunflower diary' by Yuu Asagiri (1992) representing "teen's heart" fiction is 32.73 percent. In *Tooshi Kakusei* 'The awakening of a warrior' by Yuuji Okano (1991), an example of "super fantasy" fiction, 31.49 percent of questions are commentary questions. *Dangai no Onna Kanshikikan* 'The female criminal investigator on the cliff' by Tadao Soono (1992), a mystery novel, contains 22.67 percent commentary questions.

Commentary questions are not uniquely Japanese, but it is easier to ask them in Japanese than it is in English. Languages differ in their assumptions about what kind of and in what ways questions should be or can be posed. Whether the scenario is an international business negotiation, an economic summit meeting, or a diplomatic talk, the threat of a misunderstanding as a result of an inappropriate or misguided query is very real. In cross-cultural discourse, the nature of and motivation for questioning are likely to differ. Responses emerging as answers, evasive answers, or absence of an answer largely depend on a culturally bound interpretation. Since language is a sign system reflecting more than any individual's thoughts and feelings, there is danger in treating the question-answer interaction without cross-cultural evaluation.

It is especially important to discover differences in the ways in which question-answer interactions operate or do not operate in Japan and the United States. This is because a large part of the bilateral negotiation process depends on the question-answer exchange—and increasingly it is taking on an accusatory tone. Japan–U.S. skirmishes are played out through language and rhetoric. The clash is often in the exchange of words. Language is not an epiphenomenal reflex of other relationships. As Gregory Bateson (1972) points out, the interpersonal relationship is the exchange of messages; language and rhetoric inescapably create and shape the interpersonal (as well as international) relationship.

18 Japan–U.S. Intercultural Communication

In discussing intercultural discourse I examine conversation (in English) between Japanese and American college students in the United States. One aspect of the conversation under focus is listener back-channel response. I look at its distribution, context, and functions. Although I investigate only a small part of the conversational interaction, it provides a base from which to speculate on the Japanese and American images of each other.

When inquiring into an intercultural discourse, one may ask: Will a non-native speaker of English ever be perceived to speak English as naturally as a native English speaker? Will he or she forever be treated as an estranged "other"? How about a native speaker of American English? Will that person be forever destined to be perceived as the "other" in intercultural discourse that does not take place in English?

These questions raise several important issues. After all, intercultural communication consists of far more than correct grammatical usage. It involves many factors far beyond language and communication. But even when we concentrate exclusively on ways of communication, intercultural discourse between native and non-native speakers often evokes a feeling of awkwardness, disengagement, foreignness, estrangement, and lack of respect. Sometimes this lack of respect unfortunately takes the form of sympathy—or a disguised sense of superiority—over the "weaker" non-native speaker. Analysis of listener behavior in videotaped intercultural discourse shows how some of the feelings of awkwardness can be

211

traced to certain empirically observed behavioral differences. An observable difference exists in Japanese and American communication styles, particularly in the frequency of back channels. This aspect of communication is likely to be a trouble zone and perhaps a cause for communication difficulties.

Japanese-American Intercultural Discourse

The conversations under discussion here were video- and audio-taped at Rutgers University in New Jersey in 1987. Two intercultural conversations are examined; one between two female students, Japanese and American, and the other between two male students, Japanese and American. I have excluded the first two minutes from each tape (due to the potential unnaturalness) and have collected approximately thirty seconds of conversation consisting of segments at least five seconds long. An analysis according to back channels is shown in table 8.

Clearly Japanese listeners send far more back channels (approximately once every two seconds) than their American counterparts. Head movement is the most frequent Japanese back channel. Americans prefer brief utterances.

Context and Functions of Listener Back-Channel Response

Japanese listeners send back channels frequently at the beginning of a brief pause, but they also send back channels while their American partners are speaking and where there are no recognizable pauses. In one situation, when a Japanese speaker explains how he feels about finding and quitting jobs to his American friend, the American friend listens silently. Only after he comprehends the explanation does he send the back channel. In contrast to this, when the

TABLE 8.   Frequency of Japanese and American Back Channels

	Japanese female	American female	Japanese male	American male
Duration of listener state (in seconds)	28	26	39	32
Back channels sent	12	4	18	1
Average number of seconds between back channels	2.15	6.5	2.05	32

identical Japanese student listens to his friend, he continuously sends back channels at brief intervals, near and at the pause, regardless of the grammatically significant point.

The importance of back channels clearly differs between Japanese and American listeners. In Japanese, back channels both display that the listener understands the content and act as moral support for the speaker. In English the continuer function (a signal sent by the listener to the speaker to continue talking) seems to be primary.

The difference in back-channel behavior between the Japanese and the American listener observed in intercultural discourse becomes even more obvious when the same Japanese speaker speaks to a Japanese friend. For example, when interacting with an American female, the female Japanese speaker sends frequent back channels (one every 2.15 seconds) but receives infrequent back channels (one every 6.5 seconds). When interacting with a Japanese female, the female Japanese speaker both sends (every 3.44 seconds) and receives frequent back channels (every 1.90 seconds). Also, the female speaker's head movement is simultaneously accompanied by her Japanese friend's back channel. This phenomenon of joint head movement between speaker and listener, or rhythmic ensemble, was absent from the intercultural conversations.

What we learn from these comparisons is that both Japanese and American speakers conduct themselves in intercultural discourse much as they would within their own cultural context. Although this is a conclusion based on limited data and analysis, there is reasonable empirical evidence to support the idea that listener response transfers across cultural boundaries and is relatively unaffected by the listener's identity. Japanese conduct in conversation does not significantly alter with ethnographic context. The same can be said for Americans. Each culture's preferred back-channel strategies and head movement style remain mostly intact in intercultural exchanges. It is interesting to witness Japanese listeners sending back channels in English at positions where, in Japanese, interactional particles would appear. The Japanese person listening to English continues to behave as if listening to Japanese, at least in terms of conversation management.

Differences in Conversation Management
Unlike grammatical mistakes, which are often dismissed as a lack of knowledge, interactional signs like back-channel expressions are

more likely to be interpreted as part of an individual's social style. As Frederick Erickson (1984, 82) reports in his discussion of differences in interactional styles between African Americans and white Americans, when differing interactional styles meet, interactional trouble often results. According to Erickson, "In these troublesome encounters, persons fail to understand one another's intentions, fail to get their points across and, more often than not, make unjustified negative evaluations of the sincerity, interest, intelligence and motivation of other parties in interaction" (1984, 82).

Ironically, the more competent speakers are at the phonological, lexical, and grammatical levels of the language, the more vulnerable they become when they use different conversation management styles. Part of the stereotyping of the Japanese speakers of English—that they make hesitant statements, send endless back channels, and are too anxious to please or hurry the conversation along—is likely to come from not appreciating differences in conversation management styles.

A similar misevaluation occurs when Japanese conclude that Americans are uncomfortable to be around because their interactional style lacks the warmth and the values of supportiveness and considerateness that are, in Japanese cultural terms, expressed in part by frequent back channels. This misevaluation can make Japanese people think that Americans are unkind and unwilling to cooperate in the mutual smoothing out of potential differences of opinion. Trying to close the emotional gap may even widen it if both parties escalate their culturally sanctioned behavior in a well-intended but futile effort to compensate for the perceived lack of rapport. Gregory Bateson (1972, 68) calls this phenomenon "complementary schismogenesis."

Are the negative images that Japanese and Americans sometimes have of each other caused in part by differences observed in conversation management? Sheida White concludes that she "found no evidence for the hypothesis that back-channel conventions that are not shared contribute to negative personality attributions or stereotyping" (1989, 59). She states that the frequent back channels Japanese listeners send toward Americans were interpreted as showing more signs of comprehension, encouragement, concern, and interest, resulting in Americans' "positive stereotyping" (White 1989, 72) of the Japanese. Americans perceived Japanese listeners as more patient, more polite, and more attentive than

American listeners. White also offers an explanation for Americans' sending more frequent back channels toward Japanese speakers than toward American speakers: "Americans *accommodate* to the style of their foreign interlocutors" (1989, 69; italics in original).

However positive the stereotyping of the Japanese may seem to Americans (and to the scholar who describes it), there is no doubt that differences exist in conversation management strategies. When Americans accommodate Japanese, there is an imbalance of power: the one who does the accommodating, since he or she has control and access to the socially accepted norm of the speech community, ranks higher than the one being accommodated. It is the non-native English speaker's interactional style that is marked, is viewed with strangeness, and needs special sympathy—not vice versa. Attributions like "patient," "polite," and "attentive" are inferred by Americans from their conversational interaction with the Japanese. These "positive" characteristics of Japanese—notably lacking in authority and power—only encourage the myth of Japanese "politeness."

Inspecting this phenomenon from a psychological perspective is also useful. According to Knud W. Larsen, Harry Martin, and Howard Giles (1977), listeners tend to minimize a speaker's undesirable speech traits and overrate the speaker's similarities to themselves if they anticipate meeting the speaker immediately, and if the speaker is socially significant (of higher social status, for example). This tendency is called "perceived convergence." One tends to perceive oneself as more similar to (converges with) the speaker one wishes to be identified with. When the Japanese non-native English speaker and American native English speaker interact, the strangeness in the Japanese behavior may be "positively" evaluated if the listener perceives the Japanese to be socially important. When a sharp conflict of interest occurs, however, Americans are less likely to "perceive convergence" with Japanese non-native English speakers. Evaluation of the non-native speaker's style takes place in accordance with the prestige group's (native speakers') patterns of approval and disapproval. A difference in conversation management can become an attitudinal time bomb unless parties refrain from too readily associating others' speech style with their personalities.

19 Misinformation and Media in Global Context

Potential cross-cultural communication problems may be caused not by cultural differences per se, but by the process of information transmission. Consider the powerful role the media play in selecting, manipulating, and reporting information they find newsworthy. A minor mistake in translating from Japanese into English or vice versa, for example, can sometimes cause serious damage to Japan–U.S. public relations. With the near-instantaneous dissemination capabilities of modern information technology, news about Japan spreads like wildfire. And the media play a decisive role in portraying the image of Japan abroad.

One example of media-manipulated misinformation that contributed negatively to the Japan–U.S. relationship in early 1992 concerned former Prime Minister Kiichi Miyazawa's statement made in the Lower-House Budget Committee on February 3, 1992. Miyazawa's commentary on the U.S. labor force, taken out of context, misinformed the world through international news networks, including the Associated Press and United Press International. My discussion incorporates Hiroshi Andoo's (1992) study of this issue.

The lead sentence of the Associated Press news release of February 3, 1992, read as follows: "In Japan's latest rebuke to its U.S. economic rival, Prime Minister Kiichi Miyazawa told Parliament Monday that Americans were losing their work ethic and the drive 'to live by the sweat of their brow.'" The quotation that was featured in the media, "Americans lack the work ethic," made sensational headlines in the United States. A very different picture emerges from a careful examination of exactly what the former prime minister said in Japanese that day, however. The image of the "arrogant" and "ethnocentric" Japanese that this piece of news portrayed seems unjustified.

The former prime minister was criticizing business practices of the 1980s, both Japanese and American. Miyazawa lamented that in the United States many college graduates chose to work on Wall Street. As a result, the number of capable engineers had decreased. In addition, Miyazawa summarized the dangers of the accelerated U.S. money-market economy, where investors without substantial personal resources were involved in junk bonds and leveraged buyouts. He continued his litany of worries with the observation that, as far as the U.S. economy of the last ten years or so was concerned, he had felt for some time that there was a palpable lack of the work ethic in America. But he did not stop there. Miyazawa continued by stating that Japan's bubble economy also had involved a weakening of the work ethic. He pointed out that both Japan and the United States suffered from the consequences of the 1980s, but he thought that the experience could turn out to be a lesson from which all Japanese could learn.

The particular sentence—and the most controversial one—that the Associated Press presumably quoted comes next. Miyazawa stated, "After all, it is important to create value by sweating on one's forehead." This particular sentence has no grammatical subject. In the immediately preceding clause, the word *kokumin zentai* 'every citizen of the country'—normally translated as the Japanese people—is inserted as the subject. In the clause preceding this, Miyazawa chooses the word *otagai* 'we both,' which clearly refers to both Japan and the United States. It is possible to interpret *kokumin zentai* either as (1) the Japanese, or (2) both the Japanese and the Americans. It is, however, impossible to interpret the term as Americans alone. The translator committed a fundamental error by choosing the only impossible interpretation. The media turned it into an accusation: Americans are "lazy"; Japanese are not. It is not clear to me whether the error and its consequent worldwide dissemination resulted from the interpreter's ignorance, from the media's desire to report the sensational, or from a deliberate action on the part of those who wanted to encourage two-way "bashing"— first, the Japanese bashing Americans for being lazy, and in turn Americans bashing Japanese for being arrogant.

Most Americans were (and are) completely unaware that the former prime minister's remark was taken out of context. The discourse in which the remark was made, as discussed above, was about American business culture in general, with a theme that had been frequently voiced by Americans themselves. The former prime minister criticized the Japanese business situation of the 1980s as a phenomenon parallel to the American one. But all was lost in the news coverage. The remark that "Americans were losing their work ethic" infuriated many Americans. Public opinion polls in recent years have shown one after another that the number of Americans with a positive image of Japan and the Japanese people is steadily diminishing.

The damage has been done, but there is a twofold lesson to be learned from the incident. First, Japanese political leaders should make their commentary as explicit as possible. The transmission of information across countries with a different understanding of relationality requires extra caution. The more context-dependent the information, the more likely it is that some contextual information will be lost in transmission. After all, it is more difficult to transpose the entire context—which by definition is culturally bound—into a different cultural environment than it is to transpose the words alone. Japanese leaders must also understand that reporters are perhaps too eager to seek out controversial, if not hostile, "news."

Second, news reporters must be careful when dealing with interpreters and translators of the Japanese language, and of course translators must be better attuned to the cultural and linguistic contexts of Japan. By adding "Americans" or "American workers" to a Japanese sentence in which no agent was indicated, the media made a tragic error. The meaning of the sentence was altered to such an extent that it cannot be dismissed as an innocent mistake. In order to interpret a message expressed in the Japanese (or any) language, one needs to pay close attention to its context. Carelessly taking one short statement out of a body of text does an injustice to truth.

20 Toward a New Awareness

Given the complexity of cross- and intercultural problems surrounding Japanese ways of communication, what solutions, if any, can we find?

Relationality, the theme of this book, can help us here. Relationality is not unique to Japan. Recall the samurai and the cowboy: Both are relationally committed to society, although with different emphases. Both are ambivalent in their commitment. The definition and expression of relationality in each language and society differ, yet cultures have much in common when looked at from the perspective of human existence. I would like to make this point clear because discussing differences can give the wrong impression, that differences overpower similarities. We discuss differences because they require our attention. And differences are not absolute; they vary in degree and intensity.

Over the last thirty years there has been much interest in Japan and Japanese culture, especially among Japanese, who have been developing the notion of a Japanese cultural identity. One result of this interest is the emergence of *nihonjinron*. *Nihonjinron*, which literally means 'discussions of the Japanese,' refers to the literature that Japanese elites have produced to define Japanese culture by its distinctiveness, especially from the West. *Nihonjinron* explains everyday occurrences in Japan in terms of a cultural ethos considered peculiar to the Japanese.

Nihonjinron has been criticized, most notably by Ross Mouer and Yoshio Sugimoto (1986) and by Peter N. Dale (1986). Critics of *nihonjinron* in general point out the lack of a rigorous methodology. *Nihonjinron* often relies heavily on convenient examples from personal experience and on everyday anecdotes. Many *nihonjinron* writings are not scholarly in nature, but are written as commercialized essays. *Nihonjinron* became popular in Japan in the 1970s and has remained so. When *nihonjinron* is presented carelessly in its promotional scheme, it overemphasizes differences while almost ignoring the commonality of human experience. This is a pitfall I would like to avoid.

There is no doubt, however, that profound differences exist between Japan and America. How to handle the similarities and differences between these two (and other) cultures is of critical importance. For this purpose, let us reexamine the concept of de-Orientalizing Japan, on the one hand, and reevaluating the West, on the other. These perspectives can play beneficial roles in enhancing our understanding of Japanese communication in a global context.

De-Orientalizing Japan

The term "Orientalism," as used by Edward Said (1978), refers to the western attitude of superiority and condescension toward non-western cultures. In an Orientalizing view, the Orient is placed at the polar opposite of the Occident. The Orient is exotic, fundamentally different, and forever "other" in the eyes of the West. At the same time it is viewed as an underdeveloped West, a civilization in historical limbo. According to Harumi Befu (1992), the field of Japanese study has itself suffered from Orientalism. As a result of its historical relationship with Japan, the West, including the United States, continues to Orientalize Japan. The philosophical background for Orientalism is the theory of modernization, "which comfortably and happily placed the West above Japan in terms of application of rationality and hence in terms of modernity and evolutionary development" (Befu 1992, 7). Japan has been, and continues to be, viewed as a country that can and should be evaluated by western standards.

An Orientalizing approach often portrays differences as something that ought to be changed to resemble the West. In many ways Japan *is* like the West today, yet it continues to differ in many other ways. The different relational directions, from-society-to-self and from-self-to-society, do not represent developmental stages. Emphasis may change both in Japan and in the United States over time, but the differences are simply differences, and they will continue to exist. It is important to avoid viewing cross-cultural differences as things that will be eliminated eventually through the process of modernization.

An awareness that differences are not to be "resolved" by cultural evolution or cultural colonialism is an important one. This awareness can decrease, if not stop, the tendency to Orientalize Japan. Japan will not be the other that is opposite to the West or on its periphery, or grudgingly permitted to become a member of the West when it conforms satisfactorily. De-Orientalizing Japan promises to give rise to a new image of Japanese culture as one that resembles yet differs from—in various nonpejorative ways—other cultures.

Reevaluating the West

The West has often been seen, and has seen itself, as the principal provider of "answers" for humanity. In the past Japan has often sought answers in the West. Since the beginning of the Meiji period (1868), Japan has learned much from the West, so much that it often sees and evaluates itself in the mirror of the West. In fact, the Japanese "uniqueness" asserted by *nihonjinron* has often been that it is merely "uniquely" different from the West. The West has been the dominant, if not the most prestigious, civilization in the world, which justifies its claim to represent universal values.

What is needed today is a moratorium on evaluating cultures only through western preconceptions. When multiple cultures exist, it is important that different cultures see themselves against various other cultures. For example, the United States examines itself in the mirror of Japan, and of other cultures as well. In fact, diversified views of the West and western cultures already exist in the United States. This reevaluation of the West must be conducted not only by the West, but, more critically, by the non-West as well. Avoiding automatic dependence on western ways of thinking will open up new opportunities for many societies.

The Japanese have learned and continue to learn from the West with persistent energy, while the West has shown a relatively low level of interest in learning from the East. R. Byron Bird, for example, comments: "We [Americans] need to be able to send people to technical meetings and conferences in Japan. In this country at such conferences, there are always Japanese. They go home and write up a report—so they know what we are doing, but we don't know what they are doing" (1993, 5).

In order to make mutual understanding possible, information must flow both ways between Japan and the United States. And in order to achieve this goal, Americans will have to understand Japanese ways of communication. This will enable the Americans to see Japan from the native's, or internal, point of view, rather than from the often-exercised foreign, or external, point of view. Reevaluating the West requires investment from the West. To see the West in a nonwestern mirror, one must have access to the nonwestern cultural mirror. Language and communication, as some of the most essential parts of the culture, offer a mirrorlike device to shed light on ways of speaking and thinking across linguistic boundaries.

Reflections on Relationality

Despite their similarities, languages have profound differences. The Japanese rhetoric of commentation in certain discourse is a case in point. It exerts a rhetorical force that places as much, if not more, importance on the topic-comment structure than on the propositional information. Japanese offers a structure that presents a scene as a concept. A speaker's (frequently emotional) attitude is expressed in response to society-relational cues. Understanding the attributes underlying concrete expressions (for example, interactional particles) and strategies (for example, listener responses and business negotiation style) helps create a mirror that reflects a clear image of Japan and other societies.

The idea of relationality supports de-Orientalizing Japan and reevaluating the West, especially when it is applied on a global scale. If we can identify the different orientations of relationality endorsed by varying cultures, perhaps we can tackle cross-cultural communication difficulties more equitably. And above all, if we consider cultures—with their similarities and differences—to be relationally connected in equilibrium on the same plane while influencing each other, the trap of Orientalism may be avoided. Denying this cultural relationality epitomizes ignorance and arrogance and contributes to prejudice and stereotyping.

Each culture must hold on to its identity even as it must interact with other cultures—with increasing intensity. Here we see the human desire for separation (or independence) and connectedness (or dependence) on a global scale. Two opposing forces, those pulling toward cultural individualism and those pulling toward integration and mutual cultural influence, are likely to endure. By viewing the entire world as interconnected in terms of relationality, the samurai and the cowboy may be placed together on the same plane. Ambivalent feelings toward self and society are shared by many if not all of us. We all wonder about the meanings of the similarities and differences observed across cultures and societies. And we are all interested in expressing our feelings toward others within and outside our own cultures. The samurai and the cowboy are not polar opposites, but they are burdened with different kinds of relationality.

Understanding differences between Japan and the United States (and other cultures) from the perspectives of de-Orientalizing Japan and reevaluating the West offers a new awareness. The successful integration of both approaches depends on the acceptance of a broader concept of cross-cultural relationality. Such an awareness is necessary for the coexistence of human cultures in the global context and for deepening the understanding of the contemporary world, where so many people lead cross-cultural and intercultural lives.

Appendix

The romanizations given below correspond to examples given only in English translation in the text.

CHAPTER 6

(1)

Denjiha

Jyuukyuu-seiki no koro wa hikari to denjiha wa bekko no mono dearu to kangaerareteimashita. Shikashi hikari to denpa ga kuukan o byoosoku sanjuu-man kiromeetoru de susumu koto ga wakari, Makkusuweru ga tsugi no koto o yogenshimashita. Sono daiichi wa, "Denkai to jikai no nami ga kuukan o koosoku to onaji hayasa de tsutawaru," daini wa "Hikari wa denjiha no isshu dearu" desu. Daiichi no naiyoo o zu 1–5 ni shimeshimashita. (Kamikawa 1992, 23)

(2)

Untenshu, Shisatsusareru

Chiba, Kashiwa. Chikaku ni zenshoo takushii

Hatsuka gogo juu-ji goro, Chiba-ken Kashiwa-shi Bentenshita no Tonegawa chikaku de "Shiroi kuruma ga moeteiru" to hyaku-juukyuu-ban tsuuhoo ga atta. Chiba-ken Kashiwasho de shirabeta tokoro, kojin takushii ga zenshooshi, yaku nana-meetoru waki no yoosuiro ni dansei no shitai ga uiteita. Dansei wa, kono takushii no untenshu de dooken Narashino-shi Ookubo nana-choome, Kanayama Masaru-san (60) dearu koto o kazoku ga kakunin. Doosho de wa Kanayama-san no kubi nado ni sashikizu ga atta koto kara, satsujin, shitai iki jiken to danteishi, nijuuichi-nichi, soosa honbu o setchishita. (*Asahi shimbun*, October 24, 1993)

(3)

Nanami: Hontoni Koota da!!
Nanami: "A . . . ano, Koota, atashi . . ."
Koota: "Aa . . . nan da." "Dare ka to omottara Nanami ka
            yo." "Aikawarazu inakakusee naa."
Nanami: E . . . ?
Koota: "Tookyoo ni wa chotto inakatta taipu da yo na."
Nanami: Koota!? "Anna no Koota janai!" "Koota wa motto
            yasashikatta mon!" "Tookyoo itte hito ga kawatchatta
            n da." (Orihara 1992, 122–123)

(4)

Kono kyoku to kimete kaigan zoi no michi tobasu kimi nari "hoteru
kariforunia"

Naze "hoteru kariforunia" na no ka. Kare wa naze soo kime-
teiru no ka. Omoide ga aru no daroo ka. Nan no omoide? Dare to
no omoide? Watashi ni wa mienai omoi o motte, ima kono kyoku o
kiiteiru yokogao. Kare no kako ni tsunagaru kono kyoku wa,
watashi no mirai ni tsunagatteiru.

BG ni nagareru ongaku wa, sono hi no omoide o fuchidoru
mono da. Kyoo no koto o omoide toshite, watashi mo itsuka wa
furikaeru. Sono toki ni wa kitto, "hoteru kariforunia" o kiku daroo.
Futari de tobashita kaigan zoi no, natsu no hikari no shiroi michi o,
hitoride omoidasu daroo. Dakara watashi wa sono hi no tameni,
"hoteru kariforunia" o kiiteiru. (Tawara 1988, 153)

(15)

(15.1) *Sugiya:*   Dooshita?/
(15.2) *Asami:*   Sugiya/
(15.3)   Irie sa/ Keiko-san no shashin mottenai no ka
                   naa./
(15.4)   Hora kore./ Kenkyuushitsu./
(15.5)   Minna no shashin daro?/
(15.6) *Sugiya:*   Aa/ mada tsukiatte mamonai kara./
(15.7) *Asami:*   Soo ka./
(15.8)   Samishii daroo na/
(15.9)   kono mama dattara sa./

(18)

Gin-gin no natsuzora ga machikirenai *kimi*.

Shizen no naka ni hayaku tobikomitai to *karada* wa *uzu-uzu* shi-tenai ka.

De, kono natsu no *autodoa* wa *raito* kankaku ga *kiiwaado*.

Kangaetemo goran, onna no *ko* o sasottemo, *hebii* na tozan ya nebu-kuro de nojuku nante, daremo kiyashinai ze.

Kohan de *ranchi*, kawara de *biiru*, hamabe de hirune.

Konna *pikunikku* kankaku de karuui kanji ga IN.

Fasshon datte soo da.

Ue kara shita made, zenshin honki no *hebiidyuuti* wa chito *tsurai*.

Fudan no machigi ni, fun'iki dashi ni *bishitto* itten *autodoa* aitemu o kuwaeru.

Sonna *raito* na kankaku ga *ikeru* n da na.

Natsushoonen yo, mabushii kisetsu wa moo sugu soko da.

CHAPTER 7

Ferry Port of Yagiri

Yagiri no Watashi

"Tsurete nigete yo"
"Tsuite oide yo"
Yuugure no ame ga furu
Yagiri no watashi
Oya no kokoro ni somuite mademo
koi ni ikitai futari desu.

"Misutenaide ne"
"Sute wa shinai yo"
Kitakaze ga naite fuku
Yagiri no watashi
Uwasa kanashii Shibamata sutete
fune ni makaseru sadame desu.

"Doko e iku no yo"
"Shiranu tochi da yo"
Yure nagara ro ga musebu
Yagiri no watashi
Iki o koroshite mi o yose nagara
asu e kogidasu wakare desu. (Gotooshoin 1992, 195)

(17)

Television debate

Watashi wa desu ne/ ano/ doobutsu aigo no minasan hikyoo da to omoimasu./ Naze ka to yuu to desu ne/ imamade gutaitekini doo suru n desu ka to hanashi o kiku to/ zettai ni iwanai n desu yo/ gutaitekini doo suru no ka./ Tatoeba Hirose-san desu ne/ me no mae ni raion ga desu ne/ maa iru to shimashoo/ kateishite./ Soo yuu toki ni desu ne/ anata doo suru n desu ka./ Eh/ korosanakya naranai baai datte aru kamoshirenai shi osotte-kite/ shinu kamoshirenai desho./ Sore o/ soo yuu jootai ni ima zenzen natteimasen kara toka nan toka itte desu ne/ gomakashi janai desu ka./ Moshi atana hon-tooni doobutsu aigo yaru n dattara gutaitekini hakkiri yuu beki da to boku wa omou n desu yo./ Ijoo desu./

CHAPTER 8

A Peach Boy

(8.1) Mukashi, mukashi, aru tokoro ni, ojiisan to obaasan to ga, sundeorimashita.

(8.2) Tokoroga, natsu no aru hi no koto deshita.

(8.3) Ojiisan wa yama e shibakari ni dekakemashita.

(8.4) "Itterasshai."

(8.5) Obaasan wa, ojiisan o okuridasu to,

(8.6) "Dore, dore, watashi wa, kawa e sentaku ni ikimashoo."

(8.7) to, tarai o kakaete kawa e sentaku ni dekakemashita.

(8.8) "Zabuzabu, zabuzabu."

(8.9) Obaasan wa, seidashite sentaku o shimashita.

(8.10) Sukoshi suru to, kawakami kara, ukishizumishite, nagarete kuru mono ga arimashita. (Tsubota 1975, 24)

A Cucumber Princess

(9.1) Mukashi, mukashi, aru tokoro ni, ojiisan to obaasan to ga ori-mashita.

(9.2) Aru hi, obaasan ga kawa e sentaku ni ikimashita.

(9.3) Kawakami kara hako ga futatsu nagarete-kimashita.

(9.4) Pukapuka, pukapuka.

(9.5) Kore o miru to, obaasan ga yobimashita.

(9.6) "Mi no aru hako wa kotchi koi. Mi no nai hako wa atchi ike."

(9.7) Mi no aru hako ga yotte-kimashita.

(9.8) Sokode, sore o hirotte, uchi e kaerimashita.

(9.9)   Ban ni ojiisan to futari de akete mitara, naka kara uri ga dete-
kimashita. (Tsubota 1975, 18)

(35)
Daga, moo ii kagenni shite, kiri o tsukeru to shiyoo. Benkai ni tsuite
no, benkai o, ikura kasanete mita tokoro de, doonimo naru mono de
wa nai. Sonna koto yori, daijina no wa, genni ima omae ga, kono
tegami o yomi tsuzuketeite-kureru koto na no da. Boku no jikan ga,
sono mama sokkuri, omae no genzai ni kasanariatteite-kureru koto
na no da. Soshite, hikitsuzuki, nooto no hoo ni mo, sono mama
yomi susunde-kureru koto . . . boku ga omae no jikan ni oitsuku,
saigo no peeji made, nagedasu koto naku yomisusunde-kureru
koto. . . .

  (Ima omae wa, kutsuroide-kureteiru daroo ka? Soo soo, sencha
wa take no hikui midoriiro no kan no naka da. Yu mo, wakashitate
no yatsu o mahoobin ni tsumetearu kara, so itsu o tsukatte-moraitai.) (Abe 1968, 8–9)

CHAPTER 9

(1)
  (1.1) *A:* Dakedo/
  (1.2) are atsuryoku ga tsuyoi n da yo ne hora/
  (1.3) hoogakubu jan./ ⌐
        ∕ H H H
      (*B1:* └─Aa soo ka hoo ka uun.)
  (1.4) Dakara/
  (1.5) mottainai to ka iwarete sa.
  (1.6) *B:* A mawari kara ne./⌐
      (*A1:* ∕─H)
  (1.7) Oya kara sureba kodomo ga sureba iya/⌐(laugh)
          ∕ H H H
        (*A2:* └─Soo soo soo
           soo.)
  (1.8) *A:* Demo oya oya wa ne moo saikin soo ┌─mo/
        (*B2:* └─soo)
  (1.9) iwanaku natta kedo/H/ ⌐
      (*B3:* ∕─H H)
  (1.10) Tomodachi toka wa sa mottainai yoo toka sa/ ⌐
        (*B4:* ∕─Uun)

(1.11)   Isshoni sa hora/
(1.12)   nihongo kyooshi no yoosei no kurasu no sa/⌐
                                                    (B5:╱Un)
(1.13)   tomodachi ttara nan da kedo isshoni uketeru hito ga
                ⌐iru no./
         (B6:└Un un un)
(1.14)   Kyuu juu-nin no kurasu⌐da kara/
                        (B7:└Un un)
(1.15)   moo shitashiku natte/⌐
                        (B8:╱H)
(1.16)   daitai toshiue no sa/⌐
                        (B9:╱Uun un)
(1.17)   onna no hito ga ooi wake./⌐
                                   ╱H
                        (B10:└Un)
(1.18)   Moo ooeru yamete naru toka ne./⌐
                                (B11:╱Un)
(1.19)   Soo yuu hito ga sa/⌐
                        (B12:╱Un)
(1.20)   mottainai yo to ka yuu n da yo./
(1.21)B: Aa, sono D no hoogakubu made itte./⌐
                                    (A3:╱Soo soo)
(1.22)A: Watashi nanka C datta no yo/
(1.23)B: Da dakara D D demo ne/
(1.24)   yappari naka de iru yori/⌐
                        (A4:╱Un)
(1.25)   maa ima no hyoogen de ichioo soo na n da kedo/⌐
                                            (A5:╱Un)
(1.26)   soto kara mitemo/⌐
                    (A6:╱H)
(1.27)   D no hoogakubu dattara doonidemo naru maa gen'eki
         tte yuu ka./⌐
                    ╱H H H
              (A7: └Soo soo soo)

Chapter 15

(1)

(1.1) Kore wa Ikeda-senseimo/ kokkai no   koto   wa yoku
      this T Mr. Ikeda   also Diet LK things T well

gozonjidearu to   ┌─ (?) omoimasu./
know   QT │   think
             └─ (?)

(1.2) Iya/ ano ima made/ Takahashi Eiichi ┌─ sensei no kankei
      well uhh now until Takahashi Eiichi │   Mr. LK relation
                                           └─ (Aa LAUGH)

      mo yoku/ zonjiteorimasu shi/ ┌─ ohisashiburi desu to
      also well know   and │ long time no see   QT
                                   └─ (Maitta naa LAUGH)
                                      (You got me.)

      iitai   kimochi degozaimasu ga./
      want to say feelings BE   but

(1.3) Sensei soko n   toko wa desu ne/ ┌─ kotogoto sayooni
      Mr.   there NOM place T BE   IP │ things   such as
      Aoki-kun   └─ (Haa)
      Mr. Aoki   (Yeah.)

      o watakushi ga shinraishiteotta wake degozaimasu kara/
      O I   S   trusted   fact BE   since

      sono yooni gorikaioitadakitai   mono da to   omoimasu.
      that way   want to be understood thing BE QT   think

(2)
Sono hoka no koto ni tsuite wa/ watashi wa ano/ nai   to
other   LK things about   T   I   T uhh BE-NEG QT

omotteorimasu ga/ ano/ sakihodo/ oyakusokushimashita
think   but uhh earlier   promised

yooni/ choosashiro to/ yuu koto ni tsuite wa/ sunaoni/
as   investigate QT say fact about   T   honestly

soo shimasu to/ koo   kotaeteoru wake degozaimasu.
so do   QT this way answer   fact BE

Chapter 17

Ari to kirigirisu

Aki no owari no aru hi, aritachi ga fuyugomori no junbi o shiteiru to, soko e baiorin o kakaeta kirigirisu ga yatte-kite itta. "Tabemono o wakete kuremasen ka ne."

Ojiisan ari ga, sono ootai o shita. "Anata wa naze, natsu no aida ni shokuryoo atsume o shiteokanakatta n da ne." "Watashi wa geijutsuka na n desu yo. Ongaku o kanaderu to yuu, suukoona koto o yatteita. Shokuryoo atsume nado shiteiru hima nanka, nakatta to yuu wake desu." "Tondemonai namakemono da. Fun, nani ga geijutsu da. Osukina yooni utaitsuzuketara doo desu, yuki no ue de demo . . ."

Ojiisan ari wa sokkenai. Shikashi, kirigirisu, sahodo rakutan mo shinai. "Dame nara, shiyoo ga nai. Jaa, yoso no ari-san no toko e ittemiru ka . . ."

Kaerikakeru no o, wakai ari ga yobitomeru. "Ma, matte kudasai . . ."

Sono ippoo, ojiisan ari ni setsumeisuru. "Ojiisan, kangaetemite kudasai yo. Wareware senzo daidai no kinroo aikoo no seikaku ni yotte, su no naka wa sudeni shokuryoo de ippai. Mainen no yooni su o kakuchooshi, chozoo ni chozoo o kasanete-kita wake desu ga, sore mo genkai ni kita. Sakki mo chozoo no tame ni su o hirogetara, kabe ga kuzure, mukoo kara furui shokuryoo ga dotto dete-kite, sore ni tsubusarete sanbiki hodo fushooshimashita. Kirigirisu-san ni haitte-moratte sukoshi tabete-itadakanai to, moo sumu kuukan mo nai hodo na n desu."

Kakushite, kirigirisu wa ari no su no kyaku to natta. Sono fuyu wa aritachi ni totte mo tanoshii mono to natta. Juukubokkusu ga sonaetsukerareta yoona mono na no da. Kyokumoku sae chuumon-sureba, nan demo baiorin de hiite-kureru.

Kono kirigirisu, geijutsuka dake atte, atama no hirameki mo aru. Ari no su no chozooko o mitemawatteiru uchi ni, oku no furui shokuryoo ga hakkooshi sake to natteiru no o hakkenshita. Aritachi ni yuu, "Anta gata, kore o hoppottoku koto wa nai ze. Nonde mina."

Aritachi, osoru-osoru name, ii kimochi to nari, sake no aji o oboeru. Sake to uta to kureba, odori datte shizento mi ni tsuku. Doo kurabetemite mo, kinroo yori kono hoo ga harukani omoshiroi. Kono fuyu gomori no kikanchuu ni, kono ari ichizoku no dentooseishin wa kanzenni hookaishita.

Tsugi no haru kara kono aritachi wa, chijoo ni detemo hatara-
koo to sezu, kirigirisu no baiorin ni awasete odorimawaru dake
datta. Tada, ojiisan ari dake ga gaitansuru. "Nantaru koto da, kono
daraku. Kono mama da to tookarazu . . ."

Soshite, wakai aritachi o riron de settokusubeku, shokuryoo no
zaiko o shirabe, ato dore kurai de sore ga soko o tsuku ka keisan-
shiyoo to shita. Daga, amarini chozooryoo ga oosugi, doonimo te ni
oenai. Ato suujuu-nen o odori kurashitatte, nakunari sooni wa nai
no da. Soko de tsubuyaku. "Yononaka ga kawatta to yuu beki na no
ka. Washi ni wa wake ga wakaranaku natta . . ."

Ojiisan ari wa shin'nen to genjitsu to no mujun ni nayami, sono
nayami o wasureyoo to, sake o nomi, wakai renchuu to issho ni
odorihajimeru no datta.

Kyookun.

Han'ei ni yori ikani shakai ga kawatta kara to itte, kotentekina
monogatari o kono yooni kaisakusuru koto, hatashite yurusareru
beki dearoo ka. (Hoshi 1982, 9–11)

(1)

Inokuma: Tada desu nee/ Ishii-san to yuu kata wa/ nihon no/
booryokudan/ ichibanme ka nibanme no booryo-
kudan no/ kaichoo-san deshoo./ Soo yuu kata ga
kaizaishita to yuu koto o kiita naraba/ dare ga doo
yuu koto o itte/ doo yuu fuuni kan'yoshite/ sono
kekka/ koo yuu/ gaisen katsudoo chuushi to yuu
yoona/ koto ga dekita n da to/ yuu koto o kiku no
wa toozen da to omou n desu ga/ moo sukoshi sono
Watanabe/ Hiroyasu/ shachoo no/ kaizai no mae ni/
dono yooni ukagatta ka/ moo sukoshi hakkiri
nobete kudasai./

Takeshita: Ya ima/ Inokuma-sensei wa/ soo yuu fuuni/ kiku no
ga toozen da to/ yuu/ sono toozen dearu to sureba
watakushi wa toozen no iki ni made ittattenakata to/
yuu koto o iwazaru o enai to omoimasu./ Kesshite
ano hireina kotoba da to omotte itteiru wake dewa
gozaimasen. Shooshin shoomei/ watakushi ga/ sono/
gutaitekina koto o/ toitadasu/ kankyoo ni wa nakatta
to/ yuu fuuni gorikai o itadakitai to omoimasu./

References

Abe, Kooboo. 1968. *Tanin no kao* (The face of another). Tokyo: Shinchoosha.

Aesop's Fables. 1960. Told by Valerius Babrius and translated by Denison B. Hull. Chicago: University of Chicago Press.

Andoo, Hiroshi. 1992. Masatsu no joohoo to joohoo no masatsu (Information on friction and friction of information). *Nihongogaku* 11 (December): 64–70.

Anzai, Tetsuo. 1983. *Eigo no hassoo* (Ways of expressing in English). Tokyo: Kodansha.

Asagiri, Yuu. 1992. *Himawari nikki* (The sunflower diary). Tokyo: Kodansha.

Asahi Shimbun International Satellite Edition. 1993. Untenshu shisatsu sareru (A taxi driver stabbed to death). October 24, 23.

———. 1994. Koramu Watashi no Mikata (Column, my view). January–April.

Bachnik, Jane M. 1994. Introduction: *Uchi/soto:* Challenging our conceptualizations of self, social order, and language. In *Situated meaning: Inside and outside in Japanese self, society, and language,* edited by Jane M. Bachnik and Charles J. Quinn, Jr., 3–37. Princeton: Princeton University Press.

Bachnik, Jane M., and Charles J. Quinn, Jr., eds. 1994. *Situated meaning: Inside and outside in Japanese self, society, and language.* Princeton: Princeton University Press.

Bakhtin, M. M. 1971. Discourse typology in prose. In *Readings in Russian poetics,* edited by L. Mateika and K. Pomorska, 176–196. Cambridge: MIT Press.

———. 1981. *The dialogic imagination: Four essays by M. M. Bakhtin.* Edited by Michael Holquist and translated by Caryl Emerson and Michael Holquist. Austin: University of Texas Press.

———. 1986. *Speech genres and other late essays.* Edited by Caryl Emerson and Michael Holquist and translated by Vern W. McGee. Austin: University of Texas Press.

Barnlund, Dean C. 1989. *Communicative styles of Japanese and Americans.* Belmont, Calif.: Wadsworth Publishing.

Bartlett, Sir Frederick C. 1932. *Remembering: A study of experimental and social psychology.* Cambridge: Cambridge University Press.

Bateson, Gregory. 1972. *Steps to an ecology of mind.* New York: Ballantine Books.

Befu, Harumi. 1980. The group model of Japanese society and an alternative. *Rice University Studies* 66: 169–187.

————. 1992. Otherness of Japan. *The Japan Foundation Newsletter* 20/3, 6–9.

Bellah, Robert N., Richard Madsen, William M. Sullivan, Ann Swindler, and Steven M. Tipton. 1985. *Habits of the heart: Individualism and commitment in American life.* New York: Harper and Row.

Bellow, Saul. 1944. *Dangling man.* New York: Vanguard Press.

Berque, Augustin. 1992. Identification of the self in relation to the environment. In *Japanese sense of self,* edited by Nancy R. Rosenberger, 93–104. Cambridge: Cambridge University Press.

Bird, R. Byron. 1993. Language learning and technology trade imbalance between the United States and Japan—What can be done. *Technical Japanese Newsletter,* University of Washington.

Brown, Penelope, and Stephen C. Levinson. [1978] 1987. *Politeness: Some universals in language usage.* Cambridge: Cambridge University Press.

Bruner, Jerome. 1990. *Acts of meaning.* Cambridge: Harvard University Press.

Burke, Kenneth. 1950. *A rhetoric of motives.* Berkeley: University of California Press.

Carbaugh, Donal. 1988/1989. Deep agony: "Self" vs. "society" in Donahue discourse. *Research on Language and Social Interaction* 22: 179–212.

Dale, Peter N. 1986. *The myth of Japanese uniqueness.* New York: St. Martin's Press.

Davidson, Judy. 1984. Subsequent versions of invitations, offers, requests, and proposals dealing with potential or actual rejection. In *Structures of social action: Studies in conversation analysis,* edited by J. Maxwell Atkinson and John Heritage, 102–128. Cambridge: Cambridge University Press.

Doi, Takeo. 1971. *Amae no koozoo* (The anatomy of dependence). Tokyo: Koobundoo.

————. 1976. *The anatomy of dependence.* New York: Kodansha International.

————. 1988. "Amae" riron saikoo (Rethinking the theory of "amae"). *Shisoo* no. 761 (September): 99–118.

Endoo, Orie. 1993. Josei o arawasu goku to hyoogen (Phrases and expressions referring to women). *Nihongogaku* 12 (special issue: *Sekai no joseigo, nihon no joseigo* [Women's language of the word, women's language of Japan]): 193–205.

Erickson, Frederick. 1984. Rhetoric, anecdotes, and rhapsody: Coherence strategies in a conversation among Black American adolescents. In *Conversational style: Analyzing talk among friends,* edited by Deborah Tannen, 81–154. Norwood, N.J.: Ablex.

Fishman, Pamela M. 1978. Interaction: The work women do. *Social Problems* 25: 397–406.

Furukawa, Tetsushi. 1957. *Bushidoo no shisoo to sono shuuhen* (The philosophy and thinking of *bushidoo*—the ways of samurai). Tokyo: Fukumura Shoten.

Geertz, Clifford. 1984. From the native's point of view: On the nature of anthropological understanding. In *Culture theory: Essays on mind, self, and emotion*, edited by Richard A. Shweder and Robert A. Levine, 123–136. Cambridge: Cambridge University Press.

Gotooshoin, ed. 1992. *Enka besuto nihyaku kyuu* (209 best *enka* songs). Tokyo: Gotooshoin.

Graham, John L. 1981. A hidden cause of America's trade deficit with Japan. *Columbia Journal of World Business* (fall): 5–15.

Graham, John L., and Yoshihiko Sano. 1984. *Smart bargaining: Doing business with the Japanese*. Cambridge, Mass.: Ballinger Publishing.

———. 1986. Across the negotiating table from the Japanese. *International Marketing Review* (autumn): 58–71.

Greenbaum, Sidney. 1969. *Studies in English adverbial usage*. Coral Gables: University of Miami Press.

Greenwald, John. 1983. The negotiation waltz. *Time* (August 1): 41–42.

Gumperz, John J., and Stephen C. Levinson. 1991. Rethinking linguistic relativity. *Current Anthropology* 23: 613–623.

Hall, Edward T. 1976. *Beyond culture*. Garden City, N.Y.: Anchor/Doubleday.

Hall, Edward T., and Mildred Reed Hall. 1987. *Hidden differences: Doing business with the Japanese*. Garden City, N.Y.: Anchor/Doubleday.

Halliday, M. A. K. 1967. Notes on transitivity and theme in English. Part 2. *Journal of Linguistics* 3: 199–244.

Halliday, M. A. K., and Ruqaiya Hasan. 1976. *Cohesion in English*. London: Longman.

Hendry, Joy. 1990. Humidity, hygiene, or ritual care: Some thoughts on wrapping as a social phenomenon. In *Unwrapping Japan*, edited by Eyal Ben-Ari, Brian Moeran, and James Valentine, 18–35. Honolulu: University of Hawai'i Press.

Hill, Beverly, Sachiko Ide, Shoko Ikuta, Akiko Kawasaki, and Tsunao Ogino. 1986. Universals of linguistic politeness: Quantitative evidence from Japanese and American English. *Journal of Pragmatics* 10: 347–371.

Hinata, Shigeo. 1996. Kayookyoku no daimei no bootoogo o megutte (On initial words of *kayookyoku* songs). *Nihongogaku* 15 (June): 11–20.

Hori, Motoko. 1985. Taiguu ishiki o han'ei suru gengo keishiki (Linguistic forms reflecting politeness consciousness). In *Kokugogaku Ronsetsu Shiryoo* 24/3: 196–204.

Horiuchi, Katsuaki, and Yoshiko Oomori. 1994. Wakai josei no kotoba no gokei, gogi no tokushoku (Features of young women's word forms and meaning). *Nihongogaku* 13 (October): 72–80.

Hoshi, Shin'ichi. 1982. *Mirai Isoppu* (Future Aesops). Tokyo: Shinchoosha.

Ide, Sachiko. 1992. On the notion of *wakimae:* Toward an integrated framework of linguistic politeness. In *Kotoba no mozaiku* (The mosaic of language), edited by the Mejiro Linguistics Society, 298–305. Tokyo: Mejiro Linguistics Society.

Ikegami, Yoshihiko. 1981. *Suru to naru no gengogaku* (The linguistics of "do" and "become"). Tokyo: Taishuukan Shoten.

———. 1982. *Kotoba no shigaku* (Poetics of language). Tokyo: Iwanami Shoten.

———. 1988. What we see when we see flying cranes: Motion or transition. *The Japan Foundation Newsletter* 15/5–6: 1–9.

———. 1991. "DO-language" and "BECOME-language": Two contrasting types of linguistic representation. In *The empire of signs*, edited by Yoshihiko Ikegami, 258–326. Amsterdam: John Benjamins.

Ikeno, Koi. 1992. *Tokimeki tunaito* (Thrilling tonight). Tokyo: Shuueisha.

Inagaki, Yoshihiko. 1989. Our favorite words. *Japan Echo* 16 (special issue: *The Japanese Language*): 22–25.

Ishii, Satoshi, and Tom Bruneau. 1988. Silence and silences in cross-cultural perspective: Japan and the United States. In *Intercultural communication: A reader*, edited by Larry A. Samovar and Richard E. Porter, 310–315. Belmont, Calif.: Wadsworth Publishing.

Jones, Kimberly. 1990. Conflict in Japanese conversation. Ph.D. diss., University of Michigan.

———. 1992. Ratifying conflict in Japanese interactions. Paper presented at the Association for Asian Studies Annual Meeting, Washington, D.C.

Jorden, Eleanor. 1963. *Beginning Japanese*. Part 2. New Haven: Yale University Press.

Kabashima, Tadao. 1979. *Nihongo no sutairu bukku* (Stylebook of the Japanese language). Tokyo: Taishuukan Shoten.

Kamikawa, Kiyo'o. 1992. *Reezaa igaku no kyooi* (The wonder of laser medicine). Tokyo: Kodansha.

Kaplan, Robert B. 1972. *The anatomy of rhetoric: Prolegomena to a functional theory of rhetoric*. Philadelphia: Center for Curriculum Development.

Kendon, Adam. 1967. Some functions of gaze-direction in social interaction. *Acta Psychologica* 26: 22–63.

———. 1977. Some functions of gaze-direction in two-person conversation. In *Studies in the behavior of social interaction*, edited by Adam Kendon, 13–51. Bloomington: Indiana University Press.

Kindaichi, Haruhiko. 1957. *Nihongo* (The Japanese language). Tokyo: Iwanami Shoten.

———. 1985. Nihongo no kokoro (The heart of the Japanese language). In *Nihongo no kokoro*, edited by NHK Kokusai Kyooiku Bunka Purojekuto and translated by Don Kenny, 74–89. Tokyo: Kodansha International.

Kitagawa, Chisato. 1995. *Wake* as discourse modality indicator: A type of speaker orientation in Japanese. *Japanese Discourse: An International Journal for the Study of Japanese Text and Talk* 1: 55–81.

Kokuritsu Kokugo Kenkyuujo, ed. 1964. *Gendai zasshi kyuujusshu no yooji yoogo* (Vocabulary and Chinese characters in ninety magazines today). Tokyo: Shuueisha.

Kunihiro, Narumi. 1994. The electric geisha. In *The electric geisha: Exploring Japan's popular culture*, edited by Atsushi Ueda and translated by Miriam Eguchi, 60–67. Tokyo: Kodansha International.

Kuno, Susumu. 1973. *Nihon bunpoo kenkyuu* (Studies in Japanese grammar). Tokyo: Taishuukan Shoten.

Lakoff, Robin. 1975. *Language and women's place*. New York: Harper and Row.

Langacker, Ronald W. 1987. Nouns and verbs. *Language* 63: 53–94.

Larsen, Knud S., Harry Martin, and Howard Giles. 1977. Anticipated social cost and interpersonal accommodation. *Human Communication Research* 3: 303–308.

Lebra, Takie Sugiyama. 1976. *Japanese patterns of behavior*. Honolulu: University of Hawai'i Press.

———. 1989. The cultural significance of silence in Japanese communication. Paper presented at the International Pragmatics Association Conference, Antwerp, Belgium.

———. 1992. Self in Japanese culture. In *Japanese sense of self*, edited by Nancy R. Rosenberger, 105–120. Cambridge: Cambridge University Press.

Li, Charles N., and Sandra A. Thompson. 1976. Subject and topic: A new typology of language. In *Subject and topic*, edited by Charles N. Li, 450–490. New York: Academic Press.

McCreary, Don R. 1986. *Japanese–U.S. business negotiations: A cross-cultural study*. New York: Praeger.

McGloin, Naomi H. 1983. Some politeness strategies in Japanese. In *Studies in Japanese language use*, edited by Shigeru Miyagawa and Chisato Kitagawa, 127–145. Edmonton: Linguistic Research Inc.

———. 1984. Danwa bunshoo ni okeru no desu no kinoo (Functions of *no desu* in discourse grammar). *Gengo* 13 (January): 254–260.

Makino, Michiko. 1992. *Sora yori mo setsunaku* (More sentimental than the sky). Tokyo: Kodansha.

Maltz, Daniel N. 1985. Joyful noise and reverent silence: The significance of noise in Pentecostal worship. In *Perspectives on silence*, edited by Deborah Tannen and Muriel Saville-Troike, 113–137. Norwood, N.J.: Ablex.

Markus, Hazel Rose, and Shinobu Kitayama. 1991. Culture and the self: Implications for cognition, emotion and motivation. *Psychological Review* 98: 224–253.

Maynard, Michael L. 1993. Iconic and linguistic images of America in Japanese print advertisements: A semiotic analysis. Paper presented at the American Academy of Advertising Conference, Montreal, Canada.

Maynard, Senko K. 1980. Discourse functions of the Japanese theme marker *wa*. Ph.D. diss., Northwestern University.

———. 1982. Theme in Japanese and topic in English: A functional comparison. *Forum Linguisticum* 5: 235–261.

———. 1987a. Nichibei kaiwa ni okeru aizuchi no hyoogen (Back-channel expressions in Japanese and American conversations). *Gengo* 16 (November): 88–92.

———. 1987b. Thematization as a staging device in the Japanese narrative. In *Perspectives on topicalization: The case of Japanese wa*, edited by John Hinds, Senko K. Maynard, and Shoichi Iwasaki, 57–82. Amsterdam: John Benjamins.

———. 1989. *Japanese conversation: Self-contextualization through structure and interactional management*. Norwood, N.J.: Ablex.

———. 1990. *An introduction to Japanese grammar and communication strategies*. Tokyo: Japan Times.

———. 1991a. Discourse and interactional functions of the Japanese modal adverb *yahari/yappari*. *Language Sciences* 13: 39–57.

———. 1991b. Pragmatics of discourse modality: A case of the Japanese emotional adverb *doose*. *Pragmatics* 1: 371–392.

———. 1992. Cognitive and pragmatic messages of a syntactic choice: A case of the Japanese commentary predicate *n(o) da*. *TEXT: An Interdisciplinary Journal for the Study of Discourse* 12: 563–613.

———. 1993a. *Discourse modality: Subjectivity, emotion and voice in the Japanese language*. Pragmatics and Beyond. New Series. Amsterdam: John Benjamins.

———. 1993b. Interactional functions of formulaicity: A case of utterance-final forms in Japanese. *Proceedings of the Fifteenth International Congress of Linguists*, 3: 225–228. Quebec City: Laval University Press.

———. 1993c. *Kaiwa bunseki* (Conversation analysis). *Nichieigo taishoo kenkyuu shiriizu*. Vol. 2. Tokyo: Kuroshio Shuppan.

———. 1994a. The centrality of thematic relations in Japanese text. *Functions of Language* 1: 229–260.

———. 1994b. Commentary questions in Japanese: Cognitive sources and pragmatic resources. *Studies in Language* 19: 447–487.

———. 1995. Contrastive rhetoric: A case of nominalization in Japanese and English discourse. Paper presented at the First International Conference in Contrastive Semantics and Pragmatics, Brighton, England.

———. 1996a. Contrastive rhetoric: A case of nominalization in Japanese and English discourse. *Language Sciences* 18: 933–946.

———. 1996b. Multivoicedness in speech and thought representation: The case of self-quotation in Japanese. *Journal of Pragmatics* 25: 207–226.

———. 1997a (forthcoming). Synergistic structures in grammar: A case of nominalization and commentary predicate in Japanese. WORD: Journal of the International Linguistic Association.

———. 1997b (forthcoming). Shifting contexts: The sociolinguistic significance of nominalization in Japanese television news. *Language in Society*.

Mikami, Akira. 1960. *Zoo wa hana ga nagai* (Elephants' trunks are long). Tokyo: Kuroshio Shuppan.

———. [1953] 1972. *Gendaigohoo josetsu* (An introduction to modern Japanese). Tokyo: Kuroshio Shuppan.

Miller, Mara. 1993. Canons and the challenge of gender. *The Monist* 76: 477–493.

Miller, Roy Andrew. 1977. The "spirit" of the Japanese language. *Journal of Japanese Studies* 3: 251–298.

Mizusawa, Megumi. 1992. *Himechan no ribon* (Little Hime's hair ribbon). Tokyo: Shuueisha.

Mori, Arimasa. 1979. *Mori Arimasa zenshuu* (Collected works of Arimasa Mori). Vol. 12. Tokyo: Chikuma Shoboo.

Morita, Yoshiyuki. 1995. *Nihongo no shiten* (Perspectives in the Japanese language). Tokyo: Sootakusha.

Mouer, Ross, and Yoshio Sugimoto. 1986. *Images of Japanese society*. London: KPI.

Nagano, Masaru. 1986. *Bunshooron soosetsu: Bunpooronteki koosatsu* (Theory of discourse: Grammatical approaches). Tokyo: Asakura Shoten.

Nakane, Chie. 1970. *Japanese society*. Berkeley and Los Angeles: University of California Press.

Natsuki, Shizuko. 1981. *Hikaru gake* (The shining cliff). Tokyo: Kadokawa.

Neustupný, J. V. 1983. Keigo kaihi no sutoratejii ni tsuite (On strategies for avoiding honorifics). *Nihongogaku* 2 (January): 62–67.

Nishihara, Suzuko, and Tomoyo Shibahara. 1995. Rhetorical contrast in newspaper reports: *Asahi Shimbun* and *International Herald Tribune*. Paper presented at the First International Conference in Contrastive Semantics and Pragmatics, Brighton, England.

Noda, Mari. 1992. Relation maintenance in the discourse of disagreement. Paper presented at the Association for Asian Studies Annual Meeting, Washington, D.C.

Okano, Yuuji. 1991. *Tooshi kakusei* (The awakening of a warrior). Tokyo: Shuueisha.

Okuda, Akiko. 1977. *Desu masu* in conversation. Manuscript.

Okutsu, Keiichiroo. 1983. Jujuhyoogen no taishoo kenkyuu (Contrastive studies of "giving" and "receiving" verbs). *Nihongogaku* 2 (April): 22–30.

Oota, Minoru, trans. 1971. *Chuuburarin no otoko* (translation of Saul Bellow's *Dangling man*). Tokyo: Shinchoosha.

Orihara, Mito. 1992. *Sotsugyoo made no sen-nichi* (One thousand days until graduation). Tokyo: Shuueisha.

Plath, David W. 1980. *Long engagements: Maturity in modern Japan*. Stanford: Stanford University Press.

Popeye. 1995. May 25 issue. Tokyo: Magazine House.

Prundy, Alicia M., Donald W. Klopf, and Satoshi Ishii. 1990. Japanese and American tendencies to argue. *Psychological Reports* 60: 802.

Pullum, Geoffrey K. 1991. *The great Eskimo vocabulary hoax*. Chicago: University of Chicago Press.

Reddy, Michael J. 1979. The conduit metaphor: A case of frame conflict in our language about language. In *Metaphor and thought*, edited by Andrew Ortony, 284–324. Cambridge: Cambridge University Press.

Reimen, Etsuko O. 1996. Kashi ni miru eigohyoogen no zooka genshoo (The phenomenon of increasing English expressions in song lyrics). *Nihongogaku* 15 (June): 21–29.

Reischauer, Edwin. 1970. *The Japanese: The story of a nation.* New York: Knopf.

Robertson, James Oliver. 1980. *American myth, Amerian reality.* New York: Hill and Wang.

Rosenberger, Nancy R. 1992. Tree in summer, tree in winter: Movement of self in Japan. In *Japanese sense of self*, edited by Nancy R. Rosenberger, 67–92. Cambridge: Cambridge University Press.

Royce, Josiah. 1920. *The philosophy of loyalty.* New York: Macmillan.

Said, Edward. 1978. *Orientalism.* New York: Pantheon.

Saji, Keizoo. 1991. *Nihongo bunpoo no kenkyuu* (Studies in Japanese grammar). Kasukabe: Hitsuji Shoboo.

Samarin, William J. 1965. Language of silence. *Practical Anthropology* 12: 115–119.

Sasazawa, Saho. 1983. *Kogarashi Monjiroo Nakasendoo o iku* (Monjiroo's travel along the Nakasen Road). Tokyo: Chuuookooronsha.

Satake, Hideo. 1995. Wakamono kotoba to retorikku (Youth language and rhetoric). *Nihongogaku* 14 (November): 53–60.

Saunders, E. Dale, trans. 1966. *The face of another* (translation of Kooboo Abe's *Tanin no kao*). New York: G.P. Putnam's Sons.

de Saussure, Ferdinand. [1915] 1966. *Course in general linguistics*, edited by Charles Bally and Albert Sechehaye in collaboration with Albert Riedlinger and translated by Wade Baskin. New York: McGraw-Hill.

Scollon, Ron. 1982. The rhythmic integration of ordinary talk. In *Georgetown University Round Table on Languages and Linguistics. Analyzing discourse: Text and talk*, edited by Deborah Tannen, 335–349. Washington: Georgetown University Press.

———. 1985. The machine stops: Silence in the metaphor of malfunction. In *Perspectives on silence*, edited by Deborah Tannen and Muriel Saville-Troike, 21–30. Norwood, N.J.: Ablex.

Searle, John R. 1995. *The construction of social reality.* New York: Free Press.

Shibata, Takashi. 1992. Joohooka jidai no bunshoo (Discourse in the information age). *Nihongogaku* 11 (April): 8–11.

Shimozaki, Minoru. 1981. *No dearu* construction and a theory of cohesion. *Sophia Linguistica* 7: 116–124.

Slater, Philip. 1970. *The pursuit of loneliness.* Boston: Beacon Press.

Smith, Robert J. 1983. *Japanese society: Tradition, self and the social order.* Cambridge: Cambridge University Press.

Sonoda, Kooji. 1983. Japanized English: A lexical aspect of English influence on Japanese. *Geolinguistics* 9: 33–48.

Soono, Tadao. 1992. *Dangai no onna kanshikikan* (The female criminal investigator on the cliff). Tokyo: Koobunsha.

Suzuki, Akira. [1824] 1979. *Gengyo shishuron* (Theory of language as four kinds of elements), edited by Toshio Kojima and Tsuboi Miki. Bunseisha Bunko 68.

Suzuki, Takao. 1978. *Japan and the Japanese*. Translated by Akira Miura. Tokyo: Kodansha International.

Szatrowski, Polly. 1992. Invitation-refusals in Japanese telephone conversations. Paper presented at the Association for Asian Studies Annual Meeting, Washington, D.C.

Takashi, Kyoko. 1990. A functional analysis of English borrowings in Japanese advertising: Linguistic and sociolinguistic perspectives. Ph.D. diss., Georgetown University.

Taketomo, Yasuhiko. 1988. Meta gengo toshite no "amae" ("Amae" as metalanguage). *Shisoo* no. 758 (June): 122–155.

Talbot, Mary. 1992. The construction of gender in a teenage magazine. In *Critical language awareness*, edited by Norman Fairclough, 174–199. London and New York: Longman.

Tannen, Deborah. 1990. *You just don't understand: Women and men in conversation*. New York: William Morrow.

———. 1991. *Talking voices: Repetition, dialogue, and imagery in conversational discourse*. Cambridge: Cambridge University Press.

Tanomura, Tadaharu. 1990. *Gendai nihongo no bunpoo* (Grammar of modern Japanese). Vol. 1. *"No da" no imi to yoohoo* (Meaning and use of *no da*). Tokyo: Izumi Shoin.

Tawara, Machi. 1988. *Yotsuba no essei* (The four-leaf essay). Tokyo: Kawade Shoboo Shinsha.

Tawara, Sooichiroo. 1993. *Heisei nihon no kanryoo* (Bureaucrats of Japan in the Heisei Era). Tokyo: Bungei Shunjuu.

Taylor, Charles. 1989. *Sources of self*. Cambridge: Harvard University Press.

Time. 1983. August 1 issue.

Tobin, Joseph J. 1992. Introduction: Domesticating the West. In *Re-made in Japan*, edited by Joseph J. Tobin, 1–41. New Haven: Yale University Press.

Tokieda, Motoki. 1941. *Kokugogaku genron* (Principles of Japanese linguistics). Tokyo: Iwanami Shoten.

———. 1950. *Nihon bunpoo koogohen* (Grammar of Japanese—The spoken language). Tokyo: Iwanami Shoten.

Tsubota, Jooji. 1975. *Nihon mukashibanashi shuu* (Collection of old Japanese tales). Tokyo: Shinchoosha.

Uchida, Nobuko. 1993. Kaiwa koodoo ni mirareru seisa (Gender differences observed in conversational behavior). *Nihongogaku* 12 (special issue: *Sekai no joseigo, nihon no joseigo* [Women's language of the world, women's language of Japan]): 156–168.

Usui, Yoshito. 1994. *Kureyon Shin-chan* (Crayon Shinchan), Vol. 8. Tokyo: Futabasha.

Uyeno, Tazuko. 1971. A study of Japanese modality: A performative analysis of sentence particles. Ph.D. diss., University of Michigan.

Vygotsky, L. S. 1962. *Thought and language.* Cambridge: MIT Press.

Watanabe, Minoru. 1971. *Kokugo koobunron* (A syntactic theory of the Japanese language). Tokyo: Hanawa Shoboo.

———. 1985. Kataru jibun o kataru gengo keishiki (The linguistic system that speaks about the speaking self). *Gengo* 14 (December): 38–43.

Watsuji, Tetsuroo. 1935. *Fuudo: Ningengakuteki koosatsu* (Climate and mores: A philosophical study). Tokyo: Iwanami Shoten.

———. 1937. *Rinrigaku jookan* (Ethics, the first volume). Tokyo: Iwanami Shoten.

Werner, Heinz, and Bernard Kaplan. 1963. *Symbol formation.* New York: John Wiley and Sons.

Wertsch, James V. 1991a. A sociocultural approach to socially shared cognition. In *Perspectives on socially shared cognition,* edited by Lauren B. Resnick, John M. Levine, and Stephanie D. Teasley, 85–100. Washington: American Psychological Association.

———. 1991b. *Voices of the mind: A sociocultural approach to mediated action.* Cambridge: Harvard University Press.

Wertsch, James V., ed. and trans. 1981. *The concept of activity in Soviet psychology.* Armonk, N.Y.: Sharpe.

Wetzel, Patricia J. 1994. A movable self: The linguistic indexing of *uchi* and *soto.* In *Situational meaning: Inside and outside in Japanese self, society, and language,* edited by Jane M. Bachnik and Charles J. Quinn, Jr., 74–87. Princeton: Princeton University Press.

White, Sheida. 1989. Back channels across cultures: A study of Americans and Japanese. *Language in Society* 18: 59–76.

Whorf, Benjamin Lee. 1956. *Language, thought, and reality.* Cambridge: MIT Press.

Yamada, Haru. 1990. Topic management and turn distribution in business meetings: American versus Japanese strategies. *TEXT: An Interdisciplinary Journal for the Study of Discourse* 10: 271–295.

Yonekawa, Akihiko. 1995a. Wakamonogo no sekai (The world of youth language). Part 3. *Nihongogaku* 14 (January): 114–123.

———. 1995b. Wakamonogo no sekai (The world of youth language). Part 4. *Nihongogaku* 14 (February): 98–107.

Author Index

Abe, Kooboo, 85–86, 113–114, 116–117, 127–128, 231
Andoo, Hiroshi, 219
Anzai, Tetsuo, 172
Asagiri, Yuu, 65, 208

Bachnik, Jane M., 33
Bakhtin, M. M., 3, 186–187
Barnlund, Dean C., 179
Bartlett, Sir Frederick C., 201–203
Bateson, Gregory, 209, 214
Befu, Harumi, 30–31, 222
Bellah, Robert N., 42
Bellow, Saul, 116–117
Berque, Augustin, 39
Bird, R. Byron, 223–224
Brown, Penelope, 113
Bruneau, Tom, 153
Bruner, Jerome, 194–195
Burke, Kenneth, 26–27

Carbaugh, Donal, 26
Chomsky, Noam, 193

Dale, Peter N., 34, 221
Davidson, Judy, 138
Doi, Takeo, 19, 33–34

Endoo, Orie, 74–75
Erickson, Frederick, 214

Fishman, Pamela M., 77
Furukawa, Tetsushi, 10–11

Geertz, Clifford, 37
Gills, Howard, 215
Graham, John L., 134–135, 136

Greenbaum, Sidney, 84
Greenwald, John, 155
Gumperz, John J., 4

Hall, Edward T., 22–23
Hall, Mildred Reed, 22–23
Halliday, M.A.K., 106, 112
Hasan, Ruqaiya, 112
Hendry, Joy, 115
Hill, Beverly, 57, 61–62
Hirata, Shigeo, 94–95
Hori, Motoko, 64
Horiuchi, Katsuaki, 81
Hoshi, Shin'ichi, 203–204, 234–235

Ide, Sachiko, 57–58, 60–61. *See also* Hill, Beverly
Ikegami, Yoshihiko, 112–113, 171–172, 175, 201
Ikeno, Koi, 98, 99
Ikuta, Shoko. *See* Hill, Beverly
Inagaki, Yoshihiko, 94
Ishii, Satoshi, 136, 153

Jones, Kimberly, 156–157
Jorden, Eleanor, 115

Kabashima, Tadao, 94
Kamikawa, Kiyo'o, 50, 227
Kaplan, Bernard, 176
Kaplan, Robert B., 158–159
Kawasaki, Akiko. *See* Hill, Beverly
Kendon, Adam, 144
Kindaichi, Haruhiko, 87, 130
Kitagawa, Chisato, 115
Kitayama, Shinobu, 40, 96, 194
Klopf, Donald W., 136

Subject Index

abrupt verb forms: in conversation, 120; mixed with formal verb forms, 119–122; in the novel, 121–122; in television news, 55; in the *uchi* situation, 58, 60

adverbs, attitudinal, 2, 84–87, 116, 161; English counterparts of, 90–93; English "you know," 90–93; examples of, 86. See also *doose*

amae, 5, 33–36, 156; and avoidance of honorifics, 64; conditions for, 19; in conflict situation, 156; criticism of, 33; definition of, 33; etymology of, 33; and interactional style, 36; in Japan and America, 35; and relationality, 19; vocabulary associated with, 35

back channels: contexts for, 141–142; in conversation, 140–141; frequencies of, 142; functions of American, 150, 151; functions of Japanese, 142, 151; with head movements, 141; in intercultural discourse, 212–213; kinds of, 139. See also head movements; listener responses

beautification honorifics, 63. See also honorifics

Become-language, 6, 175, 194; contrast with Do-language, 176

Bonanza, 14; as countermyth, 14

boomerang effect, 64

chinjutsu, 192; definition of, 192. See also modality

collaboration, 133, 156, 162, 166; strategies, 133. See also head movements; negotiation

commentary questions, 207–208; expressing modal attitude, 208; in written Japanese, 208. See also questions

commentary sentences: description of, 161; in newspaper columns, 161. See also *ki-shoo-ten-ketsu*

conduit metaphor, 180–181

conflict, 1, 134, 162; and *amae*, 156; in discourse of television debate, 100, 102; and myth of harmony, 156–157, 162; ratification of, 156, 157, 162, 166; in the *soto* situation, 157; strategies used in, 157; in the *uchi* relationship, 156. See also swearing

contexts, 6, 22, 33, 49, 56, 105, 108, 126, 132, 145, 162, 166, 183, 194, 219; of American back channels, 143–144; of American head movements, 150, 151; contextual cues, 165; and culture, 23; of Japanese back channels, 141–142; of Japanese head movements, 146, 159, 151; and language, 17; manipulation of, 64, 162; multiple, associated with self-quotation, 187; related to *wakimae*, 57; relationality as, 17; self in, 41. See also high-context; low-context

conversation management, 145, 146, 152, 214; contrast between Japanese and American, 213–215; by listener responses, 144; by questioning, 207

cowboy, 9, 11–12, 26, 43, 221, 225; in contemporary America, 13; contrast with samurai, 10–12; cowboy-like negotiation style, 134. See also Bonanza

da style, 55, 75. See also abrupt verb forms

data, 48; notation used, 47–48

dependence: psychological, 43; social, 43

desu / masu form, 59, 64. See also formal verb forms

249

About the Author

Senko K. Maynard is professor of Japanese language and linguistics at Rutgers University. She received her bachelor's degree from Tokyo University of Foreign Studies and her doctorate in linguistics from Northwestern University. She has published extensively in the field of Japanese linguistics, especially in the area of discourse analysis and conversation analysis. Among her books are *Japanese Conversation: Self-contextualization through Structure and Interactional Management* (1989), *An Introduction to Japanese Grammar and Communication Strategies* (1990), and *Discourse Modality: Subjectivity, Emotion and Voice in the Japanese Language* (1993). Author of numerous articles in Japanese, U.S., and international scholarly journals, Professor Maynard is the founding and current editor of *Japanese Discourse: An International Journal for the Study of Japanese Text and Talk.*